DEDICATION

To Herbert Wechsler, Alan Stone and Herbert Morris who introduced me to and furthered my long-time interest in mental health law AND to the Honorable Joseph Schneider and Honorable Stephen Yates who provided me the opportunity to observe the legal aspects of the mental health system in operation.

*

MENTAL HEALTH AND DISABILITY LAW

IN A NUTSHELL

By

DONALD H.J. HERMANN

Professor of Law and Philosophy
Director, Health Law Institute
DePaul University

ST. PAUL, MINN.
WEST PUBLISHING CO.
1997

Nutshell Series, In a Nutshell, the Nutshell Logo and the WP symbol are registered trademarks of West Publishing Co. Registered in the U.S. Patent and Trademark Office.

COPYRIGHT © 1997 By WEST GROUP
        610 Opperman Drive
        P.O. Box 64526
        St. Paul, MN 55164–0526
        1–800–328–9352

Library of Congress Cataloging-in-Publication Data

Hermann, Donald H. J.
    Mental health and disability law in a nutshell / by Donald H.J.
  Hermann.
       p.   cm. — (Nutshell series)
    Includes index.
    ISBN 0–314–06546–6 (softcover)
    1. Mental health laws—United States.   2. Insanity—Jurisprudence—
United States. I. Title. II. Series.
KF3828.Z9H47   1997
344.73'044—dc21   97–10339
                                        CIP

ISBN 0–314–06546–6

PREFACE

The intersection of the mental health system and the criminal justice system is discussed with reference to competency to stand trial, the elements of criminal charges and defenses, sentencing, imprisonment, and fitness to be executed.

The book concludes with a review of the law dealing with protection from discrimination and access to social services for the mentally disabled. Attention is directed to the areas of employment, housing and zoning, and education. Finally, the law relating to social security disability benefits is summarized.

For students studying mental health law, this book provides supplemental material on the various groups of professionals working in the mental health system. The book provides an overview of mental health treatment and diagnosis with extensive definitional material.

For the lawyer and mental health professional, this book should serve as a convenient reference to mental health law with a concise description of the broad spectrum of subjects likely to arise in practice.

In short, this book aims not only to be a study aid but a basic comprehensive reference guide to lawyer and mental health professional.

DONALD H.J. HERMANN

Chicago, May 1997

*

PREFACE

The field of mental health law is interdisciplinary in two distinct ways. It obviously draws on case and statutory law for its doctrinal structure while dealing with the subject of diagnosis, treatment, rehabilitation, and institutionalization of the mentally ill and disabled. At the same time, mental health law involves almost every other traditional subject field of law: constitutional law in establishing the parameters of involuntary treatment or prosecution of the mentally ill; tort law in dealing with issues of medical malpractice, negligence, and informed consent; contract law in dealing with matters relating to treatment and payment; administrative law in addressing matters related to commitment, reimbursement, and social services; even procedural law becomes crucial in relation to notice requirements and treatment plans in both civil commitment and criminal prosecution of the mentally ill.

This book aims to be of use not only to the student who is in need of an overview of the law of mental health and disability, but it also designed to be of use to the practicing lawyer and to the mental health professional. Those working in the mental health field or representing clients involved with the mental health system often need a quick overview and specific direction for further research. It is hoped that this volume will meet the basic needs of both professions by providing a comprehensive, but concise explanation of the law of mental health and mental disability.

This volume examines both the civil and criminal law of mental health. It deals with civil commitment, as well as hearings to determine fitness for trial or execution. Criminal defenses and sentencing as they involve issues relating to the mental capacity of defendants are examined. The book begins with an examination of the various categories of mental health professionals including the scope of their work, their licensing and discipline. Next the subject of mental illness is taken up with a consideration of the major psychiatric disorders. Then the subject of clinical psychiatric evidence is taken up with a review of such issues as admissibility of evidence, qualifying experts and establishing the basis for a clinical opinion.

Medical malpractice and negligence are examined in some detail. Several specific subjects are extensively discussed including: informed consent; confidentiality, privacy, and patient access to records; the right to counsel and advocacy services.

Civil commitment is reviewed along with the right to refuse and consent to psychiatric treatment in the civil commitment context. Special attention is given to the subject of right to mental health treatment. The various aspects of guardianship are also set out.

ACKNOWLEDGMENT

My interest in mental health law was sparked by challenging course work under Professor Herbert Wechsler at Columbia University. The National Endowment of the Humanities furthered my work in this area by a year-long fellowship at Harvard University that allowed me to study with Alan Stone, and by a summer fellowship at the University of California at Los Angeles that permitted extensive discussions with Herbert Morris.

While at DePaul University, I have had the opportunity to teach courses in the mental health field including law and psychiatry; legal aspects of the mental health system; a seminar on the homeless mentally ill; and a course on sexuality, sexual orientation and the law. This work was enriched by opportunities to represent patients, by appointment to serve as a guardian ad litem, and to contribute to the work of two state commissions revising the Mental Health Code of Illinois. These experiences were the result of the generous encouragement and support of the Honorable Joseph Schneider and the Honorable Stephen Yates, who have served in the County Division of the Circuit Court of Cook County.

Writing a comprehensive survey requires not only significant research, but a great deal of verifi-

ACKNOWLEDGMENTS

cation and cite checking. I am particularly grateful to the following research students who contributed to this manuscript: Rebecca Cerny, Kristin Dvorsky, Joan Pufunt, Paul St. John and Robert Wood.

The preparation of this manuscript was due to the skillful work of Virginia Knittle. I am grateful to Ms. Knittle and Timothy Kollar for their work in proofreading the final copy of this book and for their help in preparing the index.

Finally, I would like to acknowledge the summer research support that facilitated my work on this book which was provided under the auspices of Dean John Roberts and Acting Dean Mark Weber of the DePaul University College of Law.

OUTLINE

OUTLINE

OUTLINE

*

TABLE OF CASES

References are to Pages

TABLE OF CASES

TABLE OF CASES

United States v. _____(see opposing party)

*

MENTAL HEALTH AND DISABILITY LAW
IN A NUTSHELL

*

CHAPTER 1

MENTAL HEALTH PROFESSIONALS

A. INTRODUCTION

The mental health field involves several groups of mental health professionals. These professionals differ in their education, training, orientation, and treatment methodology. State law establishes the requirements to be met by those individuals who wish to practice as mental health professionals. In every state, boards or commissions are empaneled to oversee the licensing and regulation of mental health professionals. These agencies have authority to impose sanctions for misconduct of mental health practitioners, including breaches of confidentiality, sexual misconduct and illegal distribution of drugs. Additionally, each major group of mental health professionals also has its own organization or association that screens its membership. Finally, hospitals, clinics and other professional groups control who may practice on their medical staff and determine who may be affiliated with their facilities or receive referrals.

Today, tensions often exist between the various groups of mental health professionals over the appropriate scope of each group's practice. This has led some professional associations to attempt to influence insurance companies to limit or deny insurance reimbursement to certain mental health practitioners in particular areas of practice. For example, insurance companies may limit compensation for certain treatments to psychiatrists while denying psychologists payment for the same treatment. Similarly, hospitals often restrict admission to the medical staff to psychiatrists while placing restrictions on the practice of psychologists.

B. CATEGORIES OF MENTAL HEALTH PROFESSIONALS

1. Psychiatrists

The origin of psychiatry dates to the early nineteenth century. Early treatment of mental illness was mainly administered within insane asylums. In 1844, an organization which later became the American Psychiatric Association was established as the principal association of professional psychiatrists. The practice of modern psychiatry greatly developed during World War II. Today, psychiatry is practiced not only in mental institutions, hospital wards and clinics, but also on an outpatient basis and in private practice.

State laws and medical professional norms determine who is qualified to practice psychiatry. In most states, any licensed physician may practice psychiatry. However, as a practical matter, physicians who receive referrals and hospital privileges and who practice psychiatry must complete a psychiatric residency program. After completing residency requirements and passing specified examinations, these psychiatrists become "Board Certified" and many become members of the American Psychiatric Association.

Only licensed physicians are qualified to become psychiatrists. Upon completion of medical school, physicians may complete a psychiatric residency program usually lasting three years. Residency may focus on either general psychiatry or on a further specialized aspect of psychiatry. Academic psychiatry programs vary in emphasis, but all include formal courses and clinical training.

Psychiatrists may also become "Board Certified" by the American Board of Psychiatry and Neurology. Certification requires completing a psychiatry residency and passing an examination. This certification is a practical necessity for psychiatrists who serve as expert witnesses or work as consultants with certain agencies.

The practice of psychiatry may be divided into two general approaches: the analytical and psychological orientation, and the directive and organic orientation. The analytical approach applies psychoanalytic (often Freudian) theories to the analysis of behavior, relationships, and motivations. This approach emphasizes gaining and applying insight, rarely emphasizing manipulating or directing patients.

The directive approach focuses on changing a patient's opinions, attitudes, and behavior through guiding and supportive methods. Directive methods include assertion, suggestion, reassurance, advice, manipulation, and even coercion. Directive techniques are often combined with organic medical treatments. Directive practitioners are likely to do medical and neurological examinations and laboratory tests, prescribing drugs, administering shock treatment, and to carry out minor medical surgeries. The directive approach rarely focuses on gaining insight. Because all psychiatrists are medical doctors, they may prescribe drugs and other medically based treatments in conjunction with other therapies when appropriate.

2. Psychologists

Prior to the 1940's, psychology was primarily an academic profession. Psychologists taught in universities or conducted research. More recently psychology has emerged as a treating profession. Today, many psychologists work in institutions, clinics, and engage in private practice.

No nationwide standards exist that define who is qualified to practice as a psychologist. However, the American Psychological Association establishes national standards for education and training in psychology. Many state licensing and certification agencies have adopted these standards in order to regulate the practice of psychologists.

While educational requirements vary among states, a master's or doctorate degree in clinical psychology is usually required. Between three and five years of study is necessary to receive a doctorate degree. Traditionally, candidates must undergo a preliminary comprehensive psychology examination after two or three years. Additionally, a major piece of original research is usually required.

Psychologists perform two primary functions. The first primary function is diagnosis and psychological assessment. Assessment and diagnosis typically involve subjective evaluations and administering and interpreting standardized psychological tests. The second primary function of psychologists is psychotherapy. Psychologist directed psychotherapy may be divided into two approaches: the psychoanalytical approach and the behavioral approach. The psychoanalytical approach emphasizes gaining and applying insight. The behavioral approach focuses on abnormal behavior patterns and uses learning theory to decondition maladaptive behavior. Often, team effort between psychologists and other mental health professionals is involved. Unlike psychiatrists, psychologists may not prescribe medication or medically based treatments.

3. Psychoanalysts

Most psychoanalysts are a subset of psychiatrists. In addition, a small minority of psychologists use psychoanalytic theories and methods in treatment. Psychoanalysts may receive specialized training at one of several institutes of the American Psychoanalytical Association. The additional training usually takes six to ten years.

Psychoanalysts use a specialized approach to the understanding and treatment of emotional disorders. One of the principal groups of psychoanalysts, referred to as Freudians, base their theories on the teachings of Sigmund Freud.

4. Psychiatric Social Worker

The field of psychiatric social work is an emerging field. Social workers provide therapy in institutions, clinics and private practice.

Licensing requirements vary among states, and not all states require licensing. Most states require a Master of Social Work degree from an accredited school, usually involving a minimum of two years of study and usually including field work. Certification by the Academy of Certified Social Workers may be obtained after two years of full-time supervised practice.

Psychiatric social workers focus on the relationship between the emotionally disturbed individual and the individual's community. The social worker employs community and family resources to help the individual. Like psychologists, a social worker may not prescribe medication or other medical treatment. In many geographical areas, social workers dominate the mental health field outnumbering psychiatrists two to one.

5. Psychiatric Nurse

All psychiatric nurses must be registered nurses. Most registered nurses are educated in hospital schools of nursing. Their educational requirements range from a high school diploma and three years of training in a general hospital, or nurse training in a two year program community colleges, to nursing programs in colleges and universities. Registered nurses are licensed by individual state boards of nursing. Additionally, every state requires education in an approved or accredited institution.

Although certification is not necessary, psychiatric nurses may become certified by the American Nurses Association. Certification requires the nurse to be licensed and meet a minimum requirement of direct psychiatric nursing experience. Most psychiatric nurses work with mental inpatients. The nurse uses knowledge of the patient's mental disorder to interact with the patient and chart the patient's behavior.

6. Other Mental Health Practitioners

In addition to the major professional groups in the mental health field, many other professionals work with the mentally ill. Occupational therapists plan and supervise activities that serve treatment objectives. Clergy provide counseling and guidance to emotionally disturbed individuals. Many clergy undergo specialized training that includes counseling and study of abnormal psychology. Specialized teachers are another professional group that deals mainly with mentally ill children. These teachers work in schools or in residential homes educating mentally ill or handicapped children. Occupational therapists, clergymen and teachers are usually not required to meet any specified state licensing requirements.

7. Limited Choices

While many different professionals work in the mental health field, in reality, the patient's choice among professionals is limited. State licensing laws may limit a patients' access to some professional groups. Further, health insurance companies impose limitations on coverage, providing reimbursement only for treatment administered or supervised by specified mental health practitioners. Such limitations often have the effect of channeling patients toward psychiatrists. Additionally, a patient's economic circumstances may limit choice. Lower income individuals cannot afford costly psychiatrists or psychologists, and usually rely on mental health social workers.

C. PERSPECTIVES ON DIAGNOSIS AND DIFFERING TREATMENT METHODOLOGIES

Licensing and professional norms do not usually control the mental health practitioner's choice of treatment. The principal restriction upon a mental health practitioners' choice of treatment is that only psychiatrists may prescribe medication and medical treatment.

Mental health practitioners differ in treatment methodology. The treatment methodology chosen is usually predicated on professional training. For example, a psychologist whose training was psychoanalytically oriented is likely to employ psychoanalytic treatment methods.

The mental health practitioner's perspective on mental health treatment influences the practitioner's definition and treatment of an illnesses. For example, a mental health professional who adheres to a medical model believes that diseases are characterized by clearly defined symptoms. This belief may have an influence on the professional's definition and treatment of a disorder. Treatment methodologies practiced today may include somatic (psychotropic drugs, electro-convulsive therapy) and/or nonsomatic (nonmedical) methods. Antipsychotic drugs are often prescribed for symptoms of active psychosis. These somatic drugs are used to treat mania, acute exacerbations of schizophrenia, schizo affective disorder, paranoia, atypical disorders such as rage reactions, severe agitated major depression, and sensory deprivation syndromes, and acute psychotic episodes associated with delirium or complex partial seizures. Electro-convulsive therapy (ECT) is often used to treat severely depressed, delusional, and suicidal patients. ECT involves an application of an electrical stimulus to produce a generalized seizure in order to alleviate the symptoms of severe depression. Other somatic treatment methodologies include behavior modification, psychosurgery, and nutrition regimens.

Below are summaries of the major nonsomatic treatment.

1. *Classical Psychoanalysis.* Psychoanalysis is usually directed at neuroses or psychiatric disorders. The goal of classical psychoanalysis is to help the individual achieve psychological changes

through emotional insight into the unconscious mind. Progress is achieved when the patient becomes conscious of previously repressed psychic functions and is able to resolve the developed neurosis. The traditional technique is free association. The patient lies on a couch in front of the psychoanalyst reporting anything that comes to the patient's mind. Often, this includes dreams. The sessions are frequent and regularly scheduled, typically for four hours per week. The psychiatrist usually remains passive during treatment, and speaks only when seeking clarifications or offering interpretations.

2. *Psychoanalytic Psychotherapy.* The goal of psychoanalytic therapy is to cause psychological change through insight into the unconscious. Similar to psychoanalysis, the techniques of free association, clarification, interpretation are used. In contrast to traditional psychoanalysts, psychoanalytic therapists take a more active role in therapy sessions, and therapy usually lasts one to two hours per week.

3. *Brief Psychotherapy.* The goal of brief psychotherapy is to bring about psychological changes through insight into the unconscious. This technique, however, differs from the previously discussed techniques in that: the hours are limited, the focus is only upon specific areas of the conflict, the patient is continuously confronted with the conflict, and the therapist is very active.

4. *Supportive Psychotherapy.* Supportive psychotherapy seeks to bring about psychological change through insight into the unconscious. However, in supportive psychotherapy, the focus is upon the therapist-patient relationship which is necessary to create a stable environment. One essential aspect of this therapy is limit setting. Limit setting is a technique aimed at preventing the patient either from indulging in destructive behavior or at avoiding regression. The therapist stands as a role model for the patient who is encouraged to internalize the therapist's image, attitudes, and strengths.

5. *Behavior Therapy.* Behavior therapy attempts to alter undesirable behavior and promoting desired behavior. Unlike psychotherapy, the focus is not on the psychic; rather, the focus is on the operationally defined behavioral problems. Behavior problems include behavioral excess, behavior deficits and behavioral inappropriateness. To effect positive change, the therapist use several techniques: (1) relaxation, where the therapist instructs the patient on muscle relaxation techniques to reduce anxiety, (2) flooding, where the patient, through intense exposure to anxiety provoking stimuli, learns adverse consequences do not result from the stimuli, (3) implosion therapy, where the patient, usually suffering from an obsessive-compulsive disorder, is exposed to the anxiety provoking stimuli, but prevented from acting out the usual response, (4) behavioral rehearsal, where the patient and therapist act out

social encounters in an attempt to replace the patient's inappropriate behavior with appropriate behavior, (5) modeling, where the patient learns appropriate behaviors and responses through observing and imitating behavior, (6) aversion therapy, where the inappropriate behavior is paired with an unpleasant event in order to eliminate undesirable behavior, (7) and behavior control, where the patient is taught to control behavior through self-monitoring, self-evaluation and self-reinforcement.

6. *Sex Therapy.* Sex therapists specialize in the treatment of sexual dysfunction. One form of treatment, usually lasting two weeks, requires daily sessions between a couple and male and female cotherapists. Other therapists may accept single patients and use sex surrogates when a partner is needed. Therapy is usually limited to one hour per week over three to six months. Medication may also be used as part of the therapy.

D. EFFICACY OF DIAGNOSIS AND TREATMENT

Diagnosis of mental disorders lacks the precision found in other fields of medicine. In an attempt to classify disorders, the American Psychiatric Association publishes the Diagnostic and Statistical Manual of Mental Disorders–Fourth Edition (DSM–IV). However, scientific names of disorders change and individuals do not always neatly fit into the DSM–

IV definition of a disorder. Moreover, nomenclature often changes. The problem of lack of precision lies not with the DSM–IV, but rather is a result of the inherent ambiguities of psychiatry. Unlike other medical fields, psychiatry focuses upon multifactorial behavior, not definitive symptoms of diseases.

1.   Efficacy Issue

The efficacy of psychotherapy has been criticized for not being scientifically sound. Other researchers are optimistic about the efficacy of psychotherapy. Many researchers believe psychotherapy is effective for certain disorders and ineffective for others. For example, researchers found group psychotherapy has little or no effect on schizophrenics or substance addicted persons.

2.   Controlled Studies

Today, in general, psychotherapy is found to be effective for some symptoms and behavior problems. Recent research has revealed that some combined treatments work better for certain disorders. For example, studies on the treatment of schizophrenia demonstrate that traditional psychotherapies enhance the benefits of drug therapy.

In one controlled study, the National Institute of Mental Health researched the efficacy of psychotherapy on depression; the researchers found weekly sessions with psychologists or psychiatrists had a positive effect on depression. Researchers also found patients receiving eighteen psychotherapy sessions were psychologically more stable twenty months later than patients who did not receive any psycho-therapy. Furthermore, patients who received anti-depressant drug therapy in addition to psychothera-py showed the most improvement.

3. Capacity To Predict

Difficulty with precision in the diagnosing mental disorders is compounded by the problem of predic-tion. Several empirical studies have seriously chal-lenged the ability of mental health professionals to make valid predictions. Yet, prediction remains im-portant under civil commitment laws and in rela-tion to a therapist's obligation to warn third parties when patients may poses a threat to them.

E. ADMINISTRATIVE REGULATION AND REMEDIATION

1. Regulation of Entry

Professional entry into the field of mental health is regulated in two ways—through licensing and through certification. State licensing authorizes mental health professionals to engage in activities that would otherwise be illegal. State licensing re-quirements limit the practice of mental health to persons who meet the designated qualifications. In addition, state licensure may be a prerequisite for individuals seeking reimbursement for mental health care under private health insurance plans or governmental programs. Certification by profession-al associations limits the use of certain titles to those who meet education, examination, and experi-ence requirements.

Psychiatry is regulated by licensing in all states since psychiatrists must hold a medical license. Additionally, psychiatry may be regulated by certification. Many hospitals require physicians to complete a residency and be members of the American Psychiatric Association.

The majority of state's require a license to practice psychology. California's licensing requirement is typical of state requirements. In California, anyone who is not a licensed psychologist may not render psychological services for a fee. Psychological service are defined to include the use of psychological principles, methods, procedures, and predicting and influencing behavior.

In other states, psychology is regulated by a certification requirement. A typical certification law provides an individual may not hold himself out as a psychologist or render psychological services without both meeting specified education and training requirements and passing a psychology certification exam.

In addition to state certification and licensing laws, states have administrative bodies that establish and enforce rules of conduct. Disciplinary any sanctions are imposed upon a professional who breaches rules of conduct. The administrative bodies are usually composed of members of the mental health professions. The most common rationale for regulation is to protect the consumer from persons who are incompetent, dishonest, financially irresponsible, unsafe, or unsanitary. Some assert that the consumer protection rationale is lacking because governmental intervention to protect consumers since the market performs this function. However, defenders of regulation assert that market failure is likely where prospective patients lack ability to make educated choices because of limited knowledge about mental health treatment alternatives and individual practitioners.

A minority of mental health practitioners contend licensing is against the public interest, because licensure only creates and protects professional monopolies. In addition, licensing has been questioned, because psychotherapy is not easily defined. The licensing requirement may encroach upon educational services. Also, education and examination scores do not adequately measure the professional's therapeutic effectiveness. Furthermore, discipline is rarely evoked against professionals who breach their duties. When sanctions are imposed, the more severe penalties are enforced upon the more publicized breaches, suggesting a concern for image rather than professionalism. Finally, licensing increases health care costs to the patients.

When licensing legislation is enacted, the statutes and regulations often include "grandfather clauses" giving individuals who had private practices prior to the statute automatic rights to a license. However, restrictive grandfather clauses creating requirements beyond the qualifications of long time practitioners have been found unconstitutional.

In addition to state regulations, all major mental health professions have an association or organization with an internal regulatory system that oversees the ethical standards of the profession. For example, psychiatrists must meet the ethical standards of the American Psychiatric Association. Similarly, psychologists must meet the standards of the American Psychological Association's Ethical Principles of Psychologists. Social workers have to abide by the Code of Ethics of the National Association of Social Workers. These organizations have authority to investigate allegations of misconduct and malpractice. If the mental health practitioner is guilty of misconduct, the association may an suspend or withdraw the individual's membership.

2. Discipline and Sanctions

Almost all state legislatures empower administrative agencies to investigate complaints regarding a mental health professionals' misconduct and impose sanctions. Permissible sanctions include license suspension, revocation and fines.

An accused professional is entitled to a disciplinary hearing that conforms to basic notions of fairness and due process. The hearing is usually held before a committee or a hearing officer of the responsible agency, and the accused is given an opportunity to testify, present evidence in the accused's favor and challenge opposing evidence. Even though such hearings are often informal, the professional has a right to prior notice and to be present at the hearing. The right to counsel is sometimes permitted, but is not constitutionally required. For adverse agency decisions, an accused professional may obtain judicial review. However, the scope of review is usually limited to determining whether the professional received a fair hearing, and whether the agency's decision was based upon competent evidence. Three types of misconduct lead to sanctions such as the suspension or removal of license: breach of patient confidentiality, sexual misconduct, and illegal use or distribution of controlled substances.

3. Confidentiality

One area where sanctions are often imposed against a mental health practitioner involves a breach of patient confidentiality. In *Mississippi State Board of Psychological Examiners v. Hosford* (Miss.1987), the Supreme Court of Mississippi upheld the authority of a state-created board to impose disciplinary sanctions upon psychologists who breach patient confidentiality. A psychologist, who had treated a husband and wife during marital problems, testified against the wife in a temporary child custody hearing. The wife, however, did not give consent to the disclosure of the confidential information. The court held that the state board was permitted to suspend the psychologist's license for ninety days based on breach of confidentiality.

4. Sexual Misconduct

Another area of frequent disciplinary action is professional sexual misconduct. Sexual relations between professional and patient is viewed as unprofessional, potentially damaging to the patient, and a breach of professional ethics. Recent reports indicate many mental health professionals have become sexually involved with their patients. Efforts are being made to discourage sexual misconduct among mental health professionals. Several states impose sanctions such as license suspension for sexual misconduct. Most state licensing agencies have the authority to remove a professional's license for sexual misconduct with patient. Furthermore, civil courts have imposed liability on mental health practitioners for sexual misconduct.

5. Controlled Substances

A third area of disciplinary action is the illegal use or distribution of controlled substances by health care professionals. States may revoke a professional's license for violating controlled substances laws.

F. ALLOCATION AMONG MENTAL HEALTH PROFESSIONALS

Ongoing conflict exists between psychiatrists and other mental health professionals over the proper scope of professional practice. This is particularly evident in the area of insurance reimbursement. In 1954, psychiatrists failed in an attempt to restrict the practice of psychotherapy to include only psychiatrists. By 1977, psychologists were required in every state to be licensed to practice psychotherapy.

More recently, organizations representing psychiatrists have opposed "freedom-of-choice" laws that would permit direct insurance reimbursement to other mental health professionals. These laws limit private insurance companies' ability to restrict reimbursement for psychotherapy to treatment billed through physicians. Forty states have "freedom-of-choice" laws that require insurance companies to reimburse psychologists for treatment if the patient prefers to be treated by a psychologist. However, only California requires insurance companies to reimburse family and marriage counselors for therapy.

Psychologists in Virginia successfully brought suit attacking a restriction imposed by insurance companies that limited coverage and reimbursement for psychotherapy for services billed through a physician. In *Virginia Academy of Clinical Psychologists v. Blue Shield of Virginia* (4th Cir.1980), the United States Court of Appeals for the Fourth Circuit held that a rule requiring billing through a physician was a restraint of trade.

A successful challenge was made against physician control of diagnosis and treatment of hospitalized mental patients in *California Association of Psychology Providers v. Rank* (Cal.1988). The California Court of Appeals found invalid a state regulation prohibiting hospitals from permitting a psychologist to carry primary responsibility for diagnosis and treatment of patients. However, the appeals court noted that ultimately disputes about the competence of the treating professions must be decided by the state legislature.

G. MANAGED CARE AND HEALTH MAINTENANCE ORGANIZATIONS

Mental health services have increasingly come within the subject matter of managed care agreements. The objective of managed care is to provide clients with necessary services at a competitive price. The managed care organization selects quality health care professionals, including mental health workers, as service providers of health care and treatment. Managed care attempts to achieve lower price through volume purchasing and by minimizing unnecessary and inappropriate treatment. The result is that patients under managed care may be provided a given mix of mental health services. At the same time these patients are subject to limitations as to the particular health care providers from whom the patient may seek care, as well as restrictions on the types of services to which they have access. Patients may be limited to the number of treatment contacts and with mental health professional, and limited to the length of mental health treatment. Health Maintenance Organizations (HMO) are systems of health care providers that offer a defined, comprehensive set of services, including mental health services, to a defined population for a fixed, periodic per-person or per-family fee. Mental health care professionals may serve on the staff of an HMO, or be organized as a speciality group into a separate legal entity.

CHAPTER 2

MENTAL DISORDERS

A. THE CONCEPT OF
MENTAL ILLNESS

Laws relating to mental disability often have an uncertainty quality, because the concept of mental disability, itself, is ambiguous. There is no consensus definition of mental illness. Some disorders, such as those manifest at birth or early infancy with related physical manifestations, or with conspicuous and persistent symptoms may have a specific definition. However, many mental disorders with symptoms that develop later in life are episodic, personal, or situational. Therefore, they are diagnosed less accurately.

Four models are helpful in defining "mental illness." The medical model posits that a person's mental state is a result of organic or chemical conditions within the body. A second model, the psychological model, suggests one's personality is largely developed by patterns established during youth through interactions with one's family or those taking parenting roles. A third model, the behavioral model, treats behavior and any thoughts which may accompany it as the result of aversive or reinforcing events, rather than underlying pathology. The last model, the social model, focuses on external determinants, such as relationships with family, peers, and institutions, as the primary influences of an individual's mental condition.

Each of these views of mental disorder influences the mental health practitioner's approach to suggested proper treatment. The medical model, that views mental illness as the product of brain disorder or chemical imbalance will treat primarily with medication or surgery. The psychological model views mental illness as the product of childhood stresses; therefore, the treatment of choice is psychotherapy. Behaviorists view maladaptive behavior as a learned response to past events; treatment consists of conditioning the person against such behavior and reinforcing acceptable behavior. The social model regards mental illness as a result of social disorder—such as the death of a loved one, loss of a job, geographic displacement or poor relationships, and suggests it is best treated by adaptations in the person's social system.

A general legal definition of "mental illness" is found in the opinion of the Illinois Supreme Court in *People v. Lang* (Ill.1986): "that a mentally ill person is an individual with an organic, mental or emotional disorder which substantially impairs the person's thought, perception or reality, emotional process, judgment, behavior, or ability to cope with the ordinary demands of life."

The law seemingly prefers the medical model of mental disorders. This preference is partly a result of the deference of legal authorities to medical physicians and medical science. It is also a reflection of the view of legal authorities toward their capacity to authorize interventions which will help alleviate mental disorders. The other models primarily focus on external factors as causing an individual's behavior. Understanding these external causes is often beyond the capacity of existing legal institutions.

The United States Supreme Court has indicated, on several occasions, that the law may treat those labeled mentally disordered differently from those who are not so labeled. The Court has explicitly upheld commitment statutes (*Addington v. Texas* (S.Ct.1979); *Jones v. United States* (S.Ct.1983)). The Court has also recognized that mental illness can form the predicate for finding incompetency to stand trial (*Drope v. Missouri* (S.Ct.1975)). Moreover, the Court has implicitly endorsed the insanity defense (*Leland v. Oregon* (S.Ct.1952); *Ake v. Oklahoma* (S.Ct.1985)). Moreover, in *City of Cleburne v. Cleburne Living Center* (S.Ct.1985) the Court held that the mentally retarded (and, by implication, the mentally ill) may not claim the protection of equal protection to force high level judicial scrutiny of laws and programs which provide differential treatment to the mentally retarded. These rulings illustrate the Court's unwillingness to invalidate laws that treat the mentally disordered differently from other citizens, and imply the Court's acknowledgment of the existence of mental illness.

Many mental health professionals develop an eclectic approach toward identification and treatment of mental problems. Few clinicians are devoted exclusively to one model of mental illness. Most mental health professionals acknowledge the concept of mental abnormality. Both professionals and lay persons who have had contact with the "mentally ill", or with individuals who have experienced mental deterioration, appreciate the reality of psychopathology and mental disorder. This appreciation, however, does not imply a consensus on what mental illness "is" or what role psychiatry and law should take in dealing with the mentally ill. Nonetheless, this appreciation is a basis for formulating and refining strategies aimed at serving the mentally ill and preventing them from being subject to neglect or harm.

B. MODERN CONCEPTIONS OF MENTAL DISORDER: THE DIAGNOSTIC MANUAL

The best recognized effort to categorize human behavior for clinical purposes is the American Psychiatric Associations Diagnostic and Statistical Manual (DSM–IV). The Manual is now in its fourth edition. DSM–IV establishes concise criteria for each diagnosis and includes specific instructions with respect to differential diagnosis.

For legal practitioners the DSM–IV is an important resource, even though the DSM–IV states that: "in most situations, the clinical diagnosis of a DSM–IV mental disorder is not sufficient to establish the existence for legal purposes of a 'mental disorder,' 'mental disability,' 'mental disease or defect.' In determining whether an individual meets a specific legal standard (*e.g.*, for competence, criminal responsibility, or disability), additional information is usually required beyond that contained in the DSM–IV diagnosis. This might include information about the individual's functional impairments and how these impairments affect the particular abilities in question. Despite this type of warning in earlier editions of the DSM, the legal community has adopted the Manual's nomenclature for various legal purposes."

The DSM–IV does not specify precise boundaries for the concept of "mental disorder." It should be stressed that there is no assumption that each mental disorder is a discrete entity with sharp boundaries between it and other mental disorders, or between it and no disorder. Nevertheless, the DSM–IV Manual provides a useful presentation of a definition of "mental disorder" that includes certain conditions as mental disorders and excludes others.

Each mental disorder is conceptualized as a clinically significant behavioral or psychological syndrome or pattern occurring in a person. Each disorder is associated with current distress such as a painful symptom disability such as impairment in one or more important areas of functioning, or with a significantly increased risk of suffering death, pain, disability, or an important loss of freedom. Under DSM–IV behavior must currently be considered a manifestation of a behavioral, psychological, or biological dysfunction in the person. Therefore, deviant behavior, whether it is politically, religiously or sexually based is not classified as a mental disorder unless the deviance or conflict is a symptom of a dysfunction in the person.

Classification of mental disorders do not classify people. The DSM–IV attempts to classify disorders that people have. It is important to note is that all individuals described as having the same mental disorder are not necessarily alike. Although all the persons described as having the same mental disorder have at least the defining features of the disorder. However, they may each differ in other important respects that may affect clinical management and outcome, and may have relevance to any legal determination that is based in part on the existence of a mental disorder.

For some mental disorders, the etiology (cause or origin of disease) or pathophysiology (the study of functional disorders resulting from disease) is known. For example within one major classification, "Organic Mental Disorders," specific bodily physical factors have been identified or are presumed. Yet, for most of the disorders, the etiology is unknown. Theories and evidence are advanced attempting to explain how disorders develop; however, these explanations are not always convincing. Therefore, the approach taken by the DSM–IV is atheoretical; the Manual only describes disorders.

The major justification for the atheoretical etiological approach taken in DSM–IV with regard to the causes of disorders is that all clinicians vary in their acceptance of differing theories. It would not be possible to present all the reasonable etiologic theories for each disorder.

Definitions in the Manual of disorders are generally limited to descriptions of their clinical features. The DSM–IV systematically describes each disorder under the following headings: "Diagnostic Features"; "Subtypes and/or Specifiers"; "Recording Procedures"; "Associated Features and Disorders"; "Specific Culture, Age and Gender Features"; "Prevalence"; "Course"; "Familial Pattern"; and "Differential Diagnosis." Characteristic features of each description consist of easily identifiable behavioral signs or symptoms which provide a basis for immediate diagnosis of a disorder. Some disorders, particularly personality disorders, require more inferential conclusions on the part of the observer.

1. Diagnostic Reliability

A diagnostic category's usefulness is determined by its reliability. Reliability is a statistical measure of agreement. A diagnostic category is reliable to the extent clinicians can agree with one another on the identification of the disorder; this includes agreement on when the disorder is present and when it is not.

There are other methods for testing reliability. The simplest, but least reliable, is to ask two clinicians to independently diagnose a series of cases based on written case records, or audiotapes or videotapes of diagnostic interviews, with the subjects. Another, more reliable method is to have two clinicians interview the subject "live" either jointly or independently.

Comparative analysis of the clinicians observation on the same patient is revealing. For example, one clinician may notice psychomotor agitation, while the other may not. Interpretation variance occurs when clinicians differ in their interpretations of the signs and symptoms of the observed patient. Observation variance is minimized with training; interpretation variance is minimized when clinicians use the same definitions of psychopathological symptoms.

Another source of variance affecting diagnostic reliability is criterion variance. Criterion variance results when clinicians use different rules to form diagnoses from their observations. Criterion variance is minimized when clinicians use the same diagnostic criteria.

The reliability of a diagnostic category (for example, the relative agreement on the diagnosis of schizophrenia), a diagnostic class (for example, the relative agreement on a diagnosis of any mood disorder,) or an entire classification of disorders is calculable. One way of calculating agreement is to determine the percentage of cases that agree out of the sample. However, matching clinicians diagnoses may result in chance agreements, thus indicating a higher than actual agreement on a specific diagnosis.

2. Diagnostic Validity

A diagnosis is valid only if it serves the purpose for which it was intended. Four major types of validity are applied to psychiatric diagnoses: face, descriptive, predictive, and construct validity.

A diagnosis is facially valid if the definition of the disorder is descriptive of a particular clinical disorder and provides for professional communicating.

A diagnosis has descriptive validity if the extent to which the defining features of a diagnostic category are unique to that category. A diagnosis has high predictive validity if it is useful for predicting the natural history and treatment response of a person with the disorder.

Finally, constructural validity of a diagnosis involves the understanding of the causal or functional processes of the disorder. Where genetic, biological, social, or environmental factors are known to contribute or cause a disorder, constructural validity is present. Construct validity is the highest form of validity, and the form for which there is the least evidence for most mental disorders.

3. Procedural Validity

Procedural validity is the standard procedure, assumedly valid, by which a particular test or procedure is evaluated. There are three indices on which a new test or procedure can be measured: sensitivity, specificity, and predictive power. The sensitivity of a diagnostic procedure is the percentage of "true" cases it correctly identifies as having the diagnosis (the true-positive rate). The specificity is the percentage of non-cases that it correctly identifies as not having the diagnosis (the true-negative rate). Finally, the predictive power of a test or procedure is the percentage of total cases in which the test or procedure agrees with the standard (the total number of cases that both tests or procedures agree have the diagnosis plus the total number of cases that both tests agree do not have the diagnosis; the sum is divided by the total number of cases). The predictive power of a test can be broken down into positive predictive power and negative predictive power.

C. CLASSIFICATIONS AND DEFINITIONS OF DISORDERS

1. Disorders Usually First Evident in Infancy, Childhood, or Adolescence

Some disorders may be classified as first evident in infancy, childhood, or adolescence; however, there is no arbitrary age limit defining childhood and adolescence. Adults may be given a diagnosis using the above classification if, as infants, children, or adolescents, they had symptoms of any of particular disorders that persisted.

Essential features of pre-adulthood disorders include difficulty acquiring cognitive, language, motor or social skills. A disturbance may involve a general delay in all mental functions, such as mental retardation; or it may be a delay or failure to progress in

specific or multiple areas. In mild cases of disturbance, recovery may occur in childhood or adulthood. However, remission is rare in adulthood.

2. Organic Mental Syndromes and Disorders

Organic mental syndrome are a group of psychological or behavioral signs and symptoms without
reference to etiology. Organic mental disorders des-
ignate particular organic mental syndromes for
which causes are known or presumed. An organic
mental disorder is associated with a physical disorder or condition. For example, Organic Delusional
Disorder is an organic mental disorder which is
associated with a brain tumor.

The essential feature of all organic disorders is a
psychological or behavioral abnormality associated
with transient or permanent dysfunction of the
brain. To diagnose a person as suffering from an
organic mental disorder, there must be an organic
mental syndrome and a specific organic factor such
as a tumor or brain lesion relating to the abnormal
mental state. An organic factor may be a primary
brain disease or a systemic illness that affects the
brain secondarily. Psychoactive toxic substances
that disturb the brain, or leave long lasting impairment, may also be categorized as a factor producing
organic brain disorder.

It should be noted that there is a wide range of
emotional, motivational, and behavioral abnormalities associated with organic mental disorders (anxiety, depression, irritability, shame, avoidance, ob-
session, irritability, decreased or increased physical

and sexual aggression, etc.). It is difficult to distinguish which abnormalities are a direct result of damage to the brain, reactions to cognitive deficits, or psychologic change due to organic factors.

3. Psychoactive Substance Use Disorders

The psychoactive substance use disorder is a diagnostic class dealing with symptoms and maladaptive behavioral changes associated with regular, long-term use of psychoactive substance affecting the central nervous system. The condition is called a mental disorder and is distinguishable from nonpathological psychoactive substance use (such as moderate use of alcohol and certain drugs for medical purposes). These disorders must also be distinguished from Psychoactive Substance–Induced Organic Mental Disorders. Psychoactive substance-induced organic mental disorders describe direct acute or chronic effect of such substances on the central nervous system. Psychoactive substance use disorders refer to maladaptive behavior associated with regular use of substances.

4. Schizophrenia

Schizophrenia is a mental disorder in which delusions, hallucinations, or certain characteristic disturbances affect the form or content of thought. Delusions or hallucinations are major disturbances in perception. These disturbances may be auditory, visual, or tactile, where a physical sensation such as an electrical or burning feeling occurs. A thought disturbance is commonly observed where a "loosening of associations" occurs. This disorganized thinking involves the shifting from one subject to another, completely unrelated or only tangentially related. Content of thought disturbance involves delusions that are often multiple, fragmented, or bizarre. For example, the delusion that one's actions are controlled by a dead person may become a dominating belief.

Essential features of schizophrenia include the presence of characteristic psychotic symptoms during the active phases of the illness, and functioning below the highest level previously achieved (in work, social relations, or self-care). Psychiatrists probably know more about and can more accurately diagnose schizophrenia than any other mental illness.

Schizophrenia is also seen with "affect" and "volitional" disturbances. A person with an affect disturbance may complain of being tortured, yet give the account while laughing or smiling. Individuals with a volitional disturbance lacks self-initiation or goal orientation which grossly impairs their work or role function.

Difficulty in interpersonal relationships is almost invariably present with schizophrenia. The schizophrenic often manifests behavior that involves social withdrawal and inappropriate emotional detachment. The schizophrenic is often so preoccupied with fantastical ideas that their functioning in reality is severely impaired.

Lastly, the schizophrenic, often experiences psychomotor behavior impairment. This impairment involves an inappropriate decrease in reaction to the environment or reduction in spontaneous movements or activity. In an extreme catatonic stupor, individuals are almost completely unaware of their surroundings and maintain a rigid posture and resisting efforts to be moved.

5. Delusional Paranoid Disorder

The essential feature of delusional paranoid disorders is a persistent delusion, which on the surface may seem to be a conventional belief, but that is without any basis, that is not the result of any other mental disorder. The disorder is defined and narrowly in the requirement of duration—at least one month in broad terms of delusional themes. The following delusional themes are recognized: erotomania (delusion one is loved by another), grandiose (person is convinced that he or she possesses some great, but unrecognized, talent or insight), jealous (usually a delusion that his or her spouse is unfaithful), persecutory (the most common delusion involving an individual's belief that he or she is being conspired against, cheated, poisoned, or harassed), and somatic (delusion that one smells, is infected with parasites, or is ugly).

6. Psychotic Disorders Not Elsewhere Classified

An important group of disorders that do not meet the diagnostic criteria for schizophrenia, delusional disorder, or mood disorders are as psychotic disorders not elsewhere classified. The essential feature of these disorders is a sudden onset of psychotic symptoms lasting a few hours, but no more than one month. The occurrence usually takes place after one or more markedly distressful events, causing such reactions as outlandish dress, screaming, or muteness. Suicidal or aggressive behavior may also be present. Speech may be inarticulate, unintelligible, or repetitious; and transient hallucinations or delusions are also common. Disorientation and impairment in recent memory often occur.

7. Mood Disorders

The essential feature of mood disorders is a disturbance in mood, accompanied by manic or depressive syndromes not caused by any other physical or mental disorder. A "mood" is a prolonged emotion that colors the entire psychic life involving either depression or elation. Mood disorders should be distinguished from mood episodes, and syndromes. Mood syndrome is a group of moods and associated symptoms occurring together for a short period of time. Mood episode is a mood syndrome that is not due to a known organic factor. A mood disorder is determined by a pattern of mood episodes.

Associated features of mood disorders usually include elation or depression. Classification of an individual having a mood disorder occurs when the disturbance is so severe as to impair occupational functioning, social activities, or relationships. Mood disorders may even require hospitalization to prevent harm to self or others.

8. Anxiety Disorders

Essential features of anxiety disorders include symptoms of anxiety and avoidance behavior. These disturbances of anxiety and avoidance occur when an individual confronts a "dreaded object or situation" or attempts to resist obsessions or compulsions. Associated with these symptoms are panic attacks that are discrete periods of fear or discomfort that can last minutes or hours. Recent studies indicate that anxiety disorders are among the conditions most frequently found in the general population.

9. Somatoform Disorders

Somatoform disorders involve physical symptoms without organic factors to account for the disturbance. However, with somatoform disorders there is likely to be positive evidence, or a strong presumption, of a link between symptoms and psychological factors or conflicts. Associated features include excessive concern with some imagined or exaggerated defect in appearance, a loss or alteration in physical function, fear of having a serious disease or the belief that another has a serious disease, and/or a chronic preoccupation with pain.

10. Dissociative Disorders

Essential feature of disassociative disorders is a disturbance or alteration in the functions of identity, memory, or consciousness. Disturbances are sudden or gradual and are either transient or chronic. When the identity function is disturbed individuals may forget who they are and assume a new identity. They may also lose touch with reality and replace it with feelings of unreality. When disturbance occurs, primarily in the memory, important personal events cannot be recalled.

The classic "Multiple Personality Disorder" falls within this group. The essential feature of multiple personality disorder is the existence of two or more distinct personalities or personality states within a person. Personality is defined as a relatively enduring pattern of perceiving, relating to, and thinking about the environment and one's self that is exhibited in a wide range of social and personal contexts.

11. Sexual Disorders

The essential feature of sexual disorder is an arousal response to sexual objects that are not part of normal arousal-activity patterns. Further, the individual believes that such objects reciprocate affection and are engaged in sexual activity with the person. "Sexual dysfunction" exists with this disorder so that there often is an inhibition in sexual desire or a psychologic change in the individual's sexual responses.

12. Sleep Disorders

Sleep disorders are chronic (of more than one month's duration) and are not transient disturbances of sleep that are a normal part of life. Sleep disturbances are common to many mental and physical disorders. Such disturbance can exacerbate, or even initiate mental or physical disorders. When sleep is the main complaint, even if associated with a mental or a physical disorder, the individual's condition is classified as "sleep disorder." Sleep disorders are divided into two subgroups: those where the predominant disturbance is in the amount, quality or timing of sleep, and those where the predominant disturbance is an abnormal event occurring during sleep.

Essential features of sleep disorders include a possible contrariness in a person's sleep schedule where the individual feels sleepy while awake, and cannot sleep when at rest. In insomnia disorders, the individual is unable either to initiate or maintain sleep. With dyssomnia, the individual's function in performing everyday functions is impaired due to the deficient quality or quantity of sleep.

13. Factitious Disorders

"Factitious" means not real, genuine, or natural. Factitious disorders are characterized by physical or psychological symptoms that are intentionally produced or feigned. Since a report of a symptom is a statement of subjective feelings, intentional production of a symptom can only be inferred by an outside observer.

Most persons with factitious disorders act in ways so as not to be discovered. These individual voluntarily act out the timing and degree of their symptoms. However, the goals of persons with factitious disorders are usually involuntarily adopted and difficult to ascertain. Factitious disorders are different from malingering where a person intentionally produces symptoms, but the goals are easily ascertainable. Malingering occurs, for example, when an individual feign illness to avoid jury duty or to establish a workman's compensation claim.

14. Impulsive Control Disorders Not Otherwise Classified

The essential features of impulse control disorders are: failure to resist an impulse, drive, or temptation to perform some act that is harmful to the self or others. The act may or may not be premeditated or planned, and there may or may not be a conscious resistance to act on the impulse to act. There is usually an increasing sense of tension or arousal before committing the act. When the acts are committed, there is an experience of either pleasure, gratification, or release. Upon completion of the act, there may or may not be a genuine regret, self reproach, or guilt.

15. Adjustment Disorder

The essential feature of adjustment disorder is a maladaptive reaction to stress. The maladaptive reaction is usually impairment in occupational functioning, social activities or relationships. Stress factors may be singular, such as divorce; or they may be multiple, such as marked business difficulties and marital problems. Individuals who are sensitive to stress may have severe reactions to mild or moderate stress, while others have only mild reactions to marked or continuing stress.

16. Psychological Factors Affecting Physical Condition

Psychological factors refer to the meaning a person ascribes to environmental stimuli. Examples of environmental stimuli are involvement in a caustic argument, or receipt of news that a loved one is dead. Evidence that psychological factors effect physical condition requires a temporal relationship between the environmental stimuli and the exacerbation, or onset, of the physical condition. Common examples of physical conditions caused by psychological factors are: obesity, tension headaches, migraine headache, painful menstruation, acne, asthma, and gastric ulcers.

17. Personality Disorders

Personality "traits" are traits that affect an individual's outlook on life and others. Personality traits constitute personality disorders when they are inflexible and maladaptive, causing significant functional impairment or subjective distress. A personality disorder diagnosis requires a finding of long-term impairment with occupational or social functioning.

Typical features of this disorder are: odd or eccentric character, antisocial, dramatic, emotional, avoidance, obsessive, dependant and compulsive behaviors, or anxiety and fearfulness.

D. DSM–IV: DEFINITION OF "MENTAL DISORDER"

The DSM–IV defines mental disorder as a clinically significant behavioral or psychological syndrome or pattern that occurs in a person and that is associated with present distress (a painful symptom) or disability (impairment in one or more important areas of functioning). A disorder may also place an individual at a significantly increased risk of suffering death, pain, disability, or an important loss of freedom. For a syndrome or pattern to qualify as a mental disorder, it must not be more than expected response to a particular event such as the grief over the death of a loved one. Instead a mental disorder must be a manifestation of a behavioral, psychological, or biological dysfunction in the person. Neither deviant behavior, whether related to political, religious, or sexual concerns, nor societal or individual conflicts, are mental disorders unless the deviance or conflict is a symptom of a dysfunction in the person.

E. MENTAL ILLNESS AS MYTH

Many mental health professionals view mental illnesses (chiefly schizophrenia, manic-depression, and depression) as diseases of the brain. A series of scientific breakthroughs beginning in the early 1970s provided strong support for these views. The development of major tranquilizers in the early 1950s and their ability to transform the life of the mentally ill is also a strong indication that certain

mental illness are diseases of the brain. Nevertheless, the early 1960s brought considerable controversy generating the suggestion that mental illness
is a "myth." This argument was originally advanced by Ronald D. Laing and Thomas Szasz,
psychiatrists with a psychoanalytic approach to
treatment. The theory that mental illness is a myth
has been called "anti-psychiatry."

R.D. Laing's first book, *The Divided Self,* marked
a departure from the way many psychiatrists had
explained the source of the individuals mental illness, that is by looking at family dynamics. Laing
treated what would otherwise be regarded as psychotic behavior as intelligible, as a "rational strategy" in the face of a terrifying family environment.
Laing promoted a theory that schizophrenia is not
only a survival strategy in face of an unlivable
situation, but is also a life-enhancing experience.
Laing concluded that madness need not be seen
simply as a breakdown, it could also be seen as a
breakthrough, that it is potentially liberating instead of involving "enslavement and existential
death." According to Laing, it is the ostensibly
"normal man" who suffers from the condition of
alienation of "being unconscious, or of being out of
one's mind."

Another psychiatrist associated with the anti-psychiatry movement is Thomas Szasz. Szasz wrote
extensively, perhaps his most noteworthy mono-
graph is *The Myth of Mental Illness.* Szasz argued
for man's freedom to act and for recognition of his
responsibility for what he does. Szasz strongly ar-

gued the importance of individual autonomy, and argued against the reality of mental illness. According to Szasz, individuals diagnosed with mental illness are in fact being denied the freedom to make choices of action and to develop a sense of self without assistance. Szasz disposed of mental illness by a conceptual sleight of hand. Szasz wrote: "mental illnesses do not exist; indeed they cannot exist, because the mind is not a bodily part or bodily organ."

For a disease of the brain to exist, Szasz maintained that lesions of the brain must exist; but, to the contrary, pathologists have not found lesions in most cases where mental illness is said to occur. If lesions were found, according to Szasz, such diseases and behaviors would no longer be considered "mental" illnesses. Instead the disease or behavior would become a condition for treatment by neurologists rather than psychiatrists.

Szasz's arguments are aimed primarily at the medical model of mental disorder. Szasz argued that mental illness, unlike physical illness, has no bodily referent. This explains why mental retardation, which is commonly believed to be genetically transmitted, is exempted from attack by Szasz.

The thrust of Laing and Szasz's work is that mental illness is used as a means of stigmatizing and controlling deviant or different behavior. Szasz argued that psychiatry is "slavery disguised as therapy." Comparing witchcraft and psychiatry Szasz wrote, "the belief in witchcraft and the persecution of witches is similar to the belief in mental illness and the treatment of the supposed mental ill."

Critics of "anti-psychiatrists" claim that its proponents deny needed treatment to those incapable of making rational choices. Critics maintain that it is inconsistent to proclaim a belief in human freedom and responsibility and at the same time deny treatment which will release individuals from the grip of debilitating mental disorder. The anti-psychiatry movement has been characterized as an approach that recognizes a freedom "to be crazy" and a movement that is in part responsible for the mentally ill homeless population.

CHAPTER 3

CLINICAL PSYCHIATRIC EVIDENCE

A. INTRODUCTION

The legal system accepts the existence of mental illness and its association with legally relevant behavior. The relation of mental illness to behavior becomes legally significant when a court or jury must decide issues such as insanity, dangerousness or competence. An individual's mental condition must be evaluated when the question of capacity or competence is raised. However, the legal system is not always clear on how to identify mental illness, or in determining mental condition. In the past, the testimony of lay persons generally determined whom the court or jury would adjudicate mentally ill. Today, the determination of mental illness or condition increasingly involves the testimony of mental health experts.

The acceptance of mental health expert testimony is not without criticism. Some critics believe the opinions of mental health professional lack reliability. Other critics argue that expert mental health testimony should not be accepted in certain areas of litigation, because it is prejudicial, unreliable and often is presented in direct contradictory form by the two sides involved in litigation.

One major set of issues of mental health expert testimony involves the proper scope of the expert's testimony. What is the mental health expert's role? When should a mental health expert testify? When should such testimony be rejected?

A second set of issues deal with the formalities of testimony. Who is an expert? What is the proper basis for the expert's testimony? May an expert testify on an ultimate legal issue?

B. ADMISSIBILITY OF CLINICAL OPINION TESTIMONY

In proceedings involving deprivations of liberty, such as civil commitment, clinical opinion testimony is often offered. Under court rules evidence may typically be admitted only if it is logically and legally relevant to the issues in a case. Evidence is logically relevant if the evidence has any tendency to make the existence of any fact of consequence more or less probable than it would be without the evidence. Evidence is legally relevant if the probative value of the evidence is not substantially outweighed by its prejudicial effects. If the likely prejudicial effect of hearing the evidence substantially outweighs its probative value, the evidence is inadmissible.

Evidence is further restricted by whether the evidence is offered by lay or expert witness. A lay witnesses may testify to facts which the witness observed of which the witness or has personal knowledge. The lay witness may only testify in the form of opinion where the opinion is rationally based on the perception of the witness and helpful to obtaining a clear understanding of the facts at issue. In contrast, an expert's testimony is not so limited. An expert may testify in opinion form if scientific, technical, or other specialized knowledge will assist the trier of fact in understanding the evidence or determining a fact in issue. The witness must be qualified as an expert by knowledge, skill, experience, training, or education. Lay witness testimony concerning normality, responsibility, propensity, and competency is generally confined to describing an observed event. Expert testimony is extended to interpreting the events.

1. Diagnosis

Mental health professionals traditionally provide information about patients through their diagnoses. Most mental health professionals rely on the American Psychiatric Association's Diagnostic and Statistical Manual of Mental Disorders, Fourth Edition (DSM–IV). The diagnostic categories in DSM–IV are used by psychiatrists to make and to communicate their diagnosis of a patient to others. However, not all mental health professionals will agree on a diagnosis for a given individual. For example, a range of diagnoses were provided by mental health experts in the trial of John Hinckley. In 1981, Hinckley attempted to assassinate President Ronald Reagan.

One physician testified that Hinckley suffered from blunted or restricted affect and was legally insane. A second physician testified that Hinckley was suffering from possibly four personality disorders (dysthymic, narcissistic, schizoid and mixed personality disorders) but was legally sane. Other physicians' testimony provided alternative diagnoses.

As a result of frequent discrepancies found among mental health professionals, some commentators argue that mental health professionals' testimony should be limited to behavioral observations. Several additional criticisms exist in favor of excluding expert testimony.

One criticism of DSM–IV is that diagnostic categories are generally over-inclusive. Normal individuals can be said to readily fall into several of the diagnostic categories. A second criticism is that diagnoses do not accurately convey legally relevant information. A diagnosis can not inform the fact finder how or to what degree the individual has behaved abnormally. Often, evidence relied upon lacks objectivity. The prevailing measure of mental illness is behavior. However, reported behavior, and even observed behavior, unlike physical symptoms, often lack reliability.

Diagnostic unreliability may exist for several reasons. First, the major cause of diagnostic unreliability is criterion variance and overlap of diagnostic categories. The DSM–IV diagnostic categories are descriptions of recurring patterns of behaviors (thoughts, feelings, actions). These patterns of behavior are the basis of any particular diagnosis. However, diagnostic categories often overlap. Further, the categories are vague; mild or severe behavior may fall under the same diagnosis.

Second, the orientation and training of the examiner may strongly influence the professional's choice of diagnosis. For example, psychiatrists diagnose mental illness more often than psychologists. This is probably because psychiatrists are medically trained to be overly cautious. Additionally, the diverse psychiatry programs view mental illness differently. Schools differ as to the definition of the cause, and most effective treatment of mental illness.

Third, the social and institutional context of the individual at the time of evaluation may influence a diagnosis. A person in a jail may be diagnosed differently than he or she would be diagnosed in the comfortable surroundings of the psychiatrist's office. Moreover, an initial diagnosis may profoundly effect subsequent diagnoses. The mental health professionals may erroneously perceive what that they expect as a result of the influence of suggestion. The expert's perception of a patient is largely shaped by an earlier diagnosis of the person.

Fourth, time may influence the diagnosis. People vary in their behavior from day to day. Different aspects of behavior are observed at different times of the day. The timing of the patient's examination may influence the diagnosis.

Fifth, an individual's class and culture of the individual may influence a diagnosis. Mental health experts may be influenced by the socioeconomic backgrounds of a patient. Individuals with lower socioeconomic status are diagnosed more frequently, with more serious illnesses, poorer prognoses and are apt more often to be found violent.

Sixth, personal biases of mental health professionals will undoubtedly influence the diagnosis. Each expert comes to court with an individual personality, values, self-image, and attitudes.

Nevertheless, there are benefits to expert testimony. An expert may notice significant behavior a lay witness might overlook. For example, a lay person will probably not ask a patient if he or she hears voices or has crazy thoughts. This testimony may be relevant to determining the mental state of the individual. Moreover, some studies indicate there is reliability among diagnoses. In the past, diagnoses were thought to be less than 50 percent reliable. That is, psychiatrists were thought to agree on a diagnosis less than one out of every two times. However, recent studies show the percentage of reliability is closer to 80 percent for major disorders.

Under modern rules of evidence, an expert on cross examination may be required to disclose underlying facts or data which aided the diagnosis. Therefore, the finder of fact has the opportunity to accept or reject the professional's opinion based on the facts.

Finally, a diagnosis is not the only type of evidence with a reliability problem. Other categories of expert testimony that have validity and reliability problems are, nevertheless, admissible and heavily relied upon. For example, paint samples, blood samples, and firearm identification have low reliability rates. Yet, expert testimony on this variety of matters is accepted in court.

2. Responsibility

The issues of responsibility for one's action and the relevance of mental illness to the question of responsibility often arise in the setting of the criminal justice system. Most often, responsibility is an issue in the insanity plea. An individual may be found guilty and punished only if the court determines that the individual is responsible for his or her acts. Testimony is often admitted to determine whether the person is culpable for his or her actions.

The law focuses on the effects of mental disorder. Many states permit establishment of lack of responsibility by showing the absence of the requisite cognitive or volitional affect. Other states, and the federal law, limit establishment of lack of responsibility to showing absence of the requisite cognitive effect. The requisite cognitive effect negating responsibility is an individual's lack of awareness and perception of the unlawfulness or wrongfulness of his or her action at the time of the offense. The volitional effect is the individual's inability to control his or her behavior or conform to the law at the time of the offense.

Several screening barriers exist to admission of testimony to establish mental illness. The first obstacle is a requirement that there be an initial showing of insanity. In criminal law, there is a presumption the defendant is sane. In order for a defendant to plead insanity, the defendant must present evidence of a lack of awareness or understanding of one's actions or the wrongfulness of one's actions. Most jurisdictions require the defendant provide a "scintilla" of evidence to rebut the presumption before the court will admit any evidence of insanity. However, some jurisdictions have a higher standard, requiring the defendant make a *prima facie* case of insanity before the jury may hear any psychiatric testimony.

A second possible obstacle to admitting psychiatric evidence of mental illness is meeting the reasonable medical certainty test. Under this test, the court must decide whether the evidence is based on reasonable medical or psychological certainty. If the evidence is not based in such certainty then it will be excluded.

A third barrier to receipt of expert testimony is the *Frye,* rule. (*Frye v. United States* (D.C.Cir. 1923)). In jurisdictions that follow the *Frye,* rule, the principle from which scientific evidence is deduced must be sufficiently established to have gained general acceptance within the relevant scientific or medical field.

A fourth hurdle for those presenting psychiatric evidence is jury comprehension. Judges may exclude expert testimony if the testimony or rebuttal to the testimony will confuse the jury. However, evidence is rarely excluded on the ground that it is difficult to comprehend.

3. Propensity

Propensity is the prediction of future behavior. Evidence of propensity is particularly significant in determinations of dangerousness that arise in such contexts as criminal sentencing and civil commitment. In order to determine propensity, the mental health expert must make a prediction of the defendant's or patient's future behavior.

The most significant area involving propensity testimony arises in death penalty proceedings. In *Barefoot v. Estelle* (S.Ct.1983) the United States Supreme Court held that during a death penalty proceeding, testimony of dangerousness is admissible. The court determined the finder of fact is entitled to assess the weight to given such evidence. However, a strong dissent argued this type of testimony may be incorrect two out of three times, and presents an unacceptable risk of error when determining whether an individual should be executed.

Mental health professionals use several tools to determine an individual's propensity. One such tool is an individual's diagnosis. The presence of a patient's mental illness or specific personality disorder may effect future behavior. An individual diagnosed with certain personality disorders usually are found likely to be dangerous. However, studies differ on whether a diagnosis is valuable in determining future dangerousness.

Additionally, it is claimed by some experts that theories about aggressive behavior provide a predictive tool. These theories are the basis of tests and measures that are used to predict dangerousness. For example, one theory considers the manner in which an individual deals with stress to be predictive of future aggressive behavior.

Further, past behavior may be a predictive tool. However, when past behavior is used as a basis for prediction, critics point out that with this approach, individuals with histories of antisocial behavior have little chance to combat an inference that they are dangerous.

Finally, demographics are used as a predictive tool. Demographics include age, sex, race, intelligence quotient (IQ), socioeconomic and employment status, drug and alcohol abuse, and marital status. However, problems exist with using demographic evidence to make predictions as the basis for legal decisions potentially restricting individual liberty. The strongest argument against demographic evidence is that using this evidence violates equal protection. Demographic evidence is often racially-based or sex-based. Discrimination based on race or sex may violate equal protection. Thus, decisions based on evidence using explicit racial categorization will generally be held unconstitutional. Demographic evidence based on other criteria may invoke a lower standard of judicial scrutiny. Even with lower scrutiny, however, the use of demographic evidence must be reasonably related to a legitimate purpose. Problems with over inclusiveness and under inclusiveness will preclude most evidence based on demographics.

A second argument against the use of demographic evidence is the use of social science statistics in judicial proceedings. Statistics are susceptible to ambiguity. Further, statistics are generalizations that may not be appropriate if offered as a prediction.

A third objection is based on the use of status, instead of conduct, to punish a person. The Supreme Court has held a state may not punish a person for a status where the status is a mere condition that does not involve any conduct. When a person is labeled as dangerous based solely on demographics, this possibly leads to status being the basis of punishment.

A fourth criticism is predicated on admitting generalized characterizations into evidence. The use of class generalizations to determine an individual's behavior is inconsistent with proper standards for judicial scrutiny. Moreover, judgments based on generalizations threaten the principal of individual blameworthiness.

A final objection is the claim that demographic evidence is inherently unfair. The major difference between demographic and other psychiatric evidence is the degree to which the defendant may rebut the predictive inferences. A defendant may rebut other psychiatric evidence through evidence of personal behavior. However, a defendant cannot rebut demographic evidence unless he or she shows the demographics have been incorrectly analyzed.

4. Competency

Competency refers to an individual's capacity to carry out or perform a function. In the civil case, the question may arise whether a person is competent to manage his or her personal affairs or property. Such competence is at issue in guardianship proceedings. In the criminal context, the issue of competency may arise with regard to whether a defendant is fit to stand trial, to be sentenced or to be executed.

While proceedings to determine competency to stand trial are rare, many jurisdictions rely entirely upon reports of mental health professionals to determine whether an individual is competent to stand trial. In determining competency, many professions follow structured interview formats. For example, The "Competency Assessment Instrument" requires mental health professional to rate the individual on thirteen different functions in order to assess competency. The "Interdisciplinary Fitness Interview" requires the professional to rate the individual on his or her capacity with regard to five legal items and eleven psychopathological items. Neither test produces a score that separates the competent from the incompetent. Instead, a score is used as a guide. "The Competency Screening Tests" takes a different approach. This test consists of twenty-two partial sentences that the subject completes, that in turn the professional must evaluate. The test equates a designated score with competency.

The determination of competency by a mental health professional is very reliable. One study found mental health professionals to agree on competency determinations over 90 percent of the time. Research also shows lay persons' competency determinations are equally reliable.

C. QUALIFYING AS AN EXPERT

In order for a mental health professional to testify as an expert, the witness must fulfill certain qualifications. Under the modern rules of evidence, an expert is anyone who is qualified to testify on a specific issue by reason of specialized knowledge, skill, experience, training or education. Psychiatrists, psychologists, social workers, or psychiatric nurses may testify if they possess the necessary specialized knowledge, skill, experience, training or education. However, the legal system has been reluctant to allow the testimony of mental health professionals other than psychiatrists.

An expert may testify if the expert's experience or training provides the basis for forming an opinion that will aid the trier of fact in deciding the disputed issue. The ability of an expert to render an expert opinion depends upon the nature and extent of the expert's knowledge. In some cases, a psychologist may be as competent as a psychiatrist to testify about a patient's mental condition.

The most prevalent justification for limiting psychological testimony is the widespread adherence of judges and attorneys to the medical model. For the most part, the legal profession prefers to view mental disease as a medical problem. Under this view, only medically trained professional's, such as psychiatrist's are qualified to testify about a patient's medical condition.

While most state statutes and case law allow psychologists to testify on issues concerning insanity and mental disorders, they do not give psychologists the same testimonial scope as psychiatrists. Some courts restrict psychologists to interpreting psychological tests, degrees of cognitive or volitional impairment, causes of mental deficits or determinations of dangerousness. Many states do not allow psychologist's to testify in commitment proceedings. The states that allow psychologists to testify, require higher professional certification than required for psychiatrists.

D. RIGHT TO EXPERT EVALUATION

The right to expert evaluation may be raised in several contexts. The most common context involving criminal insanity cases. Expert assistance is also useful in other criminal contexts such as: diminished capacity, defense based on automatism, and in sentencing. Additionally, expert evaluation may be useful in civil commitment and guardianship proceedings.

In *Ake v. Oklahoma* (S.Ct.1985), the United States Supreme Court addressed the issue of whether the constitution gives an indigent defendant access to a psychiatric examination when insanity is at issue. The court held evaluation by a competent expert was an inherent part of an individual's due process right to a fair hearing. The Court restricted its opinion to situations where the defendant makes a clear showing that mental disease is a genuine issue.

The Supreme Court did not decide the issue of who qualifies as a competent mental health expert. Usually, mental evaluations are performed by state hospital employees. If the defendant is not satisfied with the state's designated expert, some jurisdictions allow the defendant to seek an independent or a secondary evaluation. However, many states do not allow for independent evaluations.

Furthermore, under the *Ake* decision, the defendant must initially establish the relevance of his or her mental condition prior to receiving an expert evaluation. This requirement poses a difficulty for indigent defendants who are unable to make an initial showing without the help of an expert.

Finally, in states providing an expert evaluation, the result of evaluations are automatically made available to both defense and prosecution. This may have a chilling effect on an indigent's exercise of the right to obtain an expert evaluation.

E.   BASES OF CLINICAL OPINION

An expert's opinion may be based on information normally relied upon by professionals in the field. This information may include test results, interviews of the subject, and information from third parties. Two major issues are implicit in expert testimony are constitutionality and admissibility into evidence.

1.   Constitutional Considerations

The Constitution protects against self-incrimination in criminal trials. The Fifth Amendment provides no person "shall be compelled in any criminal case to be a witness against himself." Several policies are fostered through this provision: preventing abuse by governmental officials, protecting a defendants' privacy, preventing the unreliability of coerced statements, protecting the an accused from self-accusation, avoiding perjury or contempt, preserving an accusatorial system and promoting a fair state-individual balance.

The United States Supreme Court has considered whether the Fifth Amendment protection applies to a state requested psychiatric evaluation. In *Estelle v. Smith* (S.Ct.1981), the Supreme Court considered the issue of whether the prosecution's use of state-requested psychiatric testimony during a sentencing hearing violated the Fifth Amendment. In *Estelle,* the defendant was forced to undergo a psychiatric evaluation. The defendant neither asked for an evaluation, nor attempted to admit psychiatric testimony at trial. Further, the defendant was never informed the information could be used against him. The Supreme Court determined the defendant's right not to incriminate himself had been violated. Under *Estelle* the prosecutor must warn a defendant that testimony derived from a requested evaluation could be used against him.

In most states, if the prosecution compels evaluation of the defendant when a determination of competency to stand trial is made, the result may be used only for competency purposes.

A final consideration the *Estelle* Court did not address is the right to have counsel present during an expert psychiatric evaluation. In *United States v. Wade* (S.Ct.1967), the Supreme Court found a right to counsel exists during any stage where the presence of the counsel is necessary to preserve the defendant's basic right to a fair trial. In *Wade,* the court found a right to counsel at post-indictment line-up identifications. However, most courts hold there is no right to have counsel present during state-required psychiatric evaluations.

2. Evidentiary Considerations

Mental health experts testify on the basis of what they observe and on the basis of statements provided directly to them, or recorded by third parties. Examples of third-party sources commonly used are interviews with family, friends, or witnesses, as well as records (medical, psychological, criminal, educational, and occupational), and clinical reports from other mental health professionals. However, hearsay problems may potentially bar a mental health professional from testifying on the basis of third party information. Hearsay is defined as an out of court statement offered for the truth of the matter asserted. Hearsay is usually inadmissible, because the declarant is not subject to cross-examination. Without the presence of the declarant, the trier of fact has no way of judging the third-party's sincerity, perceptions, truthfulness, or narration.

Traditionally, expert opinions based on information obtained from out of court statements by third parties was inadmissible. No exception existed for mental health experts. However, this rule has changed. Under the modern rules of evidence, a hearsay exception does exist for mental health experts. An expert may use third party statements in order to draw conclusions. The facts or data upon which an expert bases an opinion or an inference may be those perceived by or made known to the expert at or before the hearing. If the third party statements or records are of a type reasonably relied upon in forming opinions or inferences upon the subject, by experts in the particular field, the expert may offer an opinion based on those statements or records. The third party statements need not be introduced into evidence. The cross-examination of the witness provides sufficient opportunity to question the expert's basis of opinion or to impeach the credibility of the expert's testimony. It is believed an expert is qualified to determine the reliability of the information on which he or she bases his or her opinion. The trier of fact is then capable of judging the credibility of the expert witness.

3. Opinion on Ultimate Issue

Traditionally, a witness was prohibited from testifying on the ultimate issue of case. Courts applied this rule equally to both lay witnesses and experts. The objective of courts was to leave the ultimate decision for the finder of fact, and not for the witness.

The modern rules of evidence did away with the ultimate issue prohibition. Testimony in the form of an opinion or inference is not objectionable simply because it focuses on an ultimate issue. The rule was changed because of difficulties in enforcing the old rule, and because the old rule deprived the finder of fact of valuable information.

However, limitations are often placed on the permissible inferences an expert may draw. Psychiatrists are permitted to testify about the defendant's diagnosis, mental state and motivation at the time of the alleged act. The expert may not testify as to whether the subject meets the relevant legal tests, for example whether the defendant is legally insane.

CHAPTER 4

MEDICAL MALPRACTICE, NEGLIGENCE AND OTHER TORT THEORIES

A. MENTAL HEALTH MALPRACTICE LITIGATION AND NEGLIGENCE

Medical malpractice litigation within the mental health field has grown in recent years. This increase has led experts to make efforts to determine the underpinnings in the surge in malpractice suits. One possible reason for the rising amount of mental health related malpractice litigation is a lack of consensus among health professionals as to the proper standards for psychiatric treatment. Absent a consensus among mental health professionals on a standard of care, psychiatrists, and other mental health professionals, have difficulty agreeing on the appropriateness of individualized treatment plans. Another contributing factor to the increase in malpractice law suits is a patient's right to sue for injuries that do not manifest themselves physically. Courts have only in recent years permitted suits for psychological harm or psychic distress not related to some underlying physical harm. Within this new realm of litigation, mental health professionals often find it difficult to disprove "psychiatric injury."

Additionally, the continued development of pharmaceuticals to treat mental illness has produced new potential for medical harm to patients resulting from error in prescribing drugs and failure to anticipate harmful drug side effects. The three most common malpractice actions in the mental health area involve misdiagnosis, improper treatment, and drug reactions.

B. NEGLIGENCE

Mental health professionals like other medical professionals, have affirmative obligations to render service in conformity with mental health standards of care. In bringing a negligence action against a mental health professional, the plaintiff must prove each of these elements: 1) a duty upon the professional to conform to a specific standard of conduct to protect others from unreasonable risks; 2) the professional's failure to conform to such standard; 3) a reasonably close causal connection between the professional's conduct and the plaintiff's injury; and 4) actual loss or injury. While these criteria seem relatively straightforward, secondary issues often arise such as liability to third parties based strictly upon the professional's conduct, and liability to third parties based upon diagnostic functions performed by the psychiatrist at the request of the third party.

1. Defining the Negligence Standard: The Professional Standard of Care

In the Massachusetts case of *Stepakoff v. Kantar* (Mass.1985), the plaintiff, a mental patient's wife, brought suit against her deceased husband's psychiatrist. The plaintiff alleged that although defendant knew or reasonably should have known her husband was suicidal, defendant negligently failed to inform plaintiff or take appropriate measures to prevent the suicide. The court's discussion centered on whether defendant acted in conformance with the appropriate psychiatric standard of care. The court held a specialized physician has a duty to provide services in compliance with the standard set by other professionals practicing in his or her field. Essentially, the court suggested a failure to act may be negligent only if the act or omission is not in compliance with professional standards of the practitioner's particular field. For example, a psychologist, unlike a medically trained psychiatrist, would generally not be liable for a failure to diagnose an organic disorder presented by a patient.

2. Limitations and Defenses on Liability: The Best Judgment Rule

In the New York case of *Schrempf v. State* (N.Y. 1985), the plaintiff brought a wrongful death suit against the state for releasing a mental patient who subsequently stabbed and killed her husband. Prior to the killing, the patient had been released from institutional confinement and had became a voluntary outpatient receiving medication. The plaintiff

alleged that the treating mental health professional's knowledge, that the patient refused to take his
medication during continued outpatient care, gave
rise to a duty to intervene and prevent the patient
from harming others in his non-medicated condition.

The court in *Schrempf* found no duty to intervene. The patient's status as a voluntary outpatient
lessened the state's control over him. Psychiatric
testimony revealed the patient's refusal to take his
medication did not necessarily indicate his condition
would worsen or he would become increasingly dangerous. Moreover, the patient did not give any
warning signs of worsening condition. Finally, the
patient often reacted violently to psychiatric intervention. The psychiatrist, therefore, thoroughly
evaluated the patient's history and actions before
deciding not to intervene. However,unfortunate the
result, the court determined the state could not be
held liable for the patient's actions.

The rule articulated by the court in *Schrempf* is
known as the "best judgment rule". The best judgment rule simply states a physician is not liable for
the consequences of professional judgment made
upon sound and thorough evaluation. Basically the
best judgment rule provides no liability for "mere
error." Few states have adopted the rule, but states
such as New York have applied the rule to all
malpractice cases, including those arising in the
field of psychiatry. The result of such a rule is an
exemption for psychiatrists from liability for deciding not to involuntarily hospitalize a patient. Juris-

dictions that fail to adopt the rule may render psychiatrists liable for honest errors in judgment.

Many courts have chosen an informal or "sub silentio" adoption of the best judgment rule. In these cases, courts refuse to hold psychiatrists liable for injuries to third parties based upon a psychiatrist's decision not to involuntarily commit a patient.

Reasons for adopting some form of the best judgment rule include the uncertainty of psychiatry, the inability to make precise judgments, and a psychiatrists inability to predict with a high degree of certainty how a patient will react to commitment or to specific treatments. The standard of care in the psychiatric realm, therefore, must encompass the uncertainty accompanying diagnoses. However, it should be noted that before the best judgment rule applies, a sound psychiatric evaluation of each patient must be made. Thus, psychiatrists are not exempt from liability until they present evidence of a thorough examination of the patient.

3. "Respectable Minority Rule"

While a finding that a psychiatrist acted in compliance with the majority standard set forth by other psychiatrists usually precludes liability, a psychiatrist's decision to prescribe an alternative treatment does not necessarily imply liability or negligence. Some states allow the use of a "respectable minority rule" which protects psychiatrists from liability if evidence establishes the psychiatrist made a sound decision reflecting the views of a respectable minority of experts in the field. One court explained the "respectable minority rule" operates as a psychiatrist's exemption from liability for a particular decision so long as two or more psychiatrists find the treatment appropriate, and each expert is backed up by a responsible medical authority.

Controversy surrounds the acceptance of minority psychiatric opinion when evidence indicates the majority standard's treatment is significantly more effective. The development of new and experimental treatments is likely to give rise to a great deal of criticism of the respectable minority rule. Psychiatrists eager to experiment with new treatments not readily accepted by the majority of psychiatric professionals may cause harm to patients or third parties. On the other hand, refusal of psychiatrists to administer new treatment is likely to hinder the development of effective new standards.

In *Osheroff v. Chestnut Lodge Inc.* (Md.App.985), a case initiated before the Maryland Health Care Arbitration Panel, a patient alleged defendant failed to administer psychopharmaceutical treatment, resulting in a delay in returning the plaintiff to normal functioning, loss of income, and loss of standing in the patient's profession. The plaintiff, a physician, voluntarily admitted himself to the defendant hospital for treatment for various psychoses. The treatment administered by the hospital psychiatrist did not improve the plaintiff's condition. The plaintiff alleged the defendant should have administered a different form of therapy. The plaintiff further alleged the defendant negligently misdiagnosed his disease.

The tribunal in *Osheroff* rejected the plaintiff's allegations, reasoning that different theories used in psychological training could lead trained practitioners to different diagnoses. In essence, the tribunal determined the treating psychiatrist's theoretical orientation likely influenced his diagnosis. Therefore, another psychiatrist's conflicting diagnosis based on a separate and distinct theory did not necessarily indicate misdiagnosis. Furthermore, the tribunal found the treatment administered by defendant was appropriate for the diagnosis rendered.

The tribunal's ruling in *Osheroff* significantly reduces a psychiatrist's liability for misdiagnoses and subsequent mistreatment. Under an *Osheroff* analysis a psychiatric institution's emphasis on a particular psychological theory will justify the decision to use a particular treatment. In theory, the *Osheroff* ruling is an application of the respectable minority rule.

The tribunal's opinion in *Osheroff* is also significant for its failure to address the issue of the plaintiff's informed consent. Critics argue a patient's implicit covenant not to sue (resulting from signing the informed consent form) should not be enforced in cases involving standardized treatment. The argument for finding such an implicit agreement and the concomitant enforcement of the covenant not to sue seems strongest in instances where the procedure is experimental, and the patient has been informed of the alternatives and risks and, nevertheless, agrees to undergo the experimental treatment or therapy.

Another significant concern arising from the court's opinion in *Osheroff* is the issue of liability of general practice physicians and hospital staff physicians for failure to refer patients for needed psychiatric care, or for having referred patients to mental health professionals using innovative treatments. Some cases suggest general practitioners and hospital staff physicians, when dealing with depressed patients, may have a duty to refer patients to psychiatrists for psychological treatment. A related concern about physician liability arises, because of the fact that some psychiatrists to whom such patients may be referred occasionally will use innovative therapy, unsupported by a majority view, yet considered promising by some area of psychiatry. Some courts dismiss such cases due to evidence of the overwhelming success in the area of experimental treatment. These courts justify taking a broader view of experimental treatment for the sake of medical and scientific advancement, thus, reducing liability imposed upon psychiatrists willing to administer such treatment. Other courts, however, refuse to allow the testimony of expert witnesses in jury trials and instruct the jury that the innovative nature of the treatment constituted malpractice in itself. A balance, however, must be struck between the need to advance treatment and the need to protect patients from reckless, harmful treatment.

C. COUNSELING BY NONTHERAPISTS

The central issue in *Nally v. Grace Community Church of the Valley* (Cal.1988), decided by the Supreme Court of California, was whether persons other than licensed psychotherapists who counsel individuals on emotional and spiritual problems have a duty to refer the individual to a licensed mental health professional when the counselor becomes aware of the client's suicidal tendencies. The plaintiffs, the client's parents, filed suit for wrongful death after the counselee shot himself in the head. The client had received pastoral counseling through his church. The counseling was generally religious in nature and was conducted through prayer, instruction and study. The defendants did not hold themselves to be medical or psychiatric counselors. Following a break up with his girlfriend, the client became increasingly upset and was encouraged by the church to seek additional counseling within the church. Later the client was hospitalized for an intentional overdose of an antidepressant drug. The pastor from the client's church visited the client who spoke of his wishes that he had been able to kill himself. The defendants did not disclose this information to the attending physician. Two days after a family argument, the client was dead from a self-inflicted gunshot wound.

The plaintiffs contended the clergymen should have informed the parents and hospital staff of the client's wish to die. The court distinguished the case before it from other cases in which the evidence established a special relationship between medical personnel and a patient under medical supervision. The court determined liability for a non-therapist could only be found if a special relationship existed between the suicidal client and the defendant. However, this special relationship must be one of medical professional and patient. The court found no duty of care extends to personal or religious counseling relationships in which non-professional guidance is given. The client in *Nally* was not under a medically supervised counseling program, nor was he under any medical treatment.

The court in *Nally* cited several public policy reasons for its decision. First, imposing liability to nonprofessional counselors would have a deleterious effect on the provision of counseling services. Second, the clergy's exemption from state licensure requirements for domestic counseling recognizes that secular counseling may not meet everyone's needs, and that clergymen may provide different, but equally effective, counseling to a special population. In spite of the clergyman's exemption from liability, however, clergyman malpractice insurance has been offered to protect clergyman from suits arising from counseling. The effect and value of this insurance, however, is unknown.

Nally does not hold nonlicensed professionals exempt from liability. In fact, mental health counselors who act as professionals are held to the standard of care of licensed professionals.

D. SOVEREIGN IMMUNITY

Generally, an employer such as a clinic or hospital may be liable for damages caused by its mental health professional employees. However, governmental agencies have only a limited liability under sovereign immunity. Several reasons are cited for the existence of sovereign immunity. Perhaps the most important reason is that the doctrine is viewed as a means of maintaining the government's control over its funds, and property. Many feel the government would be unable to perform various necessary functions without the protection of its economic resources that results from recognition of the doctrine of sovereign immunity.

Nevertheless, the sovereign immunity doctrine has encountered criticism in recent years. As a result, Congress passed the Federal Tort Claims Act (FTCA) limiting federal sovereign immunity exemption to certain specified actions. In passing the FTCA, Congress aimed to compensate victims for negligent and injurious actions by employees or agents of the federal government. However, the FTCA excludes many torts from coverage, continuing to partially maintain the doctrine's existence. Specifically, under the doctrine of sovereign immunity and the FTCA, a federal employee may not be sued for any act or omission within the discretionary function of any federal agency or employee. However, suit may be brought for ministerial or nondiscretionary actions. Difficulty invariably arises in determining whether an act is discretionary in nature. As a result, some courts have provided exemption from liability only for decisions made by top-level officials. Physicians and nurses providing services in federal governmental institutions, not otherwise immune from liability, will not be able to invoke sovereign immunity as a protection from suit for negligence in cases involving direct administration of treatment to patients.

Individual states have long invoked sovereign immunity as a defense in suits brought for injuries caused through the state's activity. In most states, an individual may not sue the state government or its agencies unless there is a statutory waiver of sovereign immunity. Recently, legislation was enacted in many states that automatically waived sovereign immunity status in specified circumstances. Importantly, state agencies may be sued without a waiver of immunity in instances where that agency acted outside its governmental capacity. Hospitals established and operated by the state may be protected by sovereign immunity; however, in most states sovereign immunity has been waived for those activities directly relating to patient treatment. Even in cases where a hospital or governmental agency is immune from suit, an employee of the agency may be subject to liability for his or her negligent actions. Moreover, government employees are not exempt from personal liability merely because of their status as governmental employees.

Immunity has received special attention in the mental health field. Mental health professionals, especially psychiatrists are protected by absolute immunity from liability for diagnostic statements indicating the presence of mental illness in court proceedings, commitment proceedings, or reports and recommendations. Absolute immunity entitles the psychiatrist to complete exemption from liability for acts, unintentional or malicious, committed within the scope of employment. Absolute immunity is granted to these professionals so they are not deterred from making professional judgments in the best interests of the patient for fear of civil liability.

Most other mental health professionals providing direct treatment to patients in state institutions are protected only by a qualified immunity. Qualified immunity applies only to those actions taken within the range of professional judgment in treatment of patients and performed in good faith. Acts undertaken under administrative direction, but performed negligently will not be protected by sovereign immunity. Qualified immunity is provided to encourage mental health professionals to exercise their professional judgment in the best interest of their patients.

E. ISSUES IN THE APPLICATION OF THE NEGLIGENCE DOCTRINE

1. Proximate Cause and Suicide

One area of malpractice litigation involving numerous lawsuits is patient suicide. Here, courts have given special attention to the issue of proximate cause. In the *Weathers v. Pilkinton* (Tenn.App. 1988), a plaintiff brought suit against her husband's treating physician claiming he was liable for her husband's suicide. The husband took several over-doses of anti-depressant medication and was hospi-talized for each episode. Following the husband's fourth self-inflicted overdose of medication, the treating physician released the husband, but urged the patient to seek psychiatric counseling. During a telephone conversation with his estranged wife, the husband informed her that he was going to shoot himself. Subsequently, the husband fatally shot himself before his wife or anyone else could inter-vene. The plaintiff alleged the physician had a duty to intervene and prevent the husband's death since the physician was aware of the husband's suicidal tendencies and numerous suicide attempts.

The *Weathers* court found the physician did not have a duty to intervene and involuntarily commit the husband. The court's analysis focused on whether the deceased knew and understood the nature of his acts at the time he committed suicide. Testimonial evidence indicated the deceased was completely aware of his acts on the date of his death. The court found no evidence of depression or anxiety in the deceased at the time of his suicide. Because the deceased's act was deliberate, willful and calculated, the physician was not liable for the suicide. However, the court stated if a suicide victim was shown to be so mentally disturbed that he or she lacked an understanding of the nature or effect of his or her personal actions, then the act of suicide could not be considered willful and deliber-ate behavior. Therefore, a physician aware of the patient's mental condition could be found liable for the suicide.

Courts are more likely to find physicians liable for the suicide of patients who are inpatients of hospitals or psychiatric institutions. In these situations, physicians are held liable to the ordinary standard of care and must take precautions to protect a patient from harm if the patient exhibits suicidal tendencies.

In determining whether a defendant proximately caused a patient's harm, courts evaluate whether the death could have been prevented by reasonable steps taken by the defendant. In *Lando v. State* (N.Y.1975) mental patient wandered off the institution's grounds and died of exposure. Although an initial appeal overturned a finding of liability, a subsequent appealable review determined the institution's failure to conduct a search of the grounds as soon as the patient was discovered missing could be found to be the proximate cause of the patient's death.

2. Damages For Sexual Misconduct

A second highly litigated area of malpractice by mental health professionals involves sexual relations between the professional and the patient or client. In *Corgan v. Muehling* (Ill.1988), plaintiffs, parents of a psychiatric patient, brought suit against the child's psychiatrist for allegedly engaging in sexual relations with the child. In awarding judgment for the plaintiffs, the court pointed out that victims of psychological malpractice may bring suits for emotional or psychological injury without a need to show fear of or actual physical injury. The court stressed the subject matter of mental health treatment involves the psyche and emotions. Therefore, intentional or negligent conduct in rendering of such care would result in psychological or emotional harm. Proof of sexual misconduct by a mental health professional is sufficient to establish liability for negligence.

Contrary to the court's decision in *Corgan,* some courts require proof of intentional infliction of emotional harm, as well as physical manifestation of injury in order to sustain an emotional distress claim. Moreover, a few states do not recognize causes of action for negligent infliction of emotional distress. In such cases, an alternate theory for recovery must be established. In the state of Washington, for example, courts allow actions for assault, against therapists, even if the patient consented to sexual intercourse.

Punitive damages for sexual misconduct may be awarded if the plaintiff successfully shows an evil motive or intention on the part of the defendant. Conscious and deliberate disregard of the interests of others may qualify as wanton or wilful conduct.

Recovery in sexual misconduct cases has been extended to cases involving sexual relations between the therapist and the patient's spouse. In cases where the spouse was not a patient of the therapist, courts have relied on the theory of de facto abandonment. In abandonment cases, recovery is allowed under the premise that the therapists sexual relations with a patient's spouse interferes with treatment of the patient, and the therapist effectively has discontinued services to a patient still in need of treatment. In other cases, recovery has been allowed in cases where both spouses were patients of the therapists.

3. Liability to Third Parties

Limits on professional liability traditionally were based on privity of contract between the therapist and the patient. Recovery for negligence was not allowed without establishing a treating relationship between the plaintiff and the defendant. Privity is no longer a requirement in professional negligence cases. Courts now hold defendants liable to third parties for actions the defendant should have reasonably foreseen would injure the plaintiff.

In *Merchants National Bank & Trust Co. of Fargo v. United States* (D.N.D.1967), the estate of a mentally-ill patient's wife brought a wrongful death suit against the government. The case involved a mentally ill patient who was committed to a state institution and subsequently discharged to a community residential facility. On a weekend leave from the facility, the patient sought out his wife and killed her. The court determined the state institution had a duty to the deceased, finding the patient's psychiatrist ignored warning signals that the patient wished to harm his wife. Furthermore, the treating psychiatrist failed to warn the community facility of the patient's homicidal tendencies.

The court determined defendant's negligent failure to exercise due care was the sole and proximate cause of the wife's death.

Courts have increasingly imposed liability on institutions that release patients that are known or that should reasonably have been known to be dangerous. Debate persists, however, whether institutions should be liable to third parties for injuries caused by voluntary patients who decide to leave the institution. Courts have adopted different standards for voluntary patients. In *Hinkelman v. Borgess Medical Center* (Mich.App.1987), the Michigan Court of Appeals decided a state institution was not liable for an assault committed by a voluntary patient who had institutionalized himself for a three day period and left before any treatment was administered.

The California Supreme Court's decision in *Tarasoff v. Regents of University of California* (Cal. 1976), firmly established the imposition of liability on mental health professionals for serious injuries caused to third parties who are known to be the subject of a direct threat of injury or death by a patient. The parents of deceased Tatiana Tarasoff, brought suit against the University of California's psychiatric clinic for negligently failing to warn the parents and proper authorities of the released mental patient's expressed intent to kill Tatiana. Prosenjit Poddar, a voluntary outpatient, confided to his psychiatrist his intention to kill Tatiana. The clinic notified police who detained the patient for a short time then released him after the patient assured police he was rational and would not kill Tatiana. No further steps were taken by police nor by defendants to detain the patient. The patient later went to Tatiana's apartment and killed her.

The court found defendants owed plaintiffs a duty to inform and reasonably protect Tatiana from Poddar's verbalized intentions. Although Poddar was a voluntary outpatient, his expressed intentions to kill a specifically named individual imposed upon defendants an affirmative duty to warn Tatiana and those who may be in contact with her. Because the patient named a specific victim, no special relationship existed or needed to exist between the third party and the defendant. The special relationship between the patient and the psychiatrist imposed an obligation on the defendant to exercise reasonable care to control the patient's behavior.

In evaluating the imposition of liability, the court noted the discretion given psychiatrists in using their best judgment to determine whether a patient is dangerous. Courts will generally defer to this discretion; however, in circumstances where a patient verbally manifests an intent to cause harm to another, the psychiatrist is liable for injuries arising from a patient's who carries out his or her threats. The public interest in protecting individual safety overrides public interest in maintaining confidentiality between patient and therapist.

Some states have refused to follow *Tarasoff*. These state courts have cited the overwhelming need to protect confidential disclosure of information, barring disclosure of any information to third parties. Other states have followed *Tarasoff*, but limit third party liability to situations where the patient names a specific victim. Other states require that the victim be directly threatened by the patient himself. Nevertheless, other states have given *Tarasoff* a broad reading imposing a duty on psychiatrist to protect a group which is threatened by a patient. In these instances, psychiatrists must take action to prevent the patient from carrying out his or her threat of harm. Such action may require seeking commitment of the patient or insuring police detention.

Tarasoff has been criticized because of the inherent limitations of the therapist's ability to accurately predict violent tendencies or danger to third persons with consistency. While the identification of a specific victim in *Tarasoff* made it easier for the court to impose liability, the court failed to suggest general criteria for evaluating a therapist's professional judgment resulting in injury to a third party.

The assassination attempt against former President Reagan provided the occasion for further consideration of the nature of duty of psychiatrists to protect the public from the acts of dangerous patients. Plaintiffs in *Brady v. Hopper* (D.C.Colo. 1983), brought suit against the psychiatrist who had been treating John Hinckley, Jr., before his attempted assassination of former President Reagan. The plaintiffs alleged the psychiatrist negligently examined, diagnosed and treated Hinckley. Hinckley had been brought to the psychiatrist by his parents because of their concern for his suicidal behavior. The psychiatrist ultimately formed the opinion Hinckley was not ill, but immature and needed to be made to take responsibility for himself. Subsequently, Hinckley, in his attempt to kill former president Reagan, shot and seriously injured Reagan and the plaintiffs. The plaintiffs alleged the defendant negligently misdiagnosed Hinckley's condition and that had he performed his duties properly, Hinckley's behavior could have been controlled.

The defendant physician in *Hinckley* claimed the relationship between himself and his patient did not give rise to an obligation to prevent Hinckley from harming others nor create a duty to control Hinckley's behavior. The defendant further contended there existed no duty to protect third parties, because Hinckley had not identified a specific victim during the course of treatment with the therapist. Although the court found the psychiatrist's diagnosis fell below the reasonable standard of care, the court focused its attention on the impossibility of holding therapists responsible for every act of a patient. The psychiatrist's assertion that Hinckley had no history of violence or violent tendencies persuaded the court that Hinckley's subsequent actions were unforeseeable. Absent a threat to a specific victim and absent a foreseeable risk, the psychiatrist had no duty to control Hinckley or to warn others.

A controversial area of asserted liability to third parties involves the negligent discharge of patients from mental health facilities. In *Sellers v. United*

States (6th Cir.1989), the estate of an individual killed by a patient discharged from a veterans hospital brought suit against the government for negligent discharge. The patient was treated for manic depression and released from the hospital, but continued treatment on an outpatient basis. The patient subsequently beat and killed the deceased. Plaintiffs alleged defendants failed to administer the proper level of medication to the patient during his outpatient treatment. Plaintiffs further alleged the patient exhibited symptoms of returning manic depression which the hospital failed to detect and treat. Plaintiffs contended defendants owed a duty to the deceased as a member of the general public.

The United States Court of Appeals for the Sixth Circuit held in *Sellers* the hospital had no duty to inform the general public, absent the patient's identification of a specific victim. The court applied a *Tarasoff* analysis and decided a psychiatrist owes a duty of reasonable care to a person foreseeably endangered by his patient. Because the patient never identified a specific victim, the Court determined the decision to release the patient was based on the physician's professional judgment, and did not render the physician liable.

4. Application of the Identifiable Victim Standard and the Duty to Warn

Courts have construed the identifiable victim doctrine broadly. In cases involving mental patients with violent tendencies toward a certain group of individuals, for example women, courts may find therapists have a duty to warn women close to the patient. Similarly, threats made by patients prior to their commitment may impose liability on a therapist to protect the threatened individual when the patient is released.

Courts have also debated whether non-professionals aware of a patient's condition have a duty to warn foreseeable victims. For example, spouses, aware of a husband's condition for which he receives treatment, may have a duty to warn the husband's fellow workers of harm threatened by the husband against them.

In *Hamman v. County of Maricopa* (Ariz.1989), plaintiffs brought suit against a treating psychiatrist for failure to commit their son in spite of his violent tendencies. The son had a history of mental disturbances. On several occasions plaintiffs asked the psychiatrist to commit their son for fear he would injure himself or others. The defendant refused to commit the son and only prescribed medication. The son subsequently severely beat his stepfather. The court found defendant owed a duty to protect the plaintiffs from their son. Although the patient did not specifically identify his parents as possible victims of his violence, plaintiffs were in the zone of danger created by their son's violent threats and, therefore, were foreseeably likely to come into contact with their son. The foreseeable danger was within defendants awareness of the patient's violent tendencies. The court specifically rejected the idea that a therapist's duty to third persons is limited to those specifically threatened or identified as a potential victims by the patient, but rather advocated the zone of danger rule.

F. RECOVERY AND DAMAGES UNDER NON–NEGLIGENCE THEORIES

1. Miscellaneous Theories

A therapist's failure to exercise a reasonable standard of professional care may result in a breach of contract. This theory eliminates plaintiff's need to prove negligence. The difficulties in establishing physical and emotional manifestations of injury arising from sexual misconduct cases may be overcome by pursuing a breach of contract action.

Recovery under contract theory is limited, however. For example, in *Dennis v. Allison* (Tex.1985) the court denied plaintiff's claim for breach of contract arising from sexual assault by her therapist. The court reasoned plaintiff could not sue under an implied warranty theory, because public policy dictated plaintiffs may recover specifically for wrongs committed during treatment.

2. Claims Based on Federal Civil Rights Laws

The Federal Civil Rights Laws have been applied to provide protection for mental health patients. Civil rights actions have three requirements: 1) that the conduct complained of was committed by a person acting under color of state law; 2) this conduct deprived the patient of rights, privileges, or immunities secured by the laws and Constitution of the United States; and 3) the conduct complained of was not protected by the professional's qualified immunity.

These standards are difficult to meet; but if successfully met, federal civil rights claims have several benefits. First, the action may be removed to a federal forum where federal statutes may be more favorable than governing state law. Second, the plaintiff may qualify for attorneys' fees. Thirdly, an action in federal court may avoid state exhaustion of remedies. More importantly, a federal forum may avoid state created limitations on liability. Specifically, some states limit the amount of damages that may be recovered by a plaintiff. However, plaintiffs seeking limited recovery may choose to bring their suits in state court to avoid the additional elements of proof necessary in federal civil rights actions.

Spencer v. Lee (7th Cir.1989), raised the issue whether private physicians and hospitals act "under color of state law" when they commit a mentally disturbed person. The defendant physician decided the plaintiff needed to be involuntary committed. The plaintiff resisted and a nurse had to inject the plaintiff with a drug, whereby he sustained bodily injury. Plaintiff brought a federal civil rights action for deprivation of liberty under 42 U.S.C. § 1983, as well as reckless infliction of injury.

The court, denying plaintiff's claims, stated the purpose of involuntary commitment protecting the patient or others from physical harm. The petition to commit must be fully detailed with respect to the patient's behavior and signed by a competent professional attesting to the need for the individual's commitment. Moreover, the need for immediate hospitalization must be compelling. The court acknowledged a state's reasons for committing individuals were equivalent if not identical to a private physician's objectives: for the protection of the individual and others. The court found no reason why laws regarding commitment and liability should differ between state and private physicians.

CHAPTER 5

INFORMED CONSENT

A. INTRODUCTION

Deeply rooted in American jurisprudence is the right of every individual to determine what happens to one's own body. As far back as the nineteenth century, courts have been willing to recognize the individual's right to bodily self-determination. Individuals could bring battery cases against physicians for treatment that involved unconsented touching. However, once the patient consented to treatment, the patient was precluded from recovery for any uninformed risks.

The doctrine of informed consent emerged during the 1960's. This doctrine was based upon the principle that an individual could not give adequate informed consent unless the patient was aware of the risks of treatment and available alternatives. Therefore, even though a patient consented to treatment, the patient could still recover for uninformed risks.

Today, the doctrine of informed consent requires the physician to disclose information regarding risks and alternatives to the patient; and the patient must consent to the treatment. When a physician breaches the duty of informed consent, relief may be available under two theories: battery and professional negligence or malpractice.

The doctrine of informed consent applies only to medical treatment. Therefore, nonmedical practitioners may not be liable for failure to obtain informed consent. A cause of action for breach of informed consent requires that the injury be the direct and proximate cause of treatment; therefore, recovery cannot be predicated on lack of informed consent to medical treatment when injury is the result of a nonmedical treatment.

The doctrine of informed consent does not rest on tort liability for a failure to exercise reasonable care during treatment. Liability is based solely on a lack of appropriate consent.

B. ORIGIN OF DOCTRINE OF INFORMED CONSENT; DUTY TO INFORM

Prior to the 1960's, physicians were required to obtain a patient's consent in order for the physician to treat the patient. Physicians had no duty to inform their patients of risks or alternatives prior to treatment. A physician was only liable for injury sustained as a result of treatment where the patient did not consent to treatment. Liability could be established only when the patient consented to a procedure different from the performed procedure, or when the patient consented to treatment on one area of the body and the physician performed a procedure on another part. However, no case rested on a failure to disclose collateral risks in treatment. Physicians had a valid defense if the physician informed the patient of the procedure and the patient consented.

During the late 1950's courts began to realize that a patient's consent was not meaningful unless the consent was based on sufficient knowledge of the risks attendant to a course of treatment. Two cases significantly influenced the development of this modern doctrine of informed consent. In *Mitchell v. Robinson* (Mo.1960), a mental patient was not warned of the possible side effects of insulin "subcoma" therapy. As a result of therapy, the patient experienced a grand mal seizure and fractured several vertebrae. The court held the physician liable for the injury to the patient, because physicians have a duty to inform their patients who are competent, that is of mature age and in possession of their mental faculties, of serious collateral hazards that might accompany recommended treatment or procedures. Similarly, in *Natanson v. Kline* (Kan.1960), a physician administered radioactive cobalt therapy to a mental patient. The court expressly held that failure to disclose collateral risk data is sufficient to constitute negligence.

The doctrine of informed consent is applied under several theories. Some courts regard the underlying conduct as intentional and classify the cause of action as assault and battery. Other courts treat informed consent cause of actions as negligence. A court's choice of which cause of action for trial of informed consent claims has serious implications for the claimant. First, negligence claims have a longer statute of limitations than intentional tort actions. Second, the burden of proof is lessened with intentional tort claims, because expert testimony is not needed to prove intent. Third, intentional tort claims allow punitive as well as nominal damages without showing actual injury. Negligence requires actual injury. Fourth, some malpractice insurance policies will not cover intentional tort claims.

C. ELEMENTS OF INFORMED CONSENT

Obtaining a patient's informed consent requires adequate disclosure to the patient of all material risks of a proposed treatment, available alternative treatments and associated risks, and the option of no treatment and its risks. To recover for failure to obtain informed consent, a plaintiff must show causation. The patient must prove that but "for nondisclosure," the patient would not have consented to the treatment. Some jurisdictions require an actual physical injury, while other jurisdictions hold that mental anguish is sufficient.

1. Disclosure

The first element for a cause of action for failure to obtain informed consent is disclosure. The modern doctrine of informed consent requires the physician to disclose the collateral risks of the proposed treatment prior to initiating the treatment. The amount of disclosure necessary, however, depends on the prevailing view of the particular jurisdiction.

Two prevailing views exist; the medical professional standard and the subjective patient standard.

Under the traditional view, the amount of information necessary to satisfy informed consent is determined by the medical community. The measure is whether the physician adhered to a medical standard of reasonable care. For example, in *Aiken v. Clary* (Mo.1965), the Supreme Court of Missouri held that to recover under a theory of lack of informed consent requires presentation of evidence of failure of disclosure of information that a reasonable practitioner would make under the same or similar circumstances. This is solely a matter of medical judgment. To determine if the physician adhered to a reasonable standard of care, certain factors pertaining to the particular patient are to be taken into account. This involves a determination of the range of and particular collateral risks a reasonable physician would have disclosed. To this end, courts assess the patient's physical health and mental state, the nature of risks posed, and a medical judgement as to whether disclosure of possible risks might have an adverse effect on the patient.

Courts following the medical community standard differ on how to determine the scope of reasonable disclosure. In some jurisdictions, the scope of disclosure is determined by what a reasonable medical practitioner, on a national standard, would disclose under the same or similar circumstances to the patient. In other jurisdictions, the scope of disclosure is determined by what a reasonable practitioner in the same community would inform a patient under same or similar circumstances.

The rationale of the traditional approach is that medical decisions are neither matters of common knowledge, nor within the experience of laymen. Expert medical evidence is necessary, because only experts can determine the effect of a risk on a patient and understand the medical decision involved. Jurisdictions following the traditional approach also recognize several practical matters. First, time constraints prevent physicians from disclosing all possible risks. Second, negligence is traditionally evaluated by what a reasonable person would do in the actor's position. Finally, the courts do not want to subject the physician to hindsight determinations of patients.

The increasingly prevalent view is the subjective patient standard that was articulated by the United States Court of Appeals for the District of Columbia in *Canterbury v. Spence* (D.C.Cir.1972). Under the modern view, the scope of disclosure is measured by information that is material to an individual patient's decision to undergo or to reject proposed treatment. All risks and alternatives that may potentially affect a patient's choice to undergo or to forego treatment must be disclosed. A material risk is defined as any risk a physician knows or should know to which a reasonable person, in the patient's position, would attach significance. The "significance" at issue may be thought of as information about the risk and benefits about the treatment or procedure being recommended that would be considered by the patient in deciding whether to consent to the recommendation. Such information includes inherent and potential risks, alternative treatments and their risks, and likely results if the patient forgoes treatment.

Several benefits exist with applying the subjective patient standard that places significant responsibility for disclosure on the treating physician. By contrast, under the medical standard, physicians have unlimited discretion in determining the amount of disclosure. Critics of the medical standard argue this approach undermines the individual's right to self-determination. By contrast, the subjective patient standard takes more fully into account an individual's right to self determination. Further, many issues of disclosure are not medical in nature; yet, lay witnesses are not allowed to testify about adequate disclosure under the medical model. A lay witness is certainly competent to testify to a lack of knowledge of risks, a failure to disclose, and consequences of the failure to disclose. A lay witness is also competent to evaluate the materiality of the risk to the decision to undergo treatment and the effect of nondisclosure.

In addition to differing on the requisite amount of disclosure, jurisdictions also differ on the amount of knowledge imputed to physicians. Not all physicians are aware of the same risks. Some jurisdictions hold physicians responsible for divulging only the risks of which they are in fact aware of, while other jurisdictions hold physicians liable for risks known to a reasonable physician.

The doctrine of informed consent is not unqualified. While exceptions exist relieving physicians of the duty to give informed consent, these exceptions do not allow a physician to remain silent for fear the patient will refuse necessary treatment. Instead, the exceptions grant physicians the right to withhold information only in very limited situations.

One exception exists in emergency situations where the patient is unconscious or incapable of giving consent. In order to waive the requirement of informed consent in these situations, harm must be imminent and the prognosis of treatment must outweigh all risks.

Another exception exists where the disclosure of a risk possesses so grave a threat to the patient that the disclosure is medically unsound. Nondisclosure is justified where disclosure will cause a patient to become so emotionally distraught as to prevent a rational decision, complicate or hinder treatment, or cause psychological damage to the patient.

A minority of jurisdictions also recognize an exception where disclosing every risk may result in alarming an apprehensive patient. The physician may be excused from disclosing all material risks if the patient would be likely to refuse to treatment in which there is minimum risk. Some courts even allow the patient to waive informed consent.

2. Causation

A second element of a cause of action for failure to obtain informed consent is causation. A failure to disclose a material risk or an alternative procedure is insufficient to automatically impose liability on a physician. First, the plaintiff must prove causation. The patient must also prove that if the physician had disclosed all the risks and alternatives, the patient would not have consented to treatment or have undergone a recommended procedure In essence, the patient is required to show that "but for" the failure to be given the information attendant to obtaining the requisite informed consent, the patient would not have undergone the medical treatment or procedure. Courts use different approaches to determine causation. One approach is the objective approach. Courts determine whether a reasonable person in the plaintiff's situation would have consented if informed of all risks or alternatives. Causation may only be established if the reasonable person would have chosen to forgo treatment.

Under the subjective approach, the court must determine whether the specific plaintiff would have forgone treatment if the risks had been adequately disclosed. The focus is upon the plaintiff's testimony as to what he or she would consider relevant information for deciding on treatment.

3. Damages

A third element for a cause of action for failure to obtain informed consent is damages. Damages vary depending on the jurisdiction. In jurisdictions following a negligence theory of liability, compensation may be received for loss or injury resulting from an undisclosed risk. To recover under this approach, the plaintiff needs to show physical harm.

In jurisdictions that use an assault and battery theory, recovery may include punitive, exemplary and nominal damages. A direct injury need not be shown in order to establish a cause of action. However, for a plaintiff to receive compensatory damages, a compensable physical injury must be proven. Psychological injuries, alone such as mental distress or humiliation, are not sufficient to recover compensatory damages.

D. ISSUES OF CONSENT

Most litigation concerning informed consent centers on a physician's failure to provide adequate information. In addition to providing the information, the physician must also receive adequate consent. For consent to be valid, several elements must be satisfied. First, the patient must understand the information. Second, assent must be present. Third, the consent must be voluntary. And fourth, the patient must have the legal capacity to consent.

1. Understanding

Even when a physician informs the patient about all material risks and the patient consents, informed consent may not be sufficient. The patient may not understand the nature and degree of the disclosed risks. When this situation arises, courts take two approaches.

The majority approach focuses on the adequacy of the physician's disclosure. The disclosure must include an explanation comprehensible to the average patient. This approach does not require a showing the patient actually comprehended the risks.

An alternative approach focuses on the patient. The disclosure must be sufficiently adequate to actually inform the particular patient. It is the physician's duty to make sure the individual patient knows and understands the risks.

2. Consent

Generally, a physician cannot provide medical treatment without obtaining a patient's actual assent or agreement to accept treatment. To establish assent, a physician must prove that he or she informed the patient of all collateral risks, and the patient knowingly agreed. Consent is determined through an objective test. The patient's accord or agreement must be such that a reasonable physician would have determined that the patient accepted the proffered treatment. Generally, patients may at any time revoke their consent.

The reasonable physician must believe the patient's words and behavior manifested both awareness of risks and acceptance of the treatment. Usually assent is only an issue when determining whether the patient's acceptance of treatment was the result of sufficient knowledge and awareness. Some states have enacted statutes which list the requirements of informed consent. A typical statute will both require the physician to provide the pa-

tient with a document that lists collateral risks and
specify that the patient need sign the document as
proof of assent. Other states require an informed
consent sheet or an entry in the patient's medical
record that merely states the patient has been informed. It should be noted, most states do not
require written informed consent.

Consent may not be necessary in limited situations. One exception to the requirement of consent
is where the patient is unconscious or incapable of
consenting. In emergency situations the courts do
not impose the requirement of consent. However,
harm must be imminent and the likely benefit of
treatment must clearly outweigh any of its risks.

3. Voluntarily Given Consent

Consent must be voluntary in order to be legally
recognized. If consent is obtained through coercion
or duress, the consent is not voluntary. Consent is
not voluntary when the circumstances the patient is
in are sufficiently coercive that a fact finder is led to
the conclusion that, but for the coercion or duress,
consent would have been withheld. Consent may be
involuntary if gained through force, deceit, duress,
overreaching, or as the result of an empty promise
of a benefit. Likewise, consent may be involuntary
where derived through unequal bargaining.

Consent generally is presumed legal. Presumption
of legality or capacity to consent extends to psychiatric patients and may only be rebutted with adequate proof. However, some medical decisions do
not require a psychiatric patient's consent. In a few

states, informed consent is not required to administer psychotropic medications to civilly committed patients. However, this exception does not extend to consent in experimental or research settings.

The use of experimental treatment protocols on institutionalized patients raises the issue of voluntary consent. The issue is even more significant when the experiment is physically intrusive. The question exists as to whether a hospitalized patient may voluntarily consent to treatment of an experimental nature. The hospital setting is an inherently coercive environment, because a patient is dependent on the staff. The concern is that a patient may consent to experimentation in return for promises of early release or improved custodial conditions. Even if the researchers are not intentionally coercive, the patient may erroneously believe that consent will lead to certain benefits or favors. However, denying patients the right to consent may not be an appropriate solution. Some patients may be legally capable of giving valid consent. These patients may understand the risks involved, but may still desire experimental treatment for the psychological or medical benefits these treatments may provide without regard to any extrinsic benefit or favor.

4. Lack of Capacity to Consent

Some individuals lack the capacity to consent. Two major groups of individuals who lack capacity to give valid consent or are considered incompetent include: infants and the mentally incompetent.

The law attempts to protect minors by withholding their right to consent. Generally, minors are legally incompetent to consent to treatment. Physicians must obtain consent from a minor's parents or guardian prior to treatment. However, exceptions do exist.

One exception is in emergency situations where the parent is unavailable to give consent. The emergency situation must require treatment intervention to save a child's life or prevent the child from suffering irreparable injury.

A second exception exists when parents refuse to give consent. The court may order necessary medical treatment for a minor, even though the parents refuse, if the situation is life-threatening or risks irreparable injury to the child. A special situation arises when parent's religious beliefs are the basis for the parent's refusal to consent to medical intervention on behalf of a minor. The exception that permits medical intervention over parental objection may extend to nonemergency situations when the parent's refusal to consent to treatment is based on the parent's religious beliefs.

Some state statutes allow children to consent to treatment if the treatment is necessary, relatively risk-free, and requiring parental consent would have a chilling effect on providing health care needed by the minor. The situations such statutes are meant to deal with occur when a minor seeks treatment for venereal disease or pregnancy, or desires to obtain contraceptives. Additionally, many statutes specifically allow children to consent to mental health treatment. However, some state statutes, such as that of Illinois, specifically limit the number of mental health treatment sessions that can occur before the parents are informed the minor is receiving mental health treatment.

An exception also exists for emancipated children. Children who are no longer subject to parental control, guidance or financial support may also consent to treatment. In some jurisdictions, this exception extends to older children, not yet emancipated, who, nevertheless, display intelligent and mature judgment.

The law also attempts to protect those declared mentally incompetent by holding them incapable of giving legally effective consent to treatment. Many mentally disabled individuals suffer from impairments which diminish their ability to comprehend information, make rational judgments, or communicate intentions.

When a psychiatric patient is mentally incapable of giving consent, a judicial order or decree is required prior to performing nonemergency treatment. A judicial order may declare a psychiatric patient legally incompetent to consent and provide for the appointment of a guardian who may, then, consent to treatment on behalf of the patient. In some jurisdictions, guardians may consent to treatment on the basis of a judgment of the patient ward's best interests. In other jurisdictions, a guardian may consent to treatment through a process of substituted judgment. In some jurisdictions, a guardian's decision to consent to electroconvulsive therapy or to the administration of psychotropic medications must receive court approval.

The capacity of some patients to consent may not be clear. Some patients fluctuate in their ability to acknowledge and understand information provided to them. A court determination that a patient is incompetent to consent at a particular time may not apply to the patient in the future. Physicians seeking to obtain informed consent must be sensitive to the patient's ability to understand the disclosed information and to give effective consent. When it is determined that a patient is competent, the physician must adhere to the patient's wishes.

E. REGULATING RESEARCH

Not all research with the mentally impaired is designed for direct patient treatment. Experimentation involving the mentally ill also involves scientific research into treatment efficacy. Fear of over zealous experimentation has prompted regulation of research and experimentation. Regulations, both professional and legal, have been developed to protect the rights of mentally disabled acting as research subjects.

1. Professional Self–Regulation

A researcher's work is subject to professional self-regulation. Researchers who plan to publish their research in professional journals are required to show the procedures utilized have been approved by the proper regulatory bodies and conform to governmental and ethical requirements. Some journals require that all research submitted for publication follow the appropriate government agency guidelines. Additionally, many professional organizations have ethical and policy codes mandating researchers follow certain guidelines. These organizations may impose sanctions against members who violate their respective codes. Professional self-regulation is thus important in biomedical research.

2. Legal Regulation

Through legal regulation, states provide remedies for subjects harmed by research and further mandate punishment of those researchers who violate experimental guidelines. Legal regulations extend to both behavioral and biomedical research. Legal regulation of research is effected statutorily and administratively, and by case law.

Federal and state legislatures have enacted statutes regulating human subject research. The Federal legislation includes the National Research Act of 1974 and the Food and Drug Act of 1938. Both Acts are administered by the Department of Health and Human Services, and they apply to all researchers who obtain federal funding.

The National Research Act regulates human-subject research in two ways. First, researchers must submit a detailed description of their research plan to an Institutional Review Board that oversees all human-subject research. The board reviews the proposed research and ensures that all risks to humans are minimized. Second, the Act requires the researcher to obtain the informed consent from all subjects prior to conducting the research. Additionally, the Act imposes specific requirements governing the extent of information to be provided to subjects.

The Department of Health and Human Services also protects human research subjects through the Food and Drug Act. The Food and Drug Act requires the approval of experimental drugs and medical devices prior to their use in human research. Further, researchers using experimental drugs and procedures must provide the subjects with information about the drug or medical device when obtaining informed consent.

Many states also provide safeguards for human research subjects. Some states require researchers meet informed consent requirements prior to receiving funding. Furthermore, New York and California require all medical research, regardless of funding, involve obtaining informed consent from all research subjects.

However, federal and state regulations do not provide compensation for the injured research subject. Compensation is only available under state tort law or civil rights statutes.

F. PROBLEMS WITH BEHAVIORAL RESEARCH

The type of research often determines the extent to which informed consent must be obtained. Biomedical research involves scientific research into physical or biological changes in a subject. Biomedical research poses greater risks to the subject than behavior research, therefore, requiring more significant disclosure.

Behavioral research is directed at scientific inquiry into factors that determine human behavior and attitudes. With behavioral research, there is generally no physical risk to the subject. Therefore, the informed consent standard may be reduced. Yet, behavioral research frequently requires deception. Due to the nature of the research, disclosure of risks often would adversely affect the outcome of the research. There are primarily three types of behavioral research: passive observation studies, manipulation studies without overt deception; survey studies; and manipulation and deception studies. The type of behavioral research influences the requisite amount of necessary disclosure.

1. Passive Observation Studies

Passive observation requires no manipulation of the subject's environment. Generally, observation will not pose any risk to the subject, because subjects are frequently unaware of their participation in the study. However, the researcher may be potentially liable for invasion of privacy if the subject matter is sensitive. Liability may also result if the researcher keeps records of the subject's identity, publishes the information, and the publication causes legal liability or financial loss to the subject.

2. Manipulation Studies Without Overt Deception

Another type of study involves manipulation without deception. This type of study involves modification of the subject's environment. In manipulation studies, researchers generally do not have a duty of informed consent, because such a requirement would undermine obtaining the desired results of the research. However, the subjects involved in this type of research usually are not placed at risk.

3. Survey

Survey research does not place a subject at risk. However, the researcher must keep the subject's identity anonymous where the interview concerns sensitive or personal subjects. Failure to do so may result in a cause of action for invasion of privacy.

4. Manipulation and Deception

Manipulation and deception research is sometimes necessary. Often the subject's awareness of the researcher's goal may grossly hinder obtaining accurate results. Therefore, informed consent is often limited. The Department of Health and Human Services permits the forgoing of the informed consent requirement where the risks to the subject are minimal.

Patient risks depend on the type of deception employed. In some situations, the risks may be great. Where the researcher exposes individuals to severe artificial stress or to possible influence of their self esteem, the researcher may be held liable for failure to obtain informed consent or for intentional infliction of emotional distress.

CHAPTER 6

CONFIDENTIALITY, PRIVACY, AND PATIENT ACCESS TO RECORDS

A. THE NEED FOR CONFIDENTIAL-ITY IN MENTAL HEALTH TREATMENT

Confidentiality in mental health treatment is important to effective treatment. The objective of mental health treatment is to reduce the discomfort caused by mental illness, to stabilize the condition of, and ultimately to successfully rehabilitate a patient. Confidentiality between the patient and the mental health professional encourages the patient to reveal intimate thoughts and feelings to the mental health professional. Confidentiality also protects the patient from any embarrassment that might accompany disclosure of communications during treatment.

Confidentiality serves a public interest function as well. An individual in need of mental health treatment may be encouraged to seek treatment knowing communication with the treating professional will be confidential. Moreover, confidentiality ensures that the patient will not suffer from any social stigma attached by the public to those receiving mental health treatment.

Confidentiality of communications between a patient and treating professional extends to non-disclosure of patient records as well. Confidentiality of patient records protects the patient from the same harms as verbal disclosure of patient communications.

B. PROFESSIONAL AND ETHICAL BASES FOR CONFIDENTIALITY

Psychiatrists, as physicians, are ethically bound by the Hippocratic oath which states in part, "Whatever in connection with my professional practice, or not in connection with it, I see or hear, in the life of men, which ought not to be spoken of abroad, I will not divulge, as reckoning that all such should be kept secret."

The American Medical Association has promulgated a code reiterating the ancient maxims of professional responsibility. The Code allows disclosure by a physician only when legally compelled to do so, or when necessary to protect the safety of the patient or community. A determination of what is dangerous to the public is difficult to make. A therapist's disclosure of otherwise confidential information about a patient resulting from misjudgment about public harm, that is thought to justify disclosure, may result in legal action against the therapist. The health care professional, therefore, is discouraged from both making disclosures about patients and consenting to releases of patient records.

Psychologists are similarly bound by a set of ethical principles set out in a code promulgated by the American Psychological Association. Psychologists are required protect the confidentiality of information obtained from clients. Before divulging information, a psychologist should determine the immediacy of danger created by nondisclosure, the scope and purpose of disclosure, the client's awareness of the limits of confidentiality, and the client's consent to disclosure.

C. LEGAL REGULATION OF CONFIDENTIALITY

In addition to the professional and ethical bases for maintaining confidentiality, various licensing and certification statutes encourage treating mental health professionals to maintain confidentiality. Many states have enacted special disclosure laws which place tight controls on disclosure of information concerning the mentally ill. Such laws generally provide for a testimonial privilege. The testimonial privilege allows the therapists to refuse to testify about their patients in court. Penalties for violation of these statutes range from fines to revocation of the therapist's license.

Suits brought against the therapist for failing to maintain confidentiality are typically civil damage suits. A civil damage suit for failure to maintain confidentiality or nondisclosure can be brought under defamation, invasion of privacy, and breach of duty arising from a confidential or nondisclosure professional relationship. Generally, a therapist's wrongful disclosure results satisfies the requirements for establishing all three torts. Civil suits are the most effective method of enforcing a therapist's duty of confidentiality.

D. LEGAL REMEDIES FOR WRONGFUL DISCLOSURE

1. Breach of Privacy Actions

Breach of privacy actions are allowed in almost every state. A breach of privacy action brought by a patient against a therapist arises from the disclosure of confidential information which the patient reasonably expects to remain private. In instances where an individual is incapable of forming such an expectation or realizing harm has been done to him by disclosure of personal information, state legislatures act as *parens patriae*. The laws provide a statutory expectation of privacy for these individuals. The doctrine of *parens patriae* extends to inmates of mental institutions within the correctional system.

2. Defamation Actions

Defamation is conduct which tends to injure the plaintiff's reputation, diminish the esteem, respect, goodwill or confidence in which the plaintiff is held, or excite adverse or unpleasant feelings against the plaintiff. Defamation may be oral (slander); or it may be written (libel). In courts where malice or ill will is not required in order to bring a defamation suit, the speaker may be liable under an implied malice standard.

Various defenses to defamation actions exist including: truth, privilege and consent. Truth is always a defense to a defamatory statement or publication. Privilege may be an exemption from liability where speaking or publishing defamatory words was made in the performance of a political, judicial, social, or personal duty. For example, a therapist who makes slanderous statements in the course of judicial testimony is exempt from liability. A therapist's privilege also extends to statements about a patient made to other professionals treating that patient.

Privilege may be absolute or conditional. An absolute privilege refers to the speaker or publisher's right to make statements without regard to malice or ill will. Conditional privilege, also called qualified privilege, protects the speaker or publisher as long as malice, or knowledge of the falsity of the statement, can not be shown. State statutes address the specific requirements for actions based upon libelous or slanderous statements.

Consent is another defense. A therapist is not liable for disclosure of communications if the patient consents to disclosure. Two problems exist with consent behavior, however. It may not be clear whether the patient consented to disclosure; moreover, the scope of consent may be unclear.

3. Remedies For Breach of Patient–Therapist Confidentiality

With the exception of a therapist's statements made about a patient during trial, a therapist generally may not disclose any information concerning patient-therapist communications. The purpose of this rule is to promote trust and honesty in the patient-therapist relationship in order that the patient be successfully treated. Where the consent of the patient is not obtained, a therapist is barred from publishing materials specifically referring to a patient's experiences, feelings, or thoughts. A patient's consent may not be obtained during the course of a therapy session. Although the rule against disclosure is not absolute, the use of patient-therapist communications is not justified by showing an educational or medical purpose.

To obtain punitive damages for breach of confidentiality, the plaintiff must show that the therapist disclosed information with malice or ill will. Actual damages may be awarded where the plaintiff suffers injury as a result of a therapist's wrongful disclosure of confidential information. Yet, in some cases where the patient suffers injury resulting from the publication of confidential information, monetary damages may not be sufficient. In these instances, the plaintiff may seek to enjoin the defendant from further circulation of the publication.

Wrongful disclosure of confidential information may also lead to disciplinary measures by state agencies licensing and regulating mental health professionals. In addition to awarding the patient monetary damages, the therapist may also be fined under statutory provisions. In some instances where the therapist has acted unprofessionally in making the disclosure of confidential information, the state licensing board may revoke the therapist's license.

4. Limitations on the Duty of Confidentiality

A therapist's duty to maintain confidentiality concerning patient-therapist communications is not absolute. In some situations, disclosure of patient information is mandatory. Compulsory reporting statutes require therapists to disclose such information as child abuse or narcotic addiction. Therapists may also be required to disclose relevant information during judicial proceedings. Some states require therapists to disclose threats or danger posed by a patient to third parties.

E. STATUTORY REPORTING REQUIREMENTS

Most states require that therapists disclose specific patient information such as communicable diseases, narcotic addiction and child abuse. Some professionals believe mandatory reporting requirements detract from, if not abrogate, the therapist's testimonial privilege. Similarly, some professionals maintain such reporting requirements adversely effect the successful treatment of patients.

Some controversy centers around the situations in which the reporting statutes take effect. Generally, mandatory reporting statutes require the disclosure of certain types of patient information obtained only during therapy sessions. Most states have held disclosure of patient information obtained during court ordered therapy sessions cannot be ordered, because it is not within the reach of mandatory reporting statutes.

F. DISCLOSURES OF DANGEROUS PROPENSITIES OF THE PATIENT

Increasingly, states are requiring therapists to disclose to third parties threats of, or direct danger posed by a patient. In *Tarasoff v. Regents of the University of California* (Cal.1976), the Supreme Court of California held therapists have a duty to protect third parties from the dangerous propensities of the patient where the patient informs the therapist of intentions to bring harm to an identifiable victim. Once a therapist determines a patient poses a direct danger to a third party, the therapist must take the steps necessary to protect foreseeable victims from those dangers. The court in *Tarasoff* suggested that a therapist may have to take one or many steps to protect the threatened person, depending on the facts of the case. The duty imposed by *Tarasoff* is not merely to warn the third party, but the court's opinion imposes a duty to protect the intended victim. For the duty to protect to arise, there must be: (1) a serious threat of violence; (2) and imminent threat of harm; and (3)an identifiable third party who is at risk of harm.

Although the therapist's duty to protect third parties from foreseeable violence by a patient has not been fully developed or adopted by every state, most states have found the therapist's duty extends only to identifiable victims. The duty does not extend to the public in general. Furthermore, the patient must inform the therapist of an intention to cause bodily injury or death. In the absence of the required factors, courts will generally find disclosures of patient information to be a breach of confidentiality.

A minority of courts have recognized a broader duty to protect the public from the danger posed by a patient. Cases have been brought on theories of negligent discharge of patients or failure to institute commitment hearings because of the danger posed by a patient.

G. JUDICIAL PROCEEDINGS AND THE TESTIMONIAL PRIVILEGE

Therapists summoned to testify in court are required to disclose patient information if society's need for the information outweighs the therapists interest in protecting the patient. This need for confidential patient information arises both in civil and criminal trials. In criminal trials, society's interest in rendering a fair verdict and punishing only the guilty is strong enough to require therapists to disclose patient information. Access to factual information outside of trials may also be necessary. In these instances, courts may compel therapists to disclose patient information for legislative hearings and investigations. The necessity to compel disclosure in important situations is not absolute. The government may never compel disclosure of irrelevant information. Furthermore, the public's interest in maintaining a fair judicial system prevents unlimited disclosure of patient information. Statutory privileges may extend from excluding the disclosure of certain topics of information to barring individuals in certain relationships from disclosing information about one another. Relationships typically protected by statute are attorney and client, physician and patient, and husband and wife.

Only recently has the psychotherapist-patient relationship been recognized. In order for a relationship to be worthy of protection, four conditions must be met. First, society must have an interest in fostering the relationship. Second, the individuals must have agreed that communication would remain confidential. Third, confidentiality must be an indispensable element to achieving the purpose of the communication. Lastly, the damage caused to society by not obtaining the information must be less serious than the damage caused to the patient by compelling disclosure.

Statutory provisions governing disclosure requirements have not eliminated problems concerning testimonial privilege. Many statutes do not specify which professionals are covered by the privilege statutes. Although the psychotherapist-patient relationship is recognized as one which society should foster, only some state statutes governing testimonial privilege and professional's disclosure include psychotherapists within the list of professionals covered. Moreover, other mental health professionals including psychiatric nurses and social workers, engaged in therapeutic work often are not covered by the psychotherapist-patient privilege.

1. Defining the Treatment Relationship

Privilege statutes that specifically cover psychotherapists only extend the privilege to protect patients who reveal information in the course of treatment. Various problems arise in determining exactly what constitutes a treatment relationship. In *State v. Miller* (Or.1985), the Supreme Court of Oregon found a psychotherapist-patient treatment relationship existed when defendant telephoned a mental hospital to inform a psychiatrist that he killed someone. Although the psychiatrist had never counseled the defendant before, the information revealed to the psychiatrist during the telephone conversation was found to have established a confidential relationship. The court reasoned that the communication was based upon the psychiatrist's promise of confidentiality. The relationship extends to initial conferences made for the purposes of establishing a therapeutic relationship, even if the latter was never formed. However, the psychotherapist and patient must engage in communication with the intention of forming a treatment relationship.

2. The Presence of Third Parties During Communications

Problems arise as to the scope of testimonial privilege when patients disclose information to their therapists in the presence of others. This problem often arises in the mental health context, because of the extensive use of group therapy as a treatment mode. Courts will generally find that the privilege extends to communications made in the presence of third parties if the communication was made confidentially for the purpose of furthering diagnosis and treatment. In *State v. Andring* (Minn.1984), the Supreme Court of Minnesota found that communications made by patients during a group psychotherapy session are confidential. Since each participant is an integral part of every other participant's treatment, the information revealed during the session is privileged.

Courts determine whether communications in the presence of third parties are privileged by analyzing the surrounding circumstances to see if the patient intended the communications to be confidential. In situations where the third party is casually present and not part of the treatment, the general rule is that the communication made in the surrounding circumstances is not privileged.

3. Waiver of the Privilege

Since the purpose of the psychotherapist-patient privilege is to protect the patient from injury caused by disclosure of confidential information, the patient may waive the right to confidentiality. If the patient expressly waives the right to confidentiality, the psychotherapist may not invoke the privilege to keep the information confidential.

Privilege may be waived by the patient in two ways. First, the patient may fail to raise the privilege defense when confidential information is sought by a party in litigation. However, if the patient is unable to assert the privilege due to absence or incapacity, the psychotherapist is required to assert the privilege for him.

The second way of waiving confidentiality involves the patient-litigant exception. A patient who claims his or her mental condition as a matter in the litigation may not invoke the privilege to preclude a therapist's testimony concerning the patient's mental condition. For example, a patient who raises insanity as a defense may not prevent testimonial disclosure of confidential information by claiming that it is privileged. The same rule is followed for a patient who initiates a malpractice suit against his therapist, and for a patient who initiates an emotional distress suit against another individual.

A patient's right to invoke the privilege exists even after the patient's death. If a patient dies, the privilege may be invoked by the patient's estate. For example, a personal representative of the patient's estate may invoke the privilege in disputes over the patient's mental capacity at the time the patient signed a will.

In civil actions, a patient's failure to assert the privilege is an implied waiver of the privilege. In civil proceedings involving a patient's assertion of emotional distress, the patient-litigant exception will compel disclosure of relevant information relating specifically to the patient's emotional or mental condition. Some jurisdictions require that the patient disclose at least some patient-therapist communication to his lawyer in order to retain communication confidentiality. Many judges are critical of such a requirement, because it forces a patient to disclose confidential material to his lawyer or else waive the privilege altogether.

In criminal proceedings, if a patient raises his mental condition as a defense to his criminal conduct, his right to assert the privilege is automatically waived. The patient may even be required to disclose basic information relating to his mental illness to the prosecution in pre-trial proceedings. Generally, an attorney may consult a psychiatrist concerning the validity of the patient's mental illness without fear of mandatory disclosure. Information disclosed by the attorney in trial preparation is protected by the work product doctrine. The work product doctrine, however, does not protect other information disclosed in the course of trial preparation. It is important to recognize that waiver of the patient-therapist relationship is not a waiver of the attorney-client privilege.

A patient's expressed or implied waiver of privilege does not give a psychotherapist unlimited discretion in the disclosure of information. A waiver of privilege only allows the disclosure of relevant information. Furthermore, a therapist may not testify on behalf of the defense and the prosecution. To do so would deter patients from revealing complete and honest information to their therapists, and defeat the purpose of psychiatric treatment.

H.   THE CONFRONTATION CLAUSE AND TESTIMONIAL PRIVILEGE

The Sixth and Fourteenth Amendments give a criminal defendant the right to discover favorable evidence. The Confrontation Clause embodies this idea by guaranteeing a criminal defendant the right to confront those who testify against him and by guaranteeing the right to cross examination. However, the interests of the criminal defendant may directly conflict with interests of patient confidentiality.

Many states have statutes protecting the confidentiality of records dealing with child abuse. A criminal defendant in need of such records for his defense will encounter difficulty in obtaining the records. In *Pennsylvania v. Ritchie* (S.Ct.1987), the United States Supreme Court held the Confrontation Clause did not automatically compel the disclosure of all confidential materials for the benefit of the defendant. In *Ritchie,* the defendant was tried for child molestation and abuse. Defendant sought the disclosure of confidential child abuse records through the Confrontation Clause. The agency refused to release the records, asserting their confidentiality. The Court held the Confrontation Clause did not automatically compel disclosure or override all confidentiality laws. However, the Court found that a strong interest in maintaining confidentiality does not bar disclosure in all circumstances. Although the interest in preventing injury to the child by disclosure of information is very strong, there is an even stronger interest in ensuring that the defendant be granted a fair trial by giving him access to information that may influence the jury's verdict. The Court concluded the trial court should make a determination of whether the information requested would have affected the trial's outcome. If so, the trial court was directed to order a new trial at which the defendant could have access to the requested information.

As determined in *Ritchie,* neither confidentiality laws nor the Confrontation Clause are absolute. Many individual agencies, such as those maintaining confidential records, have provisions requiring disclosure of information upon court order. In the absence of specific provisions, the court must weigh the interest in protecting confidentiality against the interest and need for the information in conducting a fair trial.

I. PATIENT ACCESS TO RECORDS

At common law, mentally ill patients did not have a right to inspect their own records. Certain circumstances exist, however, giving patients the right of access to their records. First, patients may obtain access to their records for the purposes of litigation. However, a patient must obtain a court order for the release of his records.

Many states also have legislation providing mental patients with the right of access to their records. State statutes give recipients of mental health services the right to inspect and copy their records. A patient's right of access to his or her records does not include a right of access to the therapist's personal notes. The therapist's notes may include information between the therapist and other patients, as well as speculations and ideas injurious to the patient. A therapist's awareness that his or her thoughts may be kept separate from a patient's medical records aids the therapist in providing effective treatment and preventing injury to the patient who subsequently may wish to see his mental records.

J. CONFIDENTIALITY OF DRUG AND ALCOHOL TREATMENT RECORDS

Federal statutes provide guidelines for confidentiality and disclosure of drug and alcohol treatment records for persons treated in programs receiving direct or indirect assistance from the federal government. These statutes and the regulations adopted by the Department of Health and Human Services provide stringent protection for these records. The federal statutes require that records of the identity, diagnosis, prognosis, or treatment of any patient which are maintained in connection with the performance of any program or activity relating to alcoholism or alcohol abuse, or in connection with any drug abuse or drug abuse prevention function, which is conducted, regulated, or directly or indirectly assisted by any department or agency of the United States, are to be kept confidential. Disclosure is permitted, with patient consent, in several situations: in medical emergencies requiring information for treatment of the individual, for specified research activities, and for audit and evaluation activities. The regulations permit disclosure pursuant to a court order for criminal prosecution and investigation.

CHAPTER 7

THE RIGHT TO COUNSEL AND ADVOCACY SERVICES

A. RIGHT TO COUNSEL IN CIVIL COMMITMENT PROCEEDINGS

Civil commitment proceedings are governed by statute. In most jurisdictions, patients facing civil commitment proceedings have a right to counsel. However, the right to counsel of itself does not guarantee adequate legal representation. Most state statutes provide no more than mandatory counsel, and few statutes specify the duties such counsel must assume.

Lawyers differ in their view of the role of legal counsel in civil commitment proceedings. Generally, two opposing approaches are taken: (1) the best interest model and (2) the advocacy model. These models differ in the degree to which lawyers are willing to defer to the client's wishes. Under a best interest approach, an attorney acts in a way that maximizes achieving the client's interest even if such action involves disregard of the client's choice. Under an advocacy approach, the attorney will defer to the client's wishes.

In deciding how to represent a client in a civil commitment proceeding, the lawyer receives little guidance from either statutory or professional standards. Moreover, the ABA Model Code and Model Rules contain ambiguities in their treatment of the proper approach to conflicts of interest between counsel and mentally disabled clients.

B. CONSTITUTIONAL CLAIM TO THE RIGHT TO COUNSEL

The United States Supreme Court has never held that there is a constitutional right to counsel at civil commitment proceedings. *Vitek v. Jones* (S.Ct.1980), involved a proceeding held to determine whether a prisoner had mental disabilities requiring civil commitment. The Supreme Court refused to find a right to legal counsel for individuals involved in civil commitment proceedings. The Court held due process does not require legal counsel. Instead, due process is satisfied if the individual is provided qualified, independent assistance. Qualified independent assistance may include representation by a licensed psychiatrist or other mental health professionals.

By contrast, most state courts hold due process requires counsel at the commitment hearings. However, states differ on the meaning of the right of counsel, the degree of expert assistance, minimum qualifications and required effectiveness of counsel.

Prior to the 1970's, most states did not have statutorily mandated legal counsel for patients facing civil commitment. Today, most states have statutes mandating counsel at civil commitment hearings. Most statutes provide for one or more of the following: (1) allow counsel at hearings, (2) require counsel at hearings, (3) require adversary counsel at hearings, (4) delineate duties of counsel at hearings, or (5) provide for a separate agency to provide legal assistance.

Most states allow or even require counsel. A typical state statute, such as that of Texas mandates that after a civil commitment petition is filed, the judge must appoint a lawyer to represent the patient. Counsel must then be furnished with all necessary records and papers. Few state statutes, however, require more than the presence of counsel at hearings.

Even fewer state statutes delineate counsel's duties. An example of a state's legislation delineating duties is the Iowa statute requiring the advocate to review reports and medical records. The advocate must also communicate with the patient, visit the patient within fifteen days of the hearing and consult with medical personnel. However, the statute does not require the advocate to be an attorney.

Finally, a few states have established a separate agency to provide counsel for patients. An example is the Illinois statute that mandates an established advocacy agency represent patients at civil commitment hearings.

C. ROLE OF COUNSEL IN CIVIL COMMITMENT PROCEEDINGS

In the past, civil commitment hearings were controlled by medical personnel. During civil commitment proceedings, medical personnel, most often the examining physician, testified in favor of civil commitment. The physician usually testified that commitment was in the best interest of the patient. Little emphasis was placed upon due process.

Today, attorneys play a major role in civil commitment hearings. Generally, attorneys emphasize due process and strict compliance with statutory standards for civil commitment.

Nevertheless, the attorney representing a client in a civil commitment proceeding often feels trapped between two conflicting interests: the benefits of commitment verses the harshness of loss of liberty and confinement attendant to commitment. As mentioned above, an attorney can use one of two approaches to representing the client in the civil commitment proceeding: Counsel acts either as an advocate for the client, or acts in the client's best interests.

1. Best Interests Model

Under the best interests model, the attorney uses his or her personal assessment of the patient's best interests. Based on this evaluation, the lawyer may advocate for release, hospitalization or less restrictive alternatives. Two types of attorneys exist under the best interests model: the active lawyer and the passive lawyer.

The active attorney believes patients are unable to determine their own needs. Often such a lawyer feels a need to protect the patient's liberty interests, instead of deferring to psychiatric recommendation. The active lawyer makes his or her own decisions regarding the patient's best interests. The lawyer makes this determination through interviews with the patient, members of the medical community, family, and friends, and by reviewing the patient's records. The active attorney may advocate release, less restrictive alternatives or commitment.

In contrast, the passive lawyer defers to psychiatric recommendations implicitly assuming they are authoritative and accurate. Due to a lack of personal knowledge, the passive lawyer feels the lack of professional training necessary to determine the best interest of the patient. The passive lawyer defers to the mental health community. The passive lawyer usually encourages speedy commitment and attempts to avoid placing members of the patient's family in adversarial positions.

Two significant criticism of the best interests model exist. The first criticism of the best interest model is that this approach undervalues the patient's loss of freedom. Second, critics argue the lawyers assuming this role often fail to recognize the harms of commitment such as institutional over crowding, the stigma of the "institutionalized" label, poor medical and living conditions, and the patient's adverse reactions reaction to lack of rigorous advocacy in the effort to avoid the loss of liberty following institutionalization.

2. Advocacy Model

Advocacy lawyers primarily focus on three aspects of the commitment procedure; loss of liberty, fairness in the commitment proceedings, and the patient's wishes with regard to the ultimate issue of commitment. Similar to representation in criminal proceedings, the advocacy lawyer presents the strongest possible case to avoid commitment in an attempt to protect a patient's liberty. Strong advocacy serves to protect against loss of liberty due to erroneous commitment. The advocate believes truth will only emerge through direct confrontation in the adversarial process. As a result, the assumption is potential mistakes will be reduced. Finally, the advocate lawyer believes his client should have the freedom to decide the issue of treatment. The advocacy lawyer does not allow his or her own personal judgment as to the client's best interests determine the client's defense. After the patient decides his or her own preferred outcome, the lawyer leaves the final decision to the court.

The advocacy model has been the subject of vigorous criticism. One criticism argues an advocacy lawyer neglects the best interest of the patient and fails to recognize that commitment proceedings are not supposed to be adversarial. In this view, the state only serves an administrative role of providing access to records and medical witnesses to a court that serves as a neutral factfinder on the issue of whether civil commitment of the individual should occur. The admitting psychiatrist is generally viewed as the adversary in this approach to civil commitment. Cross examination is seen as sufficient guard against an erroneous judgment. Furthermore, it is argued that increasing the adversarial atmosphere of the commitment hearing creates undesirable trauma for some patients. Thus, it is argued adversarial proceedings may be counter-therapeutic for the patient, and deter families from involvement or participation in commitment proceedings. Also, adversarial conflict causes tension between the psychiatrist and his patient. Finally, for the lawyer's efforts to be beneficial, the attorney needs time, training and funding that is often unavailable.

D.   INEFFECTIVE COUNSEL IN CIVIL COMMITMENT PROCEEDINGS

It is not uncommon for a patient facing a civil commitment proceeding to be represented by legal counsel who is often only modestly trained and ill prepared to provide representation. Many attorneys do not acknowledge the patient's needs. Furthermore, many attorneys lack formal training in the law of civil commitment.

The law is silent as to the degree of competency required of counsel to satisfy the due process requirement in mental disability cases. The United

States Supreme Court has never addressed the question of adequacy of counsel in civil commitment proceedings. However, the Supreme Court has addressed the adequacy of counsel issue in criminal cases. In *Strickland v. Washington* (S.Ct.1984), the Court held counsel would be deemed ineffective only where the counsel denied the client his Sixth Amendment rights. The Court determined counsel was ineffective if counsel's performance was both deficient and prejudicial to the defense. Performance may be deficient if counsel fails to advocate defendant's cause, fails to consult with defendant on matters of substantive concern, fails to inform defendant of important developments, or fails to make reasonable investigations. Pennsylvania has strictly applied *Strickland* in civil commitment proceedings. By statute, Arizona grants the court power to hold an attorney in contempt if the attorney fails to perform several specified duties.

E.   RIGHT TO INDEPENDENT EXPERT EVALUATION IN CIVIL COMMITMENT PROCEEDINGS

Few courts have dealt with the issue of whether a client facing involuntary civil commitment has the right to an independent psychiatric examination. Of the courts that have ruled on the issue, most have held that the right to independent psychiatric examination exists. The rationale for granting independent psychiatric evaluation is that an attorney is not otherwise in a position to rebut a hospital's admitting psychiatric testimony. Some state courts have held the right to expert evaluation is constitutionally required through the equal protection clause or the right to effective counsel. Other states mandate expert assistance as part of the state's commitment law.

F. ABA MODEL RULES AND CODE OF PROFESSIONAL CONDUCT

The American Bar Association Model Code of Professional Responsibility and the Rules of Professional Conduct are attempts to provide guidance for attorneys representing clients with mental disabilities. The Model Code of Professional Responsibility offers little guidance for attorneys representing the mentally ill or mentally handicapped. The code requires lawyers to zealously represent their clients, within the strictures of the law. However, the rules are not very helpful in explaining what this means.

Under the Model Code, an attorney is entitled to make some decisions without consulting the client if the decision does not involve the client's substantive rights. However, if the client's substantive rights are involved, the lawyer must defer to the client's decision. Yet, the differentiation between substantive versus procedural rights is not easily determined.

Additionally, the Model Code requires the client to make informed decisions. The lawyer must exert his or her best efforts to ensure the client is adequately informed of the relevant considerations including significant nonlegal matters that may play a role in the ultimate decision about commitment. If the client chooses a course of conduct contrary to counsel's judgement, the counsel may withdraw as counsel.

Finally, under the Model Code, a legally incompetent individual must be assigned a legal guardian or representative. If a guardian already has been assigned, the lawyer must consult the client's guardian. If the patient does not have a guardian, the lawyer serves as the client's guardian throughout the legal proceedings. Regardless of whether the client is declared mentally incompetent, the lawyer must obtain all possible assistance and direction from the client.

Likewise, the Model Rules of Professional Conduct provides little guidance for lawyers in civil commitment proceedings. The Model Rules restrict a lawyer from representing clients where a general material conflict of interest exists because of the lawyer's own personal interest. Application of this requirement differs depending on whether the attorney adheres to the best interests approach or to the advocacy approach. The best interests model may be interpreted to permit a lawyer to act in what he determines the patient's best interest, or else withdraw. The Model Code requires that the lawyer to withdraw from representing a patient if the attorney cannot adequately represent the patient's wishes.

The Model Rules require that a lawyer should maintain a reasonably normal client-lawyer relationship with mentally impaired clients. The lawyer must determine the client's interest. Then, the lawyer must determine the patient's ability to act consistently with his or her interest. The client's degree of participation will depend on the lawyer's perception of the patient's mental condition. Counsel's personal judgment on this preliminary matter may lead to a lawyer-client conflict.

The Model Rules provide a client has the right to discharge his or her lawyer. However, if appointment of a succeeding counselor is unjustified, the client may then be required to represent himself. Furthermore, the client may be determined to be legally incompetent to discharge counsel. Even if the client approves of counsel, a lawyer may withdraw if the client insists on a course of action with which the lawyer does not agree.

G. PROTECTION UNDER FEDERAL STATUTORY PROGRAMS

Mentally handicapped individuals are guaranteed the right to counsel under various federal statutory programs. Three statutes that guarantee the right to counsel: the Education of Handicapped Act, the Developmentally Disabled Assistance and Bill of Rights Act, and, the Vocational Rehabilitation Services Act.

Under the Education of the Handicapped Act, the agency must inform the parent of a handicapped child of the right to counsel prior to an impartial due process hearing. This includes a right to appointed counsel at no cost, and of the availability of low cost legal and other relevant available services. At an impartial due process hearing, the child has the right to be accompanied and advised by counsel.

The Developmentally Disabled Assistance and Bill of Rights Act provides federally funded services for the developmentally disabled. However, under the Act, funds are provided only if the state has enacted a system to protect and advocate the rights of developmentally disabled persons. Under the Act, the state's protection and advocacy agency must provide direct representation for the disabled persons through specialized advocacy assistance. The goal is to provide disabled persons with protection of their rights under the law and to guarantee full access to federally funded programs.

Under the Vocational Rehabilitation Services Act, states may not receive vocational rehabilitation service funds unless the state maintains programs to provide assistance informing clients of all available benefits of the Rehabilitation act. This includes assistance in pursuing legal, administrative or other appropriate remedies. The Act also ensures the protection of the individual's statutory rights.

CHAPTER 8

CIVIL COMMITMENT

A. HISTORICAL ANTECEDENTS TO CIVIL COMMITMENT

Placement of patients in the first asylums established for the mentally ill in the eighteenth century, and for about 100 years thereafter, occurred with ease and informality. A request of a friend or relative to a member of the hospital staff for an order of admission would most often result in commitment.

Early humanitarian efforts, in this century, to secure decent care and treatment for the mentally ill focused, in part, on the inadequacy of the existing commitment laws. There was concern primarily with the possibility of wrongful commitment. Subsequently, concerns broadened to questions of treatment and rehabilitation, and identification of the best means to ensure effective medical care, protective custody and training for patients. Many states began to incorporate measures advocated by the medical profession such as institutionalization by medical certification, by an administrative authority or through a guardian.

Legal changes in the process of authorizing hospitalization did not end the concerns over commitment procedures. By the middle of the twentieth century, the preeminence of medical judgment on issues of admission and discharge was being challenged. Concern initially focused on the most drastic medical interventions, such as psychosurgery and electroconvulsive therapy, ultimately giving rise to the view that competent patients have a legal right to refuse all unwanted treatment, including medication. At the same time, there was an emerging demand for recognition of the legal right to treatment as a prerequisite for allowing the state to institutionalize an individual against his or her will.

B. THE CONTEXT OF CIVIL COMMIT-MENT LAW: DEINSTITUTIONALIZA-TION AND REINSTITUTIONALIZA-TION

The mental health system has experienced a dramatic decrease in the actual patient census of public mental hospitals since the mid–1950s. However, while the total number of patients in these facilities declined, the same period has witnessed a doubling in the annual admission rate to public mental health facilities. Many of these admissions have been readmissions. There are several explanations for this process of deinstitutionalization, and the accompanying surge in admission and readmission rates. These explanations include changes in the civil commitment laws narrowing commitment criteria, the required use of the least restrictive treatment alternative, and additional procedural protections from forced commitment. However, at the same time, shortened commitment terms make it possible a patient might be institutionalized more than once within the same year, resulting in an apparent increase in annual admission rates.

Another factor leading to deinstitutionalization was the advent of psychotropic medication in the mid–1950s. These medications suppressed the symptomatology of persons diagnosed with schizophrenia, manic-depressive psychosis, depression, and other major illnesses, and offered an inexpensive, quick treatment to a large number of mentally ill people.

Another significant factor was the growth of the community treatment movement. In 1963, Congress passed the Community Mental Health Centers Act, which provided funding for the establishment of outpatient treatment centers. Community treatment was thought to be at least as effective as institutional confinement in a mental hospital. Admission rates, however, continued to increase, because many communities had not developed adequate aftercare programs. Those patients released from the hospital as "stabilized" often returned within the year, because the community outpatient treatment was inadequate or resources were not available for adequate patient monitoring.

While deinstitutionalization has reduced the population of public mental health hospitals, it is now suggested better use of facilities must be made in order to meet the needs of the severely mentally ill. Changes in the law may be part of this trend. Some states have reacted by easing the criteria for commitment. However, civil commitment increased in New York City in the late 1980's, not attributable to a change in statutory language, but due to the city government's decision to take aggressive action against what municipal authorities judged to be a growing number of severely mentally ill homeless persons.

At least some increase in hospital admissions, independent of increases in the general population, is predictable. Resources for community treatment have been inadequate; and community programs have not always been effective, at least for certain categories of patients. There is a growing realization that treatment in the community is a complex and expensive proposition.

The relationship of the public mental health system to the criminal system must also be noted. Clearly, some of the individuals who were hospitalized in the past are now being processed through the criminal justice system, often on misdemeanor charges such as "vagrancy" violations. A debate has raged over whether this development represents the "criminalization of mentally disordered behavior" or whether, instead, deinstitutionalization and commitment law reforms have prevented further "psychologizing of criminal behavior." Whatever the outcome of this debate, the key point for present purposes is that changes in one system have usually brought about changes in the other.

C. CIVIL COMMITMENT: BASES
OF JUSTIFICATION

1. The State's Power to Commit

The state's power to commit individuals rests on inherent attributes of sovereignty: the police power and the *parens patriae* power. The police power is the authority of the state to maintain peace and order and to take action to punish or confine those whose behavior threaten the persons or property of others. The *parens patriae* power allows the state to protect those individuals who, for reasons of mental or physical disability, old age, or unsupervised minority, are unable to protect or care for themselves.

In exercising this latter protective authority, it is assumed that the state acts in the best interests of a person when that person's mental facilities or decisional capacity is impaired. The power of the state to decide on behalf of, or even against, the wishes of an individual is premised on the individual's lack of capacity to make sound decisions. An individual's decisional incompetence is, thus, the "threshold requirement" for the state to invoke its *parens patriae* authority.

A second limitation of the state's exercise of its *parens patriae* power is the imperative that it be exercised in the best interests of the individual, or in accord with what the individual would have decided had he or she been competent to make a decision. Courts often attempt to strike a balance between the deprivation of the individual's liberty interest or wishes, and the level of care and treatment the state is able to provide.

States also have authority to commit under their inherent police power. The police power allows the state to act in furtherance of the general welfare and public safety. Rather than protect individuals from themselves, or from harm by others because of the individual's vulnerability or likelihood to provoke violent act toward himself or herself, the police power tends to be invoked on behalf of society or a societal interest, and against the individual. The police power is used to isolate or confine those persons who suffer from mental disorder or disease and who, as a result of their mental disease or disorder, pose a threat to society.

The threshold requirement for invocation of the state's police power in the case of the mentally disabled individual, who has not committed a crime, is the determination that an individual's mental condition results in the incapacity to conform his or her conduct either to the requirements of the law, or to the limits of social tolerance. Moreover, such an individual often is unable to respond to the deterrent force of the law. Whether an individual's potential for dangerousness is sufficient to justify commitment is a question that involves balancing the magnitude of harm that may occur from conduct of the subject against the probability that it will occur. Effecting this balance, the type of evidence required to predict future behavior and the validity of such a prediction of future behavior, forms the base of the problems of the system of involuntary commitment.

2. Civil Commitment Standards

There are three general populations subject to today's civil commitment laws: the mentally ill, the developmentally disabled (including the mentally retarded), and persons addicted to drugs and alcohol. Many states have separate commitment laws for each category of persons. Typical statutory definitions of these three populations provide the following:

a. "Mentally Ill" means a person who, because of his illness, is reasonably expected to inflict serious physical harm upon himself or another in the near future; or (2) a person who is mentally ill and who because of his illness is unable to provide for his basic physical needs so as to guard himself from serious harm.

b. "Developmentally Disabled" means a person with a disability that is attributable to: (1) mental retardation, cerebral palsy, epilepsy or autism; or to (2) any other condition which results in impairment similar to that caused by mental retardation and that requires services similar to those required by mentally retarded persons. Such disability must originate before the age of eighteen years, be expected to continue indefinitely, and constitute a substantial handicap.

"Mental Retardation" means significantly subaverage general intellectual functioning which exists concurrently with impairment in adaptive behavior and which originates before the age of eighteen years.

c. "Addict" means a person who habitually uses any drug, chemical, substance or dangerous drug other than alcohol so as to endanger the public morals, health, safety or welfare; or who is so far addicted to the use of a dangerous drug or controlled substance other than alcohol as to have lost the power of self control with reference to his addiction. "Alcoholic" means a person who suffers from an illness characterized by preoccupation with alcohol which is typically associated with physical disability and impaired emotional, occupational or social adjustments as direct consequence of loss of control over consumption of alcohol demonstrated by persistent and excessive use of alcohol, such as to lead usually to intoxication if drinking is begun; by chronicity; by progression; and by tendency toward relapse.

Approximately two-thirds of the states have civil commitment statutes authorizing the institutionalization of persons addicted to alcohol or drugs. Most of these statutes reference the individuals habit or chronicity of abuse. The laws of some states require finding of threat of the individual's condition to others. About thirty-five states have special commitment statutes for the developmentally disabled or mentally retarded. While the general basis for civil commitment in most states statutes is extended to this special population, some state commitment statutes adopt criteria based on a finding of need for treatment, and eliminate dangerousness as a criteria.

Commitment statutes may also vary depending upon the legal context. For instance, most states both distinguish between adults and minors in commitment criteria. Most states also have separate statutes for commitment of those acquitted by reason of insanity, and for transfer of prisoners to mental hospitals for treatment.

Modern statutes governing the commitment of the adult "mentally ill" are relatively uniform. At the present time, very few states adhere to a commitment standard requiring only a showing of "mental illness and need for treatment." Typically, a person may not be involuntarily hospitalized unless the state can show, as a result of the mental disease or disorder, the person is "dangerous to self or others." About 25 percent of the states also permit commitment of a mentally ill individual who is as a result of the mental disease or disorder, "unable to provide for his or her basic needs, gravely disabled, or likely to deteriorate."

Even if the proper criteria are met, most state statutes prohibit institutionalization where a less restrictive treatment alternative is available. Every state provides for a commitment hearing, most with notice and counsel. Every state also requires periodic review of the legal status of committed persons. Additionally, most states have statutes which provide for those who have been hospitalized with various rights, including the right to communicate with persons outside the mental hospital.

3. Standard of Proof

The United States Supreme Court in *Humphrey v. Cady* (S.Ct.1972), stated (*in dictum*), that civil commitment results in a "massive deprivation of liberty." Given the consequences of involuntary commitment on a person's liberty, privacy, associational and movement interests, some commentators oppose the very process of civil commitment arguing the state should not be able to exercise its powers through civil commitment to involuntarily confine an individual or to impose treatment over an individual's objection. These critics would limit state intervention to the punishment of criminal acts and not permit the state to engage in therapeutic or custodial interventions.

Nevertheless, the United States Supreme Court in a majority opinion in *United States v. Salerno* (S.Ct.1987), found commitment to be a constitutional exercise of state power. Moreover, the Supreme Court found in *Addington v. Texas* (S.Ct.1979), that due process requires the basis for civil commitment must be established by clear and convincing evidence due to the deprivation of liberty occasioned by civil commitment. This evidentiary standard of proof while less demanding than the standard of "proof beyond a reasonable doubt" required for criminal convictions is more demanding than proof by "preponderance of the evidence" which is the

standard for a decision in civil cases. The requirement of clear and convincing proof for commitment
reflects the serious deprivation of liberty occasioned
by civil commitment.

D. JUSTIFICATIONS FOR DEPRIVING THE MENTALLY ILL OF THEIR LIBERTY

1. The Mentally Ill and Dangerousness

There is evidence that persons in certain categories of the mentally ill, solely by reason of their
condition, are notably more dangerous than others.
In addition, there is a high correlation between
dangerousness and some personality disorders, in
particular, the antisocial personality disorder. Within the psychoses there are also subgroups which
tend to be more violent prone than others. While
some studies indicate that the mentally ill as a
"class" are probably no more dangerous than their
fellow citizens, some studies in the 1990's found
persons experiencing psychotic symptoms to be over
five time more likely than those in the general
population to act violently.

2. The Mentally Ill and Treatability

The detention of the mentally ill is often justified
on the basis of the ability to provide treatment.
Although some mental illnesses at the present time
seen not to be effectively treatable, many conditions, such as schizophrenia and manic-depressive
psychosis, respond to medication or other treat-

ment. On the one hand, the state relies on the benefit of treatment to justify commitment. On the other hand, requiring a competent individual to accept treatment for his own benefit is viewed as a deprivation of liberty, rather than as a benefit.

3. The Mentally Ill and Rational Control

Some maintain commitment and treatment of the mentally ill is justified when the individual lacks the capacity for rational control and decision making with regard to treatment. Others claim the mentally ill have as much control over their behavior as do competent persons. One study of individuals diagnosed with schizophrenia concluded "it is abundantly clear that most persons identified as schizophrenics do not function differently from most persons identified as nonschizophrenics." Other studies have shown hospitalized mentally ill individuals respond to rewards and disincentives in ways consistent with rational behavior.

4. Predicting Danger To Others

A principle objection to civil commitment is based on the prediction of future dangerousness. It is argued that civil commitment should not be sanctioned, because it is not possible accurately determine who among the mentally ill is dangerous.

E. RELIANCE ON MENTAL HEALTH PROFESSIONALS TO FACILITATE INSTITUTIONALIZATION

While many individuals are hospitalized on the basis of a voluntary admission, a "voluntary decision" to enter a mental facility, particularly a public facility, is rare. Reliance by mental hospitals on the process of "voluntary" admission under the supervision of mental health professionals has declined after the decision of the United States Supreme Court in *Zinermon v. Burch* (S.Ct.1990). The Court found the process by which individuals were institutionalized under "voluntary" hospitalization involved trick and coercion. The institutionalization of incompetent patients by this process was found to involve serious deprivation of civil rights.

Commitment laws applicable to minors, and adults who are mentally disabled or incompetent, are extremely deferential to the judgments of parents of minors, and guardians of adults. These laws forgo many of the processes and procedures that protect other mentally disabled persons from wrongful commitment.

Several state and federal courts have held third-party commitment of minors without the procedural protections that are applied to other types of commitments violates the minors' due process rights. These decisions have either prohibited such procedures or have prescribed pre and post commitment procedures to minimize wrongful commitment. The procedures imposed by these courts include probable cause hearings to justify the initial detention, a full hearing on the need for treatment, written notice, representation by counsel, personal presence at the commitment hearing, and the right to confront and cross examine witnesses.

In *Parham v. J.R.* (S.Ct.1979), the United States Supreme Court limited many of the procedural requirements other courts had found were guaranteed to minors by the federal constitution. The Court held "voluntary" admission of minors by parental application with the final decision made by a neutral medical fact-finder, was constitutionally adequate. The fact finder need not be a judge, and may be a physician. The Court concluded children's rights were sufficiently protected, particularly with periodic medical review mandated by the statutes. The Court felt little is gained by requiring an adversarial judicial hearing.

F. ESTABLISHING MENTAL ILLNESS AND DANGEROUSNESS

1. Mental Illness

Aside from definitional provisions excluding "developmental disability" "mental retardation" and conditions resulting from drug or alcohol "addiction," most civil commitment statutes lack precision in their definitions of mental illness. Many state statutes contain language such as: "[m]ental disorder means the substantial disorder of the person's emotional processes, thought or cognition, which grossly impairs judgment, behavior or capacity to recognize reality."

Judicial interpretation of these standards varies. One of the more controversial issues connected with the definition of mental illness is whether the definition includes sociopathology or psychopathology, also known as personality disorder. For example, in *Johnson v. Noot* (Minn. 1982), the Supreme Court of Minnesota held an antisocial personality is not within the definition of mental illness unless the individual has "lost the ability to control his actions." Most state statutes require proof the person's dangerousness is "caused by or is the result of mental illness" before commitment may occur.

2. Dangerousness

The term "dangerousness" involves at least four elements: (1) magnitude of harm, (2) probability that harm will occur, (3) frequency with which harm will occur, and (4) imminence of harm. A determination that a person is dangerous is a prediction about potential future behavior. Such a prediction involves balancing relevant factors. For example, a harm which is not too likely to occur, but which is very serious, may satisfy the "dangerousness" standard. The same holds true for a relatively trivial harm that is very likely to occur with great frequency. However, trivial harm which is less likely to occur may not amount to "dangerous."

Many state statutes do not identify the type of danger to oneself or others that must occur in order to justify commitment. For example, Massachusetts permits commitment upon a showing of "a substantial risk of physical harm to other persons as manifested by evidence of homicidal or other violent behavior or evidence that others are placed in reasonable fear of violent behavior and serious physical harm to them." The question remains whether more specificity is desirable or should be required.

The application of the "void for vagueness" test developed in the context of the criminal law is probably not applicable to the civil commitment processes. Nevertheless, the considerations which require a clear definition of such harms in the criminal process would seem to require some level of specificity in the criteria for civil commitment. It is clear both criminal imprisonment and civil commitment involve a level of deprivation of liberty.

The state may act to prevent the commission of homicide or infliction of serious bodily harm by a mentally ill person. Even infliction of minor physical harm will likely be sufficient to justify commitment. A few states permit commitment if the court finds a person may cause "emotional or psychic" harm to others. Some states include "harm to property" as a commitment criterion.

No state statute explicitly requires the factfinder to assess the frequency of the anticipated harm. Perhaps, this is because any magnitude of harm analysis necessarily includes an assessment of frequency. Most states also prohibit commitment as "dangerous to others" unless the danger is "imminent"; but these statutes are not specific as to time, *i.e.*, whether the predicted harm is likely to occur in two weeks or two days.

3. The Overt Act Requirement

Some state statutes prohibit commitment unless the person is found either to be dangerous to self or others "based upon a finding of a recent overt act, attempt or threat to do substantial harm," or, that "imminent threat of injury to others shall be evidenced by overt acts, sufficiently recent in time as to be material and relevant as to the respondent's present condition." The rest, well over half of the states, do not require proof of an overt act. At least one state court requires the overt act to be "recent." Some states (*e.g.*, California) do not explicitly include a requirement of a recent act.

Although proof of dangerousness need only be made by clear and convincing evidence, Montana's statute uniquely requires proof beyond a reasonable doubt of "physical facts or evidence" of an overt act, but "clear and convincing proof as to all other matters, except that mental disorders shall be evidenced to a reasonable medical certainty."

4. Subject to Treatment

Civil commitment of those found not dangerous to themselves or others is justified by the state's duty to provide care and treatment for persons unable to care for themselves. However, the United States Supreme Court, in *O'Connor v. Donaldson* (S.Ct.1975), held a state cannot constitutionally confine, without more, a nondangerous individual capable of surviving safely in the community by himself, or with the help of others who are willing to provide needed assistance. The significance of the Court's ruling relates to questions of treatment efficacy and justification for commitment of non-dangerous persons. If the treatment does not fulfill its remission objective, then the person is being confined without the state fulfilling the *parens patriae* requirement that provides the basis for the commitment and attendant deprivation of liberty.

G. THE BASES FOR INTERVENTION UNDER *PARENS PATRIAE* POWER

State authority to intervene under parens patriae power can be classified under two general categories: direct physical harm to self and self-neglecting behavior. The first category includes: suicide, self-mayhem, and harm to self caused by provocation of others. Self neglect categories can be subdivided into an inability to provide for one's survival needs, a present ability to survive but inattention to deteriorating mental and/or and physical health or, most broadly interpreted, a "need for treatment."

Most state statutes do not explicitly differentiate between these categories. In several states, the only parens patriae ground for commitment is "danger to self," which actually can be viewed as a police power concern for preventing suicide. While "danger to self" encompasses suicidal behavior, it is often found to cover other self-harming or self-neglecting behavior.

State statutes with specific *parens patriae* commitment criteria provide for commitment on the basis of danger to self or inability to care for self. A few states permit commitment on a showing of a "potential for deterioration." Most states use a standard of an inability to care for oneself. Some states permit commitment if a person needs treatment as a result of mental illness. A few statutes even permit commitment for a person's "welfare."

H. VAGUENESS DOCTRINE APPLIED TO PARENS PATRIAE CRITERIA

Some courts have held the particular language implementing the parens patriae authority is so vague that it violates the due process clause of the United States Constitution. In *Commonwealth ex rel. Finken v. Roop* (Pa.Super.1975), a Pennsylvania court struck down a state statute permitting commitment of any person who was "believed to be mentally disabled and in need of care or treatment of such mental disability." The court stated: "in need of care" was so broad as to be virtually meaningless. Furthermore, once a finding of mental illness was made, it would be impossible not to find the individual was in "need of care."

I. THE OVERT ACT IN RELATION TO *PARENS PATRIAE* COMMITMENT

Usually a state statute requiring both a recent overt act and a prediction of imminent danger, when determining danger to others, also requires such findings when defining danger to oneself. Similarly, when statutes do not require a determination of danger to others, they are silent regarding a determination of danger to oneself.

Most state statutes do not require an overt act, but require evidence showing the person is unable to provide for his or her basic needs. States using a "deterioration" standard do not contemplate any explicit overt act requirement. Lastly, the imminence requirement for the treatment of the mentally ill is rarely associated with any *parens patriae* criterion.

When considering the appropriateness of an overt act requirement for determining danger to oneself, it is helpful to examine one study that found the majority of patients who attempt suicide do not go on to commit suicide. Generally, only one-quarter to one-half of successful suicides have had a past history of suicidal behavior.

J. THE LEAST RESTRICTIVE ALTERNATIVE

Whether the basis of state intervention is the police or *parens patriae* power, almost all state statutes require consideration of the least restrictive treatment alternative to hospitalization before the individual can be committed. This doctrine has also played a significant role in regulating treatment plans imposed on persons after they have been committed particularly, and in demands by patients that the government meet its obligation to provide community-based services. Although the United States Supreme Court has not adopted the least restrictive alternative doctrine for civil commitment orders, forty-seven states require involuntary patients be committed to treatment in the least restrictive setting.

The United States Supreme Court has not accorded the least restrictive alternative doctrine general constitutional status. Although the Court has limited state action taken to achieve the government's objective most notably in cases involving the First Amendment. Yet, the Court has been reluctant to apply the doctrine of "lease restrictive alternative" as mandatory standard for Supreme Court judicial review of other areas of state action. In *Youngberg v. Romeo* (S.Ct.1982), the Supreme Court considered the minimal conditions that due process requires the state to provide hospitalized mental patients. The Court expressly adopted the view that the constitution only requires that the courts ensure that professional judgment in fact is exercised. The Court found it inappropriate for the judiciary to specify which of several professionally acceptable choices should have been made for a particular patient.

According to the general view of the least restrictive alternative doctrine, it requires placement of an individual in the least restrictive setting that will both facilitate treatment and eliminate the threat of danger to the patient or others. A related view is the doctrine requires the least intrusive treatment which will meet the patient's treatment needs. Nevertheless, some scholars have argued the least restrictive doctrine means that the most effective treatment should be provided, and that the physical restrictiveness of therapy should be of a secondary concern. When the significance of a patient's treatability diminishes after the maximum benefits of care have already accrued, or the patient has not responded to the institution's programs and is untreatable in that chosen setting, concern with treatment or institutional restrictiveness emerges.

A number of studies comparing hospital and community treatment have found treatment in community-based facilities emphasizing outpatient care is more effective and less costly than hospitalization in traditional state mental health facilities. However, there is a growing consensus the findings of the efficacy of community care over hospital treatment may not apply to all patients. This is particularly true of patients with intractable severe mental illness.

Over half of the states have statutes explicitly authorizing commitment on an outpatient basis. Most other states implicitly allow such commitment by requiring treatment be provided in the least restrictive environment. Statutes authorizing outpatient commitment, although differing significantly, follow three general models. The first model permits outpatient commitment following some form of inpatient commitment, either in a hospital or in the community. The second model authorizes outpatient commitment to a community facility at the front-end of the commitment process, if the traditional commitment criteria are met, without any preliminary requirement of inpatient treatment. The third model, sometimes called preventive commitment, permits outpatient commitment at the front end, under broader commitment standards than those required for involuntary hospitalization.

Although outpatient commitment is available and arguably more desirable than institutionalization, several factors have precluded states from relying on outpatient commitment to any great degree: (1) lack of appropriate community mental health programs, (2) obstacles to compelling compliance of outpatients to treatment plans, (3) belief that few persons will comply with court-ordered treatment or voluntarily participate in community programs, (4) reluctance of mental health providers to treat clients involuntarily under judicial supervision, (5) absence of judicial mechanisms and personnel to adequately supervise outpatient care, (6) resistance of neighbors and public officials to accept mental health facilities in their community, (7) fears concerning liability for inadequate treatment or foreseeable harm to third parties, and (8) opposition to the establishment of a governmental obligation to fund a comprehensive system of community services.

K. EMERGENCY DETENTION AND SCREENING

A person initially may become subject to involuntary commitment through one of several ways: apprehension by police, commitment by a relative or friend, being taken into custody as a result of a legal petition submitted to and validated by a court, or conversion from voluntary to involuntary patient. Such conversion from voluntary to involuntary status usually occurs when a patient attempts to leave against the advice of the facility staff. Most persons, however, become involuntary patients by means of "emergency" commitments resulting from apprehension by police or by appearing on the doorstep of the institution.

All states permit emergency commitment. In such situations, immediate treatment can be provided without a formal legal hearing and without a showing the individual meets the standard of proof needed to involuntarily commit the individual. The reliance on medical judgment and the lack of legal process associated with the initial emergency admission has rarely been challenged, since it is widely held a more formal process would be counterproductive. However, the question has been raised whether a "detention hearing" should be held before the ultimate adjudication of whether the individual is subject to involuntary commitment. If such a hearing should be provided, the next question is how soon and with what procedural requirements. Preliminary hearings are required in the criminal process under certain circumstances. In *Gerstein v. Pugh* (S.Ct.1975), the United States Supreme Court held, although the Constitution does not require an adversary determination of probable cause, for any significant pre-trial restraint of liberty, a fair and reliable judicial determination of probable cause must be made either before or promptly after an arrest or when a person is taken into custody.

Although the *Gerstein* Court did not set a time limit for a criminal probable cause hearing, in *County of Riverside v. McLaughlin* (S.Ct.1991), the Supreme Court required a hearing to be within forty-eight hours after the arrest. In those states that provide detention hearings, following an emergency commitment, the analogous time periods from initial detention to hearing vary significantly. Most states require a post-admission check after an emergency admission to a mental health facility. In all states, habeas corpus review is available during the initial detention period, but only upon the patient's request and usually only after some delay.

L. INVOLUNTARY ADMISSION

Every state has established formal procedures for involuntary commitment. Depending on the jurisdiction, these procedures ensure an individual's right to a judicial hearing, notice, confrontation and subpoena of witnesses, the assistance of counsel and to remain silent in response to government questions.

In *Mathews v. Eldridge* (S.Ct.1976), the United States Supreme Court formulated the standard analysis for determining the procedural due process required when a significant action is taken by the government that affect an individual's interests. In *Mathews v. Eldridge*, a case involving the administration of social security benefits, United States Supreme the Court outlined the three basic factors to be considered. These include a showing that there is: (1) a private interest that will be affected by the official action; (2) a risk of an erroneous deprivation of such interest through the procedures used, and the probable value, if any, of additional or substitute procedural safeguards; and (3) the government's interest, including the function involved and the fiscal and administrative burden additional or substitute requirements would entail. *Mathews* is usually cited by courts considering due process requirements in civil commitment cases.

According to some studies, the use of extensive procedural requirements as a condition for civil commitment, has reduced hospital admissions. However, a number of studies indicate little change in outcome finding many commitment hearings are adversarial in name only.

The establishment of legal safeguards in civil commitment is based on two basic assumptions about "involuntary" commitment: (1) without procedural safeguards inappropriate institutionalization may occur; and (2) involuntary commitment can involve a real opposition in interest between the party applying for institutionalization, usually the state, institution or family, and the individual who does not want to be institutionalized. Critics of the adequacy of these legal safeguards point out approximately two-thirds of involuntarily committed patients are passive, stuporous, uncommunicative, or simply agree with the physician's recommendation.

Moreover, it is reported that others who initially protest, usually consent to commitment within a few days of admission.

A common argument against legal safeguards is they are anti-antitherapeutic because: (1) time is lost in the courtroom which could be used for treatment; (2) revelation of embarrassing material occurs in a public setting; (3) a serious diagnosis or poor prognosis is revealed to the patient; (4) optimistic hopes of cure are falsely created in the patient; (5) confirmation is made of delusions of persecution, particularly in paranoid individuals, (6) the psychiatrist's ability to work is impaired due to the impact of directives given by the courts; (7) trauma and exasperation occur as a result of the length of the hearing; (8) the therapist reveals statements made by the patient in treatment sessions; (9) opinions of close family members are revealed to the prospective patient; (10) material that the patient thought was revealed in confidence is disclosed; (11) likelihood of the patient's rejection of any further attempts at treatment increases and (12) experience of trauma occurs for family members testify about their medical assessment of a relative.

However, others argue that advocacy in the civil commitment process has considerable potential for therapeutic benefit. First, if properly conducted the hearing, represents an open acknowledgment that the patient's hospitalization is involuntary. Second, the hearing can improve the treatment of the patient and his or her relationship with the treatment staff. Third, the commitment hearing may provide an opportunity for the therapist to clarify his or her role. Fourth, a face-to-face confrontation occurring as soon as possible after the crisis arises that involves all major participants in the crisis may be beneficial. Finally, the hearing can improve the patient's relationship with the family and assist in developing an understanding of that relationship.

1. Prehearing Screening

A number of states have established "screening" agencies that are charged with referring mentally disabled people to the most effective treatment program available. Such programs can reduce the number of people subject to involuntary commitment, including emergency detention. According to one report, in localities with prescreening, a majority of persons entering the commitment process never see a courtroom. Further, many persons who are diverted to a more suitable treatment alternative elect to enter the mental health system voluntarily, or are discharged shortly after arrival at a mental health facility.

Although "emergency" cases are specifically exempted from this pre-screening procedure, it nonetheless appears that significant number of individuals, who otherwise, would have been handled through "emergency admissions" under the old system, are able to avoid the involuntary commitment process altogether.

2. Standard of Proof

In *Addington v. Texas* (S.Ct.1979), the United States Supreme Court clarified the standard of proof required by the Fourteenth Amendment for involuntary civil commitment. The Court recognized civil commitment for any purpose constitutes a significant deprivation of liberty requiring due process protection. Given the seriousness of involuntary civil commitment, the Court found such action could only be taken upon "clear and convincing evidence." In regard to the "beyond the reasonable doubt" standard of the criminal law, the Court stated there are significant reasons why different standards of proof apply in civil commitment proceedings. According to the Court, different standards for civil commitment and criminal law are mandated due to the differing objectives of punishment and treatment. The Court noted subtleties and nuances are characteristic of a psychiatric diagnoses. Such diagnosis is, to a large extent, based on medical "impressions" drawn from subjective analysis and filtered through the experience of the diagnostician.

Finally, the Court held the "reasonable doubt standard" is inappropriate in civil commitment proceedings; because it would impose a burden the state cannot meet and, thereby, erects an unreasonable barrier to needed medical treatment. Nevertheless, the Court found the "preponderance standard" falls short of meeting the demands of due process. Consequently, the Court determined the middle level of "clear and convincing evidence" as a burden of proof strikes a fair balance between the rights of the individual and the legitimate concerns of the state.

3. The Decision Maker

In criminal proceedings, the Sixth Amendment guarantees the right to a jury trial. This right may be waived, in which case a judge presides over the trial. Unlike the criminal justice system, at the adjudicatory hearing stage of civil commitment, at least four different types of ultimate decision makers have been authorized by state statutes: (1) a judicial officer (2) a jury (3) an administrative board which does not include a judicial officer, and (4) a psychiatric board. Most states rely on a legally trained judicial officer to make its long-term commitment decisions. However, several states provide the person subject to civil commitment with the right to request a jury trial. A small number of states permit commitment based on a decision of an administrative board. No state, today, authorizes a psychiatric board to order commitment even though it was the dominant method of commitment prior to 1970.

4. Jury Trial

The United State Supreme Court in *McKeiver v. Pennsylvania* (S.Ct.1971), citing the need to maintain the "intimacy" of the proceeding and to avoid the "clamor" of the adversarial process held there is no right to a jury trial in juvenile proceedings.

Most courts have relied on *McKeiver* to hold the right to a jury trial is not required at civil commitment proceedings.

While the United States Supreme Court has not directly addressed the "decision maker" issue in civil commitment proceedings, at least two Supreme Court opinions are relevant. In *Vitek v. Jones* (S.Ct. 1980), the Court considered the proper procedures for transferring prisoners allegedly in need of psychiatric care from correctional facilities to psychiatric facilities. The Court refused to require judicial oversight in such hearings. Instead, the Court mandated only that an independent decision maker fulfill this role. Moreover, the Court found an independent decision maker need not come from outside the prison or hospital administration. According to the Court, to hold otherwise would cause unnecessary intrusion into either medical or correctional judgments.

The second relevant Supreme Court decision is *Parham v. J.R.* (S.Ct.1979). In *Parham*, the Court held the decision to admit a child to a mental facility may be made by a mental health professional, even if that professional is the evaluating clinician. The Court, in support of its decision, identified a "significant interest in not imposing unnecessary procedural obstacles that may discourage the mentally ill or their families from seeking needed psychiatric assistance and a genuine interest in allocating priority to the diagnosis and treatment of patients as soon as they are admitted to a hospital rather than to time consuming procedural minutes before the admission."

M. THE ADVERSARY PROCESS: NO-TICE PUBLIC TRIAL & CONFRON-TATION RIGHTS NOTICE

Federal constitutional requirements are satisfied if notice is "reasonably calculated to inform the person to whom it is directed" of the nature of the civil commitment proceeding. Therefore, notice must be given prior to the commitment hearing and must include: the time and location of the hearing, the reasons being given for the need for commitment, the standards for commitment, and a copy of the petition itself.

The most fundamental issue connected with the right to notice in civil commitment is whether the state can forego such notice because of concern about the reaction of the putative patient. Concern arises that the subject of a commitment petition would be so affected by the notice that he or she might harm himself or herself, or another person such as the individual who initiated the commitment petition. Some states provide for special methods of giving notice to allegedly mentally disabled individuals. For instance, Vermont's statute states "if the court has reasons to believe that notice to the proposed patient will be likely to cause injury to the proposed patient or others, it shall direct the proposed patient's counsel to give the proposed patient oral notice prior to written notice under circumstances most likely to reduce the likelihood of injury."

A second issue is when notice should be given. The general rule is that notice shall be given "sufficiently in advance of the proceeding to afford one a reasonable opportunity to prepare." Considering the time frame between initial admission and the detention hearing, notice usually must be given immediately. If a detention hearing is held when the person is taken into custody, notice of the adjudicatory hearing can be, and often is, given at the time of the hearing itself.

A final issue which may arise is whether notice should be given to anyone other than the respondent and the attorney. Many states provide notice to the parents, guardian, spouse or next-of-kin of the patient.

N. PUBLIC TRIAL AND CONFRONTATIONAL RIGHTS

Commitment hearings usually involve disclosure of intimate, personal information. Assuming respondents have a right to a public hearing, they may often want to waive this right. The state may also want to exclude the public to protect "confidential" information and to expedite the process. State statutes addressing this right have preferred private proceedings.

The right to be present at one's criminal trial may be waived if made "knowingly and intelligently." Individuals may be excluded from trial if their action is so disruptive that an orderly proceeding cannot take place. In contrast, a large number of state commitment statutes grant the right to be present at the commitment hearing only if such presence will not "harm" the patient.

The principal issue connected with the right to cross-examine adversarial parties at civil commitment proceedings is the extent to which hearsay is admissible. Since hearsay involves out-of-court statements, the confrontation clause could be construed to exclude all hearsay evidence. However, even in the criminal context, the Supreme Court has held many types of hearsay are admissible, especially when a "firmly rooted" common law exception to the hearsay rule is applicable. Such exceptions include the party admission rule, which permits testimony of the respondent's out-of-court statements about his or her mental state or intended actions by the person who heard them; and the "business records" exception that permits admission of evidence of virtually all observations of the respondent's mental state made by clinicians and recorded as a routine matter in medical and psychiatric records.

Several courts have held the rules of evidence, including the hearsay rule, apply in commitment proceedings. Some state statutes take this stance as well; however, many others are silent on this issue, and some provide the hearing shall be conducted as informally as is consistent with "orderly procedure."

If a respondent in a civil commitment proceeding has a wide-open right to subpoena witnesses, circumvention of any state attempt to rely on hearsay occurs by serving process on the relevant out of court witness. Some state statutes explicitly grant individuals the right to subpoena persons and documents. Whether such a right is constitutionally required and the extent to which it can be exercised as a discovery mechanism is unclear. However, in *Vitek v. Jones* (S.Ct.1980), a case involving the process due prisoners who are transferred to psychiatric facilities, the United States Supreme Court held the state must give prisoners an opportunity to present witnesses and to confront and cross-examine witnesses called by the state, due to the significant deprivation of liberty inherent in psychiatric hospitalization. However, upon a finding of good cause for not permitting such presentation, confrontation, or cross-examination, limitations are permissible if the circumstances justify such limitations. The Court recognized the interests of the State in avoiding disruption in the prison setting as the basis for its decision.

The Supreme Court has clearly established the right of both the criminally accused and delinquent juveniles to counsel at trial, and the duty of the state to provide counsel to indigents. The right to counsel in civil commitment proceedings is not so firmly established. Although virtually every modern court has held the due process clause requires counsel at the commitment hearing, a few state statutes do not provide indigent individuals with counsel at any point in the process. Moreover, the Supreme Court may not agree with the lower courts on this matter. In both *Parham v. J.R.* and *Vitek v. Jones,* the Court refused to find a right to legally trained counsel for persons subjected to proceedings designed to determine the existence and extent of their mental disability.

Most state courts have not recognized a right to remain silent at any point in the commitment process. However, some states, including Illinois, require persons who are the subject of civil commitment proceedings be advised they may refuse to talk to examining experts. Those who oppose recognition of the subject's right to remain silent in a civil commitment proceeding argue such a right makes it difficult to ascertain the patient's mental state, and prevents assessment of both the need for treatment and potential for dangerousness. It is argued that recognition of a subject's right to remain silent at a commitment hearing would transform commitment decisions at the conclusion of the hearing into judgments based solely on overt acts, similar to decisions made in the criminal context.

O. RELEASE PROCEDURES

Most states require a review hearing be held after a certain period of involuntary commitment. Typically, a hearing must be held within six months after the initial admission. Other common review periods range from three months to a year.

Judicial review through habeas corpus is always available at any time if the patient requests it. The average length of stay in the hospital for a majority of patients is usually under ninety days. Nonetheless, substantial numbers of patients are still not voluntarily discharged by the hospital staff within a short period of time. Moreover, release via habeas corpus is hampered in that patients must initiate the proceeding, and the petitioner bears the burden of proving that the challenged detention is illegal.

One reason for the short hospitalization of many patients is the development of conditional release programs. A patient is released on convalescent or conditional status to a community mental health center, halfway house, or other community service in an effort to ease the transition to normal life. This release is conditioned on the finding the patient adheres to a particular treatment regimen and remains stable. Immediate rehospitalization is permissible if required. In practice, these programs have been hampered by a lack of adequate community resources and poor communication between hospitals and community service providers.

The most significant litigation involving conditional release programs has assumed their constitutionality and has focused instead on procedural questions. In particular, courts are concerned with provisions permitting conditional release to be revoked on the authority of the hospital director, with little or no judicial supervision.

P. VOLUNTARY ADMISSION

Mental health professionals have long favored avoiding involuntary commitment proceedings by encouraging "voluntary admission" of people with mental disorders. Virtually every state allows an individual to be admitted voluntarily for psychiatric treatment. Voluntary admissions comprise just under 50 percent of the mental hospital population and about 85 percent of the population in psychiatric units of general hospitals.

However, studies show "voluntary admission" is a misnomer. In the majority of cases, voluntary admission is used by persons who are already in some form of official custody. Those favoring use of voluntary admission stress the fact that it avoids procedural complexity and argue it provides patients control over the treatment process. Nevertheless, most individuals agree to voluntary commitment, as a result of the threat of involuntary commitment.

There are generally two different procedures for voluntary admission to mental hospitals. Under the first, known as "informal admission," an individual is admitted to a mental hospital without the formal application and is free to leave at any time during normal hours. Under the second, known as "voluntary admission," an individual is admitted to a mental hospital on formal application and is free to leave within a specified time, for example within three to ten days after giving notice of a desire to leave to the facility. However, during that specified notice period, hospital officials may seek certification for involuntary commitment of the individuals. A voluntary patient usually continues to be hospitalized pending a final order of the court at the hearing. Some courts have struck down such advance notice provisions, holding forced treatment during the period between the request for discharge and the involuntary commitment hearing violates the Due Process Clause. One court has stated such treatment violates the Thirteenth Amendment, which prohibits involuntary servitude except as punishment for crime.

Despite conceptual and practical problems, voluntary admission may benefit the mentally ill. In several states, commitment statutes go far to require advice to a prospective patient on the availability of "voluntary admission" before involuntary procedures are undertaken. According to mental health professionals, a person who voluntarily seeks admission recognizes his or her need for treatment. Such a person is more prone to cooperate with the staff and participate conscientiously in a treatment program. Therefore, a voluntarily admitted patient is more likely to benefit from institutional treatment than would an unwilling patient. In addition, the availability of voluntary procedures may encourage a person to seek help for his condition at an early stage of illness, at a point where the chances of successful treatment are best.

Most states have voluntary admission procedures not only for the mentally ill, but also for the developmentally disabled and substance abusers, or those who are addicted. Under one approach, the reach of statutes covering mentally ill persons is extended to other groups by defining their disability of addiction as included in the category "mental illness." The modern trend, however, has been to enact separate legislation specifying the inclusion of other groups.

Given the potential for inappropriate coercion in obtaining the "voluntary admission" of a patient, the question arises as to whether a "voluntary admission" is in fact voluntary. Under one view, voluntarily admission applies to anyone who is "suitable for admission and fails to object to it." Several states permit such "nonprotesting" admissions. However, concern arises because many voluntary admissions involve senile persons who make no objection to psychiatric hospitalization.

An alternative to a "consent" model of voluntary admission is the appointment of a guardian for all persons who assent to or do not protest hospitalization. The guardian's function is to determine the individual's actual performance, or to decide whether hospitalization is in the person's best interests, considering all relevant factors, including the person's wishes. This "substituted judgment" approach is widely used for determining whether treatment should be administered to incompetent patients, institutionalized minors and severely developmentally disabled patients. Usually a guardian is one of the patient's relatives, but the guardian can be a person appointed by a court or statutorily authorized. A final approach is simply to prohibit admission into a public mental facility unless the person meets the criteria for involuntary commitment. Presumably, however, this would prevent some people who desire or need treatment from obtaining it.

The United States Supreme Court in *Zinermon v. Burch* (S.Ct.1990), concluded there are constitutional barriers to the voluntary admission of incompetent persons. In *Zinermon,* the plaintiff was asked to sign forms giving consent to admission and treatment, even though staff evaluation showed upon his arrival at the evaluating facility, the patient was hallucinating, confused, psychotic, and believed he was in heaven. Within the next three days, the patient signed voluntary admission forms on two other occasions. Following discharge from the facility, the patient brought federal civil rights actions against the state of Florida. The patient alleged his due process rights were violated by the staff when they admitted him as a voluntary patient knowing he was incompetent, rather than affording him the procedural protections granted those subjected to involuntary commitment. The Supreme Court found the patient could maintain a claim for violation of his procedural due process rights. The Court held that proper procedures are to be afforded both to those patients who are unwilling and to those who are unable to give consent. The Court's opinion suggests that constitutional due process rights are violated when an incompetent patient is involuntarily admitted since such a person lacks the capacity to give the requisite consent. Consequently, admission of persons lacking the capacity to consent to admission can only be effected after compliance with the involuntary commitment procedures.

Many voluntary patients never request release, especially those admitted under the non-protesting admissions statutes. It has been argued there should be judicial review of such voluntary admissions after some specified period of time. Some courts have considered the review issue in the context of conversion of involuntary patients to voluntary status. Many states authorize such conversion whenever the hospital staff believes the change is indicated, in the belief a voluntary relationship enhances therapy. At least one court found a patient subject to such conversion in status is entitled to a judicial hearing to review the change, as well as the same periodic review provided involuntary patients.

CHAPTER 9

THE RIGHT TO REFUSE AND CONSENT TO PSYCHIATRIC TREATMENT IN THE CIVIL COMMITMENT CONTEXT

A. THE CONTROVERSY OVER MENTAL HEALTH PATIENTS RIGHT TO REFUSE AND CONSENT TO TREATMENT

A committed patient's right to refuse psychiatric treatment, including psychotropic medication, electroconvulsive therapy or psychosurgery has been widely contested in state and federal courts. For some, this issue appears to place the interests of the individual asserting such a right in direct opposition to the interests of the mental health facility and society at large whose purpose is to restore mentally disabled persons to a condition in which they can return to being fully functioning members of the community.

Committed patients often refuse treatment because of an objectionable past experience with the treatment, or because patients are concerned with possible side effects of the proposed treatment. Patients maintain they should have a right to refuse treatment if they pose no danger to themselves or others.

Many psychiatrists and mental health care workers maintain that the right of mental health patients to refuse treatment is both a barrier to meeting the patients medical needs and an impediment or intrusion upon the physician-patient relationship. Administrators of mental health programs maintain the funds that could be used for effective treatment are diverted to proceedings and to adhering to regulations within the institution effectuating the right of refusal of medically recommended treatment, or in court adjudications of treatment refusals.

Some professionals argue, even if a patient is recognized as having a right to refuse treatment, treating physicians within the mental health care facility should have an ability to override the patient's refusal in certain circumstances. Today, courts recognize a need of institutions to override a patient's objection and administer treatment on an emergency basis if the patient's medical condition requires treatment, or if it is necessary to prevent the patient from harming himself, herself or others. Some mental health practitioners argue their ability to override "irrational" refusals of treatment, including medication, should be broadened.

B. INFORMED CONSENT AND THE RIGHT TO REFUSE TREATMENT

Under the modern law of informed consent, a physician is required to provide a patient with all relevant information concerning the risks of any medication or procedure as well as alternative treatment modalities. Informed consent must be obtained from a patient before the patient is subjected to any treatment, including any treatment or procedure that could have adverse effects. The traditional standard for determining what information is relevant regarding a proposed treatment is what a reasonable physician would regard as medically relevant. Increasingly, courts use a standard based on what a reasonable person would regard as relevant. And more recently, courts have considered what the patient himself or herself regards as relevant.

Patients who are incompetent or lack the capacity to make a rational decision about treatment under proper circumstances may be treated or medicated regardless of their objection. With incapacitated patients, it is the *parens patriae* power of the state that allows administration of treatment to those who lack capacity to make rational decisions about their treatment. When a state administers treatment on a *parens patriae* rationale, the state ideally acts "in the interests of the individual."

If a person is mentally disabled and incompetent, some state statutes provide a guardian should be appointed to decide whether treatment should be

administered to the ward. In such a case, the decision to administer treatment to incapacitated persons is made under one of two standards: the best
interests of the patient or substituted judgment.
Under the best interests approach, the surrogate
decision maker decides whether treatment is in the
best interest of the patient by weighing the benefits
and burdens of the proposed treatment. Under a
substituted judgment approach, the surrogate decision maker looks to the preferences of the patient to
determine what treatment the patient would choose
if competent to do so.

In *Guardianship of Roe* (Mass.1981), the Massachusetts Supreme Court held a declaration of incompetency and consent by a guardian based on the
ward's best interests cannot justify treatment over
the ward's objections; that is, where a ward, even
though legally incompetent, objects to a specific
treatment. The court found only substituted judgment adequately protected the patient; that is only
after a judicial finding, using substituted judgment
to determine that the ward would have consented to
such treatment had he been competent, can medication be administered. *Roe* represents only one
approach to surrogate decision making in regard to
the refusal of treatment by a ward; it established
the court as the final decision maker for an incompetent to be forcible medicated. However, other
courts, considering an incompetent person's refusal
of medication, have held that the ward's refusal
could be overridden by the consent of the guardian

without further judicial approval, after a declaration that the ward is incompetent.

Today, the law rejects the presumption that involuntarily committed individuals are necessarily incompetent to refuse treatment. This conclusion is supported by psychiatric studies suggesting no necessary connection exists between the need for hospitalization and the ability to make rational decisions regarding psychiatric treatment.

C. RIGHT TO REFUSE PSYCHOTROPIC MEDICATION: CONSTITUTIONAL CHALLENGES

The discovery of psychotropic medication in the 1950s brought great potential for amelioration of mental patient's symptoms. After administration of anti-psychotropic medication, many mental patients were released, and overall commitment time of most involuntary patients was reduced. Unfortunately, it soon became apparent that side effects often accompanied these medications. Moreover, researchers also reported what they perceived to be misuse of these medications that were often used to control behavior rather than to treat the symptoms of institutionalized persons. The dangers of misusing psychotropic medication led to legislation and court rulings prohibiting use of these psychotropic medications over the objections of mental patients.

1. Fourteenth Amendment

The primary constitutional basis for recognizing the right of the mentally disabled to refuse medication is the individual's Fourteenth Amendment interest in liberty. Privacy and freedom from unwanted bodily intrusion are liberty interests recognized by courts when they find a competent mental patient may not be treated over the patient's objection. Freedom from bodily intrusion gave rise to a right to refuse treatment and was recognized in the decision of the United States Supreme Court in *Cruzan v. Director, Missouri Department of Health* (S.Ct.1990). In *Cruzan,* the Court suggested a fundamental right exists for a competent person to refuse treatment.

The question of an incompetent patient's right to refuse unwanted treatment was addressed in two leading cases which took very different approaches. The first case *Rennie v. Klein* (3d Cir.1981) and (3d Cir.1983), decided by the United States Court of Appeals for the Third Circuit, recognized that although a patient has a right to refuse medication absent an emergency, an in-hospital determination that a patient poses a danger to self or others, resulting in subsequent forced medication satisfies due process requirements. The decision in *Rennie* relied on *Youngberg v. Romeo* (S.Ct.1982), in which the United States Supreme Court balanced the competing interests of an institutionalized retarded person and those of the hospital staff, and held that medical decisions involving such persons are presumptively valid.

In the second case, *Rogers v. Okin* (1st Cir.1980) the First Circuit Court of Appeals determined institutionalized individuals have a right to privacy, and the requirement of informed consent can only be overcome by an emergency or after a finding of incapacity followed by appointment of a guardian who subsequently consents to treatment.

Most federal courts, following the approach of *Rennie* and *Youngberg* hold an in-hospital determination finding that forced medication is necessary satisfies due process requirements. Professional judgment is emphasized in these decisions, rather than the requirement of informed consent when evaluating the scope of the constitutional protection afforded to a mental patients who refuse treatment. Procedural due process is satisfied when the decision to treat over the patient's objection is a matter of professional judgment and is not made arbitrarily.

Courts also have relied on two other United States Supreme Court decisions to support the conclusion that judicial determinations are properly limited to whether medical decision making was arbitrary or not. In *Parham v. J.R.* (S.Ct.1979), the United States Supreme Court authorized psychiatric hospitalization of minors based upon the decision of medical professionals, rather than requiring a judicial determination.

In *Parham* the Supreme Court relied on its earlier decision in *Mathews v. Eldridge* (S.Ct.1976), to determine the amount of due process to be accorded involuntarily committed individuals. The *Eldridge* case involved contested social security benefits. In that case, the Supreme Court set forth criteria to determine if a governmental action violates procedural due process. The court identified the relevant criteria as including: (1) the private interest that will be affected by the official action, (2) the risk of an erroneous deprivation of that private interest through the procedures used, and the probable value, if any, of additional or substitute procedural safeguards, and (3) the government's interest, including the function involved and the fiscal and administrative burdens that the additional procedural requirements would entail.

Using *Parham* and *Eldridge* most courts hold that certain "base-line" decision are appropriately made by professionals. Capacity to consent to treatment is only one factor to be considered when deciding to forcibly medicate a patient. Courts using the *Parham* and *Eldridge* rationale find that although there is a liberty interest in being free from unwanted medication, the state has an interest in treating the mentally ill; and with professional decision making, the chance for erroneous decisions are limited. Most courts, therefore, hold that although mental health patients are entitled to the exercise of professional judgment before being subject to forcible medication, due process is only denied if the decision to medicate is not actually based on professional judgment.

The basis for these decisions, therefore, was not whether it is correct or appropriate to involuntarily medicate a patient, but whether the decision to medicate was made in a "professional" rather than an "arbitrary" manner.

Until the Supreme Court specifically addresses whether a right exists for an institutionalized mental incompetent to refuse treatment, courts will continue to decide treatment refusal case with reference to either a *Rennie* or *Rogers* approach. Each opinion recognizes a patient's right to refuse medication absent emergency circumstances. However, each opinion defines differently the scope of the right, and the focus of the final decision making authority. *Rennie* preserves the right of mental health professionals to decide whether an emergency exists and when forced medication is necessary. *Rogers*, however, places the ultimate authority in the courts' hands, rather than with the mental health professionals. It should be noted, however, that *Rogers* relied principally on a Massachusetts state law, whereas *Rennie* was based on constitutional principles. The law which *Rogers* interpreted, defined an "emergency" broadly, thus allowing courts to forcibly medicate a patient more readily than permitted by most other states' laws and regulations.

The United States Supreme Court has addressed whether a right to refuse treatment exists in the prison setting. In *Washington v. Harper* (S.Ct.1990), the Supreme Court held, although a liberty interest exists in being free from the arbitrary administration of psychotropic medication, substantive due process is satisfied if administration of such medication is limited to those prisoners who are mentally ill, and gravely disabled, or who represent a danger to themselves or others. The Court rejected the contention a prisoner is entitled to a finding of incompetency prior to treatment. Instead, the Court held the state's interest in providing medically appropriate treatment to reduce the threat of dangerous behavior by a prisoner was a sufficient ground for administering medication over the prisoner's objection. Furthermore, the Court concluded procedural due process did not require a judicial hearing, because the prisoner's liberty interest was adequately protected by allowing mental health professionals to decide the medication issue.

Involuntary institutionalization in a mental health facility, or civil commitment, is often thought of as comparable to imprisonment. Both forms of institutionalization involve: loss of liberty, separation from family and friends, stigma of being institutionalized, and reliance on the state to satisfy basic needs. Similarity between the situations leaves open the question whether the arguments *Harper* advanced can be used to compel medication over a patient's objection in the context of institutionalization in a mental health facility. Moreover, involuntary civil commitment is always partly justified by the benefits of treatment that will render the patient able to return to normal functioning. Any benefit obtained by a prisoner from the experience of incarceration is merely incidental to the retributive and isolating objectives of imprisonment.

State court decisions to forcibly medicate incompetent patients are generally based on the requirement of informed consent, not on the requirement of professional judgment, except in cases of emergency involving the condition of the patient or safety in the institution. State decisions requiring a "judicial determination" to impose treatment also require the appointment of a guardian who may then consent to the treatment. In some jurisdictions, the court ultimately determines whether treatment should be imposed.

Most states mandate more than a finding of mental illness or need for involuntary hospitalization is needed before making a finding that a person is incompetent to make treatment decisions, including decisions relating to treatment of the person's mental illness. Some courts view the rights of an incompetent person to refuse such treatment as having a constitutional basis. In *In re K.K.B.* (Okl.1980), the supreme court of Oklahoma held legally competent adults, involuntarily committed to state mental hospitals, have a right to refuse medication based on a constitutional right of privacy.

In *Davis v. Hubbard* (N.D.Ohio 1980), a federal district court in Ohio rejected the notion that the state's police or *parens patriae* powers automatically permit a state to medicate institutionalized mentally ill persons against their will. In *Davis* the court held there cannot be "forced drugging of a patient for the purpose of doing good absent a determination the person is not capable of rationally deciding what is good for himself." Basing its decision on a liberty interest analysis, the court found the state's interest must be "sufficiently grave and imminent to justify the significant invasion of fundamental interests that the forced use of psychotropic drugs represents." The court articulated a narrow standard for determining that a state may override a patient's refusal, stating "the state must have at least probable cause to believe that the patient is presently violent or self-destructive and, in such a condition, presents a present danger to himself, other patients or the institution's staff before it may disregard the patient's interests in refusing treatment."

2.   First Amendment: Freedom of Religion

Under the First Amendment's freedom of religion clause, most courts allow a competent patient to refuse treatment based on religious grounds if religion is recognized as a legitimate sect, and the religious objection is not part of a delusional system.

The First Amendment also provides the basis for an institutionalized mentally ill patient to refuse treatment. A court will look to whether the individual's life is at stake; whether the patient is incompetent; whether prior to becoming incompetent, the individual refused such treatment on religious grounds; and whether the individual strongly adhered to the tenets of his faith before becoming incompetent.

3.   First Amendment: Freedom of Thought

The appeals court in *Rogers v. Okin* acknowledged First Amendment protection of "freedom of thought" is violated by forcible medication; "whatever powers the Constitution has granted our government, involuntary mind control is not one of them, absent extraordinary circumstances ... medically sound treatment of a mental disease is not, itself, an extraordinary circumstance warranting an unsanctioned intrusion on the integrity of a human being."

The argument that disabled persons ought to be free to "think psychotic thoughts" has not been found valid under a First Amendment analysis. However, a stronger argument has been made that psychiatry is an imprecise science and should not be permitted to override an individuals constitutional interest in being free from mind control. Nevertheless, most arguments in support of a "fundamental right to freedom of thought" as a barrier to involuntarily medicating a patient have failed; because courts, using strict scrutiny, find the state has a compelling interest in preventing the mentally ill from harming themselves or others.

4. Eighth Amendment

Commitment in a mental hospital has been compared to criminal incarceration. This, in turn, has raised questions about the relevance of the Eighth Amendment to forced medication in a mental health facility. However, Eighth Amendment concerns arise in the mental health setting only when medication is used for punishment instead of treatment. The intent or purpose of those administering medication over a patient's objection is the touchstone for establishing whether medication is being wrongfully applied as punishment. Where medication is imposed for therapeutic reasons, uncomfortable side effects do not raise relevant concerns under the Eighth Amendment.

D. STATE STATUTORY BASIS FOR A RIGHT OF REFUSAL OF MENTAL HEALTH TREATMENT

Increasing concern over the rights of the mentally ill and specific concern over the administration of psychotropic medication have led a number of states to enact legislation granting institutionalized individuals the right to refuse treatment. Some statutes generally prohibit "excessive or punitive use of medication." Others only allow voluntarily admitted mental patients to refuse treatment. States granting a specific right to the involuntarily committed patient to refuse treatment allow the state override the objection in order to prevent injury to self or others.

E. RIGHT TO REFUSE ELECTRO-CONVULSIVE THERAPY

Historically, electroconvulsive therapy (ECT) was resisted treatment by patient advocates through litigation because of ECT's perceived harsh side effects. Today, ECT is recognized as a valid treatment in the psychiatric community. Improved techniques for administering ECT, along with the development of muscle relaxants, have eliminated many injurious and unpleasant side effects that accompanied earlier administration of ECT. In fact, some argue ECT is now less intrusive and less likely to cause harmful side effects than psychotropic medications.

Some state statutes grant a patient a specific right to refuse ECT. However, ECT can be administered in all states if informed consent is obtained. The same constitutional and informed consent arguments used to establish a right to refuse psychotropic medication may be used to justify the right to refuse ECT.

F. RIGHT TO REFUSE PSYCHOSURGERY

Psychosurgery is regarded as an experimental treatment. Its use is considered hazardous, and its benefits are believed to be outweighed by the substantial risk of significant side effects or injury to the patient. Lobotomy, a common type of psychosurgery, has not been used as a treatment on involuntary patients since the 1950s.

State statutes define psychosurgery as "brain surgery" "lobotomy" or other "experimental and hazardous" procedures. Some states place broad restrictions on psychosurgery. For example, some states allow psychosurgery only when an informed consent is obtained from the patient. Thus, mentally disabled individuals who cannot give consent are precluded from the procedure. Other states require that if a person is incompetent, surgery may be performed only following a court order.

Kaimowitz v. Department of Mental Health for the State of Michigan (Mich.1973), involved proposed experimental surgery on a prisoner to determine whether aggression could be reduced. In *Kaimowitz*, a Michigan court held psychosurgery should never be undertaken on an involuntarily committed patient when a high-risk to low-benefit ratio exists. Moreover, the court found it would be impossible for physicians to obtain fully informed consent for this type of procedure from persons institutionalized against their will. The court held neither a guardian nor a parent could give the requisite substituted consent.

Only a few courts have addressed issues involving psychosurgery. One court required informed consent as a precondition to psychosurgery. Other court opinions parallel the result in *Kaimowitz* and totally prohibit psychosurgery, lobotomy, or other unusual, hazardous or intrusive surgical procedures on institutionalized patients.

G. BEHAVIOR MODIFICATION PROGRAMS

Behavior modification involves techniques to alter specific behavior. Some of these techniques, such as aversive conditioning involving a program in which the person is subjected to unpleasant experiences after being induced to exhibit inappropriate behavior, raise serious questions of appropriateness and effectiveness. One question is whether the conditioning is employed as treatment to modify behavior, or as punishment for inappropriate behavior. One court held the use of nausea causing drugs on prisoners as part of the aversive conditioning program constituted cruel and unusual punishment in violation of the Eighth Amendment. Most courts prohibit the use of such drugs in prisons except under very limited circumstances, including allowing an inmate to withdraw consent to its use at any time.

CHAPTER 10

RIGHT TO TREATMENT

While many commentators have argued involuntarily civilly committed individuals have a constitutional right to treatment, the United States Supreme Court has not directly ruled on this issue. Although the United States Supreme Court avoided the right to treatment issues in *O'Connor v. Donaldson,* Chief Justice Burger, in his concurrence, argued no such right should be recognized. Nevertheless, several federal appeals and district court decisions have provided a constitutional law analyses that establishes the theoretical underpinnings for a right to treatment for these persons involuntarily civilly committed.

A. THE RIGHT TO TREATMENT

In *Donaldson v. O'Connor* (5th Cir.1974), the United States Court of Appeals for the Fifth Circuit held a person involuntarily civilly committed to a state mental hospital has a constitutional right to receive appropriate treatment that will provide the individual with a reasonable opportunity to be cured or to improve his mental condition. The appeals court found an involuntarily civilly committed individual suffers severe curtailment of liberty. The infringement on liberty can only be justified by showing that this denial of liberty is necessary to achieve a permissible governmental interest or objective. Where the state's rationale for involuntarily confining an individual falls under a *parens patriae* rationale, the appeals court held the state is obligated to provide treatment that will achieve therapeutic results.

According to the Fifth Circuit analysis, if treatment is not provided governmental detention can justified only upon establishment of three criteria: (1) the detention is in retribution for criminal activity; (2) the detention is limited to a specified term; and (3) the detention is mandated following formal proceedings observing due process or procedural safeguards. In absence of these criteria, detention may only be justified by a *quid pro quo* based upon an individual's need for rehabilitative detention. Under such circumstances, minimally adequate habilitation and care, beyond subsistence level, are necessary to justify detention. This is true in the mental health setting as it is in the public health setting where it is argued detention by quarantine can only be maintained where the detainee is receiving treatment for a contagious disease.

It should be noted that the United States Supreme Court in *O'Connor v. Donaldson* (S.Ct.1975), found that the case did not require the court to consider the issues addressed by the Fifth Circuit, namely the constitutional issue of whether mentally ill persons dangerous to themselves or to others have a right to treatment upon compulsory confinement by the state, or whether the state may compulsory confine a nondangerous individual person for the purpose of treatment. Instead, the Supreme Court held that a state cannot constitutionally confine without more a nondangerous mentally ill person who is capable of surviving safely in freedom by himself, or with the help of willing and responsible family members or friends.

B. RIGHT TO SAFE CONDITIONS OF CONFINEMENT AND HABILITATION

The United States Supreme Court in *Youngberg v. Romeo* (S.Ct.1982), held an involuntary civilly committed individual has a right to safe conditions of confinement, freedom from bodily restraint, and adequate habilitation. *Youngberg* involved an institutionalized mentally retarded young man who was injured several times both by himself and by others reacting to him within the institution. The young man's mother asserted that her son had a right to a safe environment, to be free from bodily restraint during the course of treatment, and to be taught self-care or habilitation.

The Supreme Court conceded without further discussion that an institutionalized residents have a right to food, shelter, clothing and medical care. Further, the court found the residents, have a right to safe confinement conditions which are an "historic liberty interest." The court held detention of individuals in unsafe conditions is deemed cruel and unusual punishment under the Constitution. Similarly, the Court found an individual's right to freedom from bodily restraint is embedded in the Fourteenth Amendment right to freedom of movement. Finally, the court found an individual has a constitutional right to minimally adequate habilitation.

The Court's determination of a constitutional right to minimally adequate habilitation stemmed from both the Due Process clause and the Fourteenth Amendment. In *Youngberg*, the plaintiff sought to expand the requirement of adequate habilitation beyond "minimal habilitation." This was more than the Supreme Court would require. The Court concluded that a state is under no constitutional obligation to provide anything beyond "self care" techniques. The Courts position recognized that in order for state institutions to guarantee safety and freedom of movement to its patients, self care must be taught to the patient. A patient's ability to perform basic daily activities without the aid of hospital staff minimizes the patient's restraint of movement.

Moreover, the Court observed that the patient's right to safety, freedom from restraint and right to habilitation were subject to limitation given a significant enough state interest. Situations where the patient poses a physical threat of violence, to others or to himself, justify a state's restraint of institutional residents. Restraints may also be a necessary element of a patient's training program. The Court's opinion indicated the amount of self-training needed was an amount sufficient to prevent self-destructive behavior.

The Court also cited the proper standard for determining whether a patient's rights have been violated. The Court determined judicial authority must exercise a minimal amount of scrutiny and defer to the professional judgment exercised in individual cases. A court may not substitute its evaluation of the appropriateness of measures taken to meet a patient's needs for the professional's evaluation. In situations where a professional exercises judgment in accordance with budgetary constraints, the professional is exempt from liability on good faith grounds.

While the Court established immunity from liability for professionals exercising judgment in light of budgetary constraints, the question remains whether inadequate funding or unreasonable budget restraints may give rise to valid patient legal attacks regarding their confinement involving charges of inadequate care resulting from a state's inadequate funding. The good faith defense used by the professional might not be a sufficient defense for the state. Several courts have rejected the budgetary defense in injunction suits against a governmental body, finding a patient's treatment must be based upon medical or psychological criteria and not nonmedical or administrative criteria based on inadequate funding.

C. IMPLEMENTING THE RIGHT TO TREATMENT

Wyatt v. Stickney (M.D.Ala.1972), decided by a federal district court in Alabama in 1972, was the first major class action suit brought by involuntarily civilly committed patients to enforce the right to treatment.

Plaintiffs in *Wyatt* sought injunctive relief against mental health institutions to ensure adequate treatment. In granting plaintiffs' request, the court drafted specific minimum standards for adequate treatment of the mentally ill which were found to be constitutionally required. The court cited specific rights guaranteed to patients, including the right to the least restrictive conditions necessary to achieve the objectives of commitment.

Wyatt had the impact of reducing patient abuse, increasing the number of supervisory personnel, and improving the quality of treatment. Following the *Wyatt* decision, many states enacted legislation securing patient rights. The greatest impact of *Wyatt* appeared in the adoption of individualized treatment plans which have become standard in most states.

D. LEAST RESTRICTIVE MEANS APPROACH

The *Wyatt* court's articulation of a "least restrictive means" approach to treatment prompted many courts to adopt a presumption that all patients are to be restricted only to the extent that clinical therapy can be effectively administered. It must be noted, however, that *Wyatt* dealt with treatment plans *within* the state institution. Subsequent application of this theory has led many courts to interpret "least restrictive" as an institution's duty to attempt to move residents from 1) larger to smaller facilities; 2) larger to smaller living units; 3) group to individual residences; 4) segregated from the community to integrated community living; and 5) dependent to independent living. Other courts have interpreted the doctrine to restrict a patient only to the extent clinically necessary for the hospital to maintain order and security.

E. RESTRAINTS AND SECLUSION

Some states have enacted statutes allowing restraint and seclusion only when necessary to administer treatment and protect the patient from harm to self or others. Other states permit institutions to use restraints and seclusion as modes of punishment, or in place of supervision in understaffed hospitals. However, states permitting restraint and seclusion as punishment require a scheduled timed release from the constraint and a complete psychiatric evaluation before continued detention is allowed.

F. PATIENT LABOR

Most states require that a program of involuntary patient labor must satisfy a compelling governmental interest. Generally, a patient's involuntary labor is permissible if it is therapeutic in nature. Interestingly, many courts have placed the burden on the plaintiff to demonstrate a particular task is not therapeutic.

Patients have not had great success in attacking work programs under the Thirteenth Amendment prohibition against involuntary servitude or slavery. Patients are more successful bringing claims under the Fair Labor Standards Act. The Act requires workers to receive minimum wage and places a maximum on the number of hours an individual may work. However, the Act was amended in 1966 specifically to allow below minimum level wages for individuals unable to work at "normal" levels due to a physical or mental handicap.

G. ENFORCING THE RIGHT TO TREATMENT

Courts have applied several sanctions for institutions violating a patient's right to treatment. One sanction is to close down the institution altogether. Economic sanctions are less severe, and more common. Some state courts make a per patient, per day assessment of damages for constitutional violations. Perhaps the most effective enforcement mechanism is an information-gathering and advocacy system. Courts have mandated the establishment of institutional human rights committees to report to the court on whether institutions have complied with treatment orders. Some states allow residents unrestricted right to attorney consultation.

H. REIMBURSEMENT FOR TREATMENT

Every state has legislation holding voluntary and involuntary patients responsible for the cost of their treatment. Most states extend this responsibility to the patient's relatives, generally the immediate family. Increasingly, states are attempting to obtain reimbursement from family members for costs incurred in treatment of civilly committed patients. Insurance company and Medicaid reimbursement are also being looked to as sources of payment for institutionalized patients.

The Equal Protection Clause prohibits charging the cost of patient treatment and facility maintenance to one particular class, whether the commitment is incidental to an alleged criminal violation, or the result of a civil commitment. Courts disagree, however, on a state's right to levy earnings of residents involuntarily committed.

I. THE RIGHT TO COMMUNITY SERVICES

Most courts and health agencies view the right to treatment to include a patient's right to community placement and services following psychiatric treatment within the institution. Courts and health experts also agree a patient's treatment is not effective unless it includes proper aftercare and provision of the means to adapt to society following psychiatric treatment. It is also the view of mental health professionals that a patient may lose the benefit gained from treatment or be unable to apply acquired coping strategies when placed in stressful surroundings. Recently, courts have begun requiring state institutions to place their residents in community homes and treatment centers.

Early court decisions guaranteed a patient's right to treatment only insofar as the patient was a resident of a state institution. However, family members brought suits on behalf of former patients to provide a smooth and effective transition to community living.

In *Lelsz v. Kavanagh* (5th Cir.1987), the United States Court of Appeals for the Fifth Circuit set out criteria for transferring residents to community centers. Each patient was found to be entitled to an individualized placement plan taking into account the patient's age, degree of retardation, and handicapping conditions. Furthermore, the court required the State to provide patients being released with the least restrictive alternative living condition. As a continuation of a patient's treatment within the institution, the state was directed to provide each patient with adequate skills to adapt and live as independently as possible in a community environment.

Much of the courts' reasoning behind a patient's right to community treatment services stems from the judicial recognition of a right to treatment within the institution. A patient's right to the least restrictive treatment means of detention includes a patient's right to be placed within a community residential facility if that sort of treatment would be the most effective and least restrictive means given his retardation and other handicaps. Many mental health professionals maintain that any showing of a patient's ability to function outside of the institution warrants placement in community facilities.

J. CONSTITUTIONAL STANDARDS OF CARE FOR THE MENTALLY RETARDED

The United States Supreme Court has not found the requirement of least restrictive treatment alternative to be constitutionally required in cases involving the placement of the mentally ill and mentally retarded. In *Society for Good Will to Retarded Children v. Cuomo* (2d Cir.1984), the Court of Appeals for the Second Circuit followed the Supreme Court's ruling in *Youngberg* and found that a court should defer to professional's decision regarding a patient's placement. Thus, even though experts may not agree on an individual's need to continue residence in an institution, a least restrictive means approach is not mandated nor required as long as professional judgment was used in making the decision. The court reasoned that if judges were to evaluate the decisions of psychiatric professionals, psychiatric evaluation would become useless. So long as professional judgment is exercised, a patient's placement, whether it be in a community residential facility or in an institution, is not subject to constitutional attack.

K. RIGHT TO TREATMENT FOR NONINSTITUTIONALIZED PATIENTS

To the extent that a patient's right to treatment has been recognized by courts, that right has been linked to involuntary institutionalization. The issue arises whether patients in community facilities possess the same right as if they have never been institutionalized.

In *Thomas S. v. Morrow* (W.D.N.C.1984), a federal district court in North Carolina found individuals placed directly in community facilities possess an implied liberty interest in appropriate treatment. The case involved an individual who was transferred to over forty facilities. The court rejected the state's argument that as a noninstitutional patient, plaintiff was not entitled to minimally adequate treatment. The court instead found the state's position that it was required only to provide a patient available treatment, rather than appropriate treatment, was unacceptable. The court concluded where the State intentionally made an adult a ward of the state and placed the individual in a community facility, the individual had a right to treatment. A right to minimally adequate treatment within the community, therefore, may be invoked by individuals involuntarily committed to community facilities with resulting restrictions on their individual liberty.

L. STATE AND FEDERAL STATUTORY BASES FOR RIGHT TO COMMUNITY TREATMENT

Some federal district courts have relied upon state statutory grounds to broaden interpretations and limitations on right to treatment. For example, in *Dixon v. Weinberger* (D.D.C.1975), the District of Columbia District Court relied exclusively on a local statute to order the reallocation of federal and district funds to create community facilities.

Reliance upon federal statutory law also enhances a patient's right to treatment. Federal statutes establishing a disabled child's right to access to the public school system if he qualifies may assist a child's placement within the community. Similarly, the Developmentally Disabled Assistance and Bill of Rights Act aids enforcement of a patient's right to treatment by providing funds to states willing to provide habilitation programs for the mentally retarded.

CHAPTER 11

GUARDIANSHIP

A. THE GUARDIAN AND THE WARD

A guardian is a person designated to act for a ward, that is a person who is unable to manage his or her own affairs. The legal basis for guardianship laws, which mandate the state to care for a person who is unable to care for himself or herself, is the state's *parens patriae* power. Although a guardian can be given the authority to protect an incompetent ward and to manage the ward's property, a guardian does not succeed to the ward's legal rights.

B. GUARDIANSHIP PROCEEDINGS

Guardianship is established through a judicial proceeding. A court receives a petition to determine the incompetency of the ward and to appoint a guardian. Until the guardian's duties terminate, a probate court retains jurisdiction over the ward and the ward's estate.

1. Initiating a Guardianship Proceeding

Although state statutes vary, most states allow "any interested person" to initiate guardianship proceedings. Over half of the states allow an incompetent person to initiate his or her own proceeding. A few jurisdictions allow a state or local official to file an application for guardianship, and only one state allows the court itself to begin a guardianship proceeding. Furthermore, a few states allow a guardianship proceeding to be initiated at the same time as a civil commitment hearing.

Questions concerning the authority to initiate guardianship proceedings may arise in the absence of a clear statutory authority providing for standing to initiate a guardianship proceeding. For example, New Jersey provides authority only for relatives to initiate guardianship proceedings; not even a "best friend" has standing. Nevertheless, clear cases will arise where incompetent persons need the protection provided by a guardian. Thus, for example it was necessary for a New Jersey court in *In re Bennett* (N.J.1981), to authorize a state official to initiate proceedings to establish a guardianship for an elderly homeless woman.

2. Need for Individualized Proceedings

It is recognized a guardianship proceeding should be an individualized matter, taking into account the particular circumstances and needs of the person for whom guardianship is sought. Failure to provide such individualized proceedings has led to litigation. For example, in *Michigan Ass'n for Retarded Citizens v. Wayne County Probate Judge* (Mich.App. 1977), a Michigan appeals court held that a seventy-five minute guardianship hearing for over one hundred mentally retarded persons violated due process.

3. Required Notice of Guardianship Proceeding

After guardianship proceedings are initiated, federal due process and most state statutes require that notice be given to the prospective ward. A majority of jurisdictions require the incompetent person's closest relative must also receive notice. Several states require the individual who has custody of the incompetent person must receive notice.

4. Requirement of the Guardianship Proceeding

After a court finds a person is incompetent, the majority of states provide for a hearing to determine whether he or she needs a guardian. Most courts require clear and convincing evidence of a need for a guardianship before a court appoints a guardian. A majority of state statutes mandate legal representation at a guardianship hearing. Upon request, approximately half the states provide jury trials for guardianship proceedings.

5. Scope of Guardianship Determination

A court may appoint a guardian to make all legal decisions, or the court may limit the guardian's authority to make only specific decisions. Traditionally, the guardian's function was to prevent mentally disabled persons from dissipating their estate and to protect persons who could not care themselves.

Historically, this was an all or nothing determination. If a person was found unfit to either manage his or her affairs or care for themselves, a "plenary" guardian was appointed to make personal or financial decisions, or both, for the incompetent person. Today, most states mandate a more specific determination of incompetence. Following, this approach a court determines the exact nature of the individual's inability to care for himself or herself or manage his or her affairs. A guardian is then appointed with only enough power as is needed to meet the ward's particular needs.

C. APPOINTING A GUARDIAN

State statutes typically focus on a ward's mental status or ability to function in society. Some states require a threshold finding of "incompetency," to appoint a guardian, while other states require "incapacity." Although the definition of incompetency varies by state, most definitions include consideration of mental retardation or developmental disability, mental illness, age, alcoholism, drug abuse, or physical disability. A minority of jurisdictions provide a court may appoint a guardian only when the appointment is necessary, that is, when the person needs supervision, or the appointment is in the person's "best interests."

To determine when a person is incompetent, most statutes include criteria that is less concerned with the effects resulting from an individual's particular decisions, but instead focuses on the individual's ability to go through the cognitive process of making rational decisions. One suggested approach would provide guardianship for adults whose ability to receive and evaluate information effectively and/or to communicate decisions is impaired to such an extent that they lack the capacity to manage their financial resources and/or meet essential requirements for their physical health or safety.

Challenges have been directed against the specificity of guardianship statutes, and particularly toward the criteria for determining incompetence or incapacity. For example, a California statute provided a court must appoint a conservator for an individual who is likely to be deceived or imposed upon by artful or designing persons. In *Katz v. Superior Court* (Cal.App.1977), a California appeals court held the California statute unconstitutionally vague, because "[i]n an age of subliminal advertising, television exposure, and psychological salesmanship, everyone is exposed to artful and designing persons at every turn. It is impossible to measure the degree of likelihood that some will succumb."

1. Qualifications of a Guardian

Court usually appoint guardians who are "competent," "suitable," or "qualified." To be qualified, the proposed guardian must meet the appropriate standards both in character and in relation to the ward that includes moral character, age, ability to formulate plans for the ward, residence in the same state as the ward, professional qualifications, experience with finances, and understanding of the religious beliefs of the ward. If several qualified guardians are available, courts usually give preference to close relatives. Many states do not allow convicted felons, judges, suspended lawyers, or spouses to serve as guardians. Moreover, a conflict of interest between the ward and the recommended guardian may disqualify the proposed guardian. The grounds for a conflict of interest vary and may include indebtedness to the incompetent person. Additionally many jurisdictions allow trust companies and banks to act as guardians for the estates of incompetent adults.

2. Powers of Guardians

A court may appoint a guardian for a person's property and personal interests. In a guardianship of the person, a guardian may have responsibility for any of the ward's non-financial personal decisions. Typically, a personal guardian is a friend, relative, or state agency.

Guardianships of the estate affect property. A guardianship or conservatorship of property has responsibility only for the ward's property and income, finances, bank accounts, trusts, and debts.

D. CONTROL OF THE WARD'S PERSON

Usually, a guardian of an incompetent person retains custody of the ward. However, it is well a settled doctrine as recognized by the California Supreme Court in *Browne v. Superior Court of San Francisco* (Cal.1940), that a guardian cannot deny a ward his or her freedom without good reason. A guardian of the person has the duty to decide matters related to the ward's health, education, and support. For example, the United States Supreme Court in *Cruzan v. Director, Missouri Department of Health* (S.Ct.1990), suggested the guardian of a ward in a terminally ill, vegetative state could obtain a court order to remove a respirator upon clear and convincing evidence that the ward, if competent, would have had the respirator removed.

E. CONTROL OF THE WARD'S ESTATE

Most statutes provide a court may endow a guardian with extensive power over a ward's personal and real property. A guardian of the ward's estate can be given possession, control, and management of the ward's personal and real property. However, the ward retains legal title to his or her property, and title is not conferred to his or her guardian.

1. Selling Property

A guardian usually can sell a ward's personal property. By contrast, the guardian cannot sell the ward's realty without court approval. A guardian's sale of a ward's real estate may be ratified by the ward when he or she becomes competent. In many states, a guardian has the power to lease the ward's real estate without a court authorization.

2. Expenditures for the Ward's Maintenance

In most cases, a guardian must receive court approval to use income from the ward's estate for the ward's maintenance. However, a court may approve a guardian's expenditures when the expenditures are appropriate for the ward's interests. A guardian has a duty to keep the ward's money, property, and investments separate from the guardian's assets. Unless restricted by statute, a guardian retains authority to compromise or release the ward's debts.

3. Making Donations

A guardian has the authority to donate gifts to a specific charity from the ward's estate if the guardian can establish that the ward previously contributed to the designated charity. Some statutes limit charitable gifts to a fixed percentage of the ward's estate. All deposits and investments of the ward's funds made by a guardian must be in the ward's name, or be indicated as property of the ward.

4. Making Investments

Unless prohibited by statute, a guardian has the authority to invest the ward's funds without court approval. In the case of court authorized investment, a guardian is not liable for the loss of funds. Retroactive court approval also removes liability. Many jurisdictions require a guardian to receive more than a court's verbal approval to avoid liability for losses on investments. A guardian who complies with the states' statutory provision for investment approval is not personally liable for any loss of a ward's funds that the guardian prudently invested in good faith.

A guardian may not invest a ward's funds in speculative investments. Instead, the funds must be invested with the reasonable expectation the investment will produce income. Many state statutes specify the type of investments and securities a guardian may buy or sell. A guardian and his or her surety are liable for a conversion of funds if the guardian invests the ward's funds in the guardian's business ventures. In most states, a guardian is personally liable for any losses arising from an unsecured investment.

Some statutes allow a guardian to temporarily deposit a ward's funds, in the ward's name, in a bank. However, courts generally hold a guardian violates the duty to invest the ward's funds if the guardian deposits the funds for a fixed time in a bank.

Under statutory authority, a guardian may invest a ward's funds in a first mortgage. However, before a guardian invests in real estate, the guardian must ascertain the value of the property and the ability to sell the property in the event of foreclosure. A guardian should value the property according to the estimate of a person of ordinary prudence who would safely invest his or her own money in that property. Some statutes recognize a mortgage is an appropriate investment if the property is worth twice the amount of the mortgage.

F. CONTRACTS

Unless a statute or court authorizes a guardian to execute an agreement, a guardian cannot bind the ward or the wards's estate by any contract. A court, however, will enforce contracts for necessary services (such as food or medicine) against the ward's estate. A guardian who enters a contract simply "as guardian" does not limit his or her liability. Instead, a guardian may limit his or her personal liability only by obtaining an agreement from the other party to the contract not to hold the guardian personally responsible.

G. LIMITS ON THE GUARDIAN'S POWERS

A court grants plenary or full guardianship only when a person has an irreversible mental in capacity. A court will limit a guardian's powers if a person is incompetent only with respect to certain specific matters.

State statutes specify limits to a guardian's authority. Approximately half of the states define "limited guardianship" as a relationship in which the guardian is responsible for "only those duties and powers which the individual is incapable of exercising." Even plenary guardians rarely have unrestricted authority. Statutory limitations serve to protect various rights of the ward; for example, sterilization and abortion generally require court approval.

Statutes often mandate court supervision of a guardian through the judicial process. Moreover, a court may retain jurisdiction to modify a guardian's decisions. For example, a court may request an accounting of all financial transactions and hold a guardian liable for any unexplained losses of the ward's income. If a guardian is legally unqualified to continue his or her fiduciary responsibilities, a court may remove and replace the guardian. In *Parker v. Barefoot* (N.C.App.1983), a North Carolina court replaced a guardian because he paid his incompetent mother rent substantially below the market rate. In another case, *In re Ronstrom, 436 So.2d 588 (La.App.1983),* a Louisiana court replaced a bank guardian, because the bank was financially "imprudent" when it spent $80,000 of the ward's $158,000 estate for a guard service. In some states, a conflict of interest in and of itself is not sufficient to penalize a guardian. Instead, the guardian's decisions must also involve fraud, bad faith, or dishonesty.

In any guardianship proceeding, a judge should structure the guardian's fiduciary relationship subject to two limitations. First, the guardian should only act in the ward's "best interests." Some jurisdictions determine the ward's "best interests" from the perspective of the decision maker. However, other courts determine a ward's "best interests" by what the ward would decide if competent; actually, such courts are using the substitute judgment criteria developed in the area of medical decision making for incompetent patients. This latter standard is more difficult to apply, because the ward's preference may not be in his or her best financial interest.

Second, courts often limit a guardian's surrogate decisions. For example, a guardian cannot waive the ward's legal rights or exercise the ward's personal elective rights.

H. A GUARDIAN'S ELECTIONS ON BEHALF OF THE WARD

Statutes often forbid a guardian of the estate from executing a will for the ward. Moreover, since the right to take under a will is a personal right, a guardian of an incompetent person cannot make an election for the ward to take under a will without express statutory authority. However, a court with jurisdiction over the ward's estate may consent to an election made on behalf of the incompetent person.

Additionally, an incompetent person has a personal right to change the beneficiary of his or her life insurance. Therefore, a guardian cannot change the ward's beneficiary unless a court determines a different beneficiary is in the ward's best interests. Courts will approve a change in beneficiaries when the facts merit change. For example *United States v. Tighe* (S.D.Miss.1964), a federal court held a guardian could change the beneficiary of the ward's life insurance policy from a person unrelated to the ward, to a sister of the ward who cared for the ward before he died.

I. EXTRAORDINARY PROCEDURES

A guardian of the person usually needs court approval before consenting to and or subjecting the ward to "extraordinary" procedures which include abortion, sterilization, or organ transplants.

A legislative scheme absolutely precluding a sterilization deprives developmentally disabled persons of privacy and liberty interests protected by the First and Fourteenth Amendments of the United States Constitution. In *Conservatorship of Valerie N.* (Cal.1985), a California court determined a guardian has the power to consent to sterilization if there is evidence the ward requires contraceptive protection, and no less intrusive method of contraception is available.

A court's decision to approve sterilization of an incompetent ward can only be made in a proceeding in which (1) the ward is represented by a disinterested guardian ad litem; (2) the court has received independent opinion based upon a comprehensive medical, psychological, and social evaluation of the individual; and (3) the court has considered the incompetent individual's view.

Within this framework, the judge must find by clear and convincing evidence the individual is (1) incapable of making his or her own decision concerning sterilization, and (2) unlikely to be able to make an informed judgment in the foreseeable future. The judge additionally must find the individual is (3) physically capable of procreation, (4) likely to engage in sexual activity at the present time or in the near future under circumstances likely to result in pregnancy, and (5) the nature and extent of the individual's disability, as determined by empirical evidence, and not solely on standardized tests, renders him or her permanently incapable of caring for a child, even with reasonable assistance.

Finally, there must not be an alternative to sterilization. The judge must find (1) all less drastic contraceptive methods, including supervision, education, and training, have been proved unworkable or inapplicable, (2) the proposed method of sterilization is the least invasive of the individual's body, and (3) the current state of scientific and medical knowledge neither suggests a reversible sterilization procedure or other less drastic contraceptive method will shortly be available, nor that science is on the threshold of an advance in the treatment of the individual's disability.

J. RIGHT TO REFUSE TREATMENT

In most jurisdictions, a guardian of an adult ward may not decide to medicate a ward after the ward leaves a hospital, unless an "emergency" occurs. However, a court may force a ward to receive medication either where a substituted judgment determination indicates the incompetent individual would, if competent, accept antipsychotic drugs; or where there exists a state interest of sufficient magnitude to override the individual's right to refuse. If the asserted state interest is the prevention of violent conduct by noninstitutionalized mentally ill individuals, upon a showing equivalent to that of involuntary civil commitment, the state may compel the individual to choose, through the use of substituted judgment, either involuntary commitment or medication with antipsychotic drugs.

K. TESTAMENTARY GUARDIAN

State statutes provide the authority for testamentary guardianship through a will or a deed. Testamentary guardianship allows a parent to appoint a guardian for his or her children if one parent dies or becomes disabled. The same fiduciary relationship applies to a husband or a wife as a guardian for his or her disabled spouse. A probate court may overrule the testator and appoint a different guardian to improve the ward's welfare. If a will does not indicate a successor to the original guardian, several state statutes specify spouses as the successors.

L. TEMPORARY GUARDIANS

A court uses temporary guardianship when the initial guardian dies, or is disabled, during the process of appointing a permanent guardian, and when an incompetent person immediately requires a guardian.

Requests by parents to be temporary guardians in order to remove emancipated children from religious or political groups generally fail. These parents often allege that their children are acting incompetently due to the influence of a zealot group.

In *Taylor v. Gilmartin* (10th Cir.1982), the United States Court of Appeals for the Tenth Circuit refused such a parental request reasoning that authority for determining whether a child has been "brainwashed" was not provided for in the applicable state's guardianship statute.

M. GUARDIAN *AD LITEM*

A *guardian ad litem* represents a person's interest in a single judicial action. The majority of states provide a *guardian ad litem* to protect an incompetent person during litigation. The *guardian ad litem* is responsible only for decisions on behalf of the ward that pertain to legal proceedings including the appointment of a permanent guardian or involuntary commitment.

N. PUBLIC GUARDIANS

A few states provide public guardians when private guardians are not available. However, conflict of interest problems often arise with public guardians. The guardian has dual responsibility to coordinate delivery of services needed by the ward, as well as to monitor the delivery of services to the ward.

O. GUARDIANS FOR THE PHYSICALLY DISABLED

Old age or physical infirmity usually does not warrant a court appointment of a guardian for the estate of the person. Some state statutes allow a physically disabled person to select his or her guardian. In *In re Guardianship of Gallagher* (Ohio App. 1981) an Ohio appeals court held a guardian was not appropriate for a physically disabled person without the person's consent. However, in a few states, a court may appoint a guardian for a person who is physically disabled if such appointment is determined to be necessary for assisting the disabled person to meet his or her basic needs.

P. REPRESENTATIVE PAYEES

A representative payee manages specific transactions of a ward. Often, a disabled person is unable to allocate his or her social security, pensions, and other income for payment to the facility where he or she resides. Thus, a representative payee often makes payments for the disabled person. A court may appoint anyone who operates a nursing home or institution where the disabled person resides as the representative payee to manage the ward's finances. However, the dangers of using a representative payee include overpayment to the facility and misuse of funds.

Q. LITIGATION

A guardian may initiate litigation to protect a ward's person and property. However, courts vary as to whether a ward may sue independently of his or her guardian. If a guardian executes a contract in the ward's name or the agreement does not indicate who is to receive the contract's benefits, then the ward is to receive the benefits of the contract and is liable for the contract. In some jurisdictions, a guardian is the only party who may initiate a lawsuit for breach of contract; whereas, the ward is the only party who may file suit after the guardianship ends.

Furthermore, a party may sue a ward and name the ward's guardian as a party defendant. However, a ward and the ward's guardian cannot have adverse positions in a lawsuit. Where there is a conflicting interests of guardian and ward in litigation, special measures must be taken. For example, in *Rupe v. Robison* (Wash.1926), the Washington Supreme Court found a husband who is the general guardian of an insane wife may bring an action for divorce so long as a court appoints a *guardian ad litem* for the wife.

R. LIABILITY OF GUARDIANS AND SURETIES

A guardian is liable for any loss incurred from his or her negligent care or handling of the ward's property. For example, a guardian may be personally liable for damages or injuries resulting from a tort committed while the guardian administered the ward's estate. A guardian is not usually liable for the ward's torts, unless the guardian negligently allowed the ward to commit the torts.

The guardian must faithfully perform his or her duties according to the law. Most states require a guardian of the estate upon appointment to provide a bond, as security, to preserve the estate of his or her ward. Furthermore, most statutes require a guardian to provide a special sale bond upon court authorization to sell the ward's property. Accordingly, the guardian must account for the proceeds from the sale of the ward's real estate. Usually, a guardian appointed by a deed or will is not required to provide a bond if the instrument relieves him or her of that duty.

Regardless of the liability the law imposes upon the guardian, a surety is bound to the extent stated in the guardianship bond. Unless authorized by a statute, a surety for a guardian's bond cannot terminate any future liability which a guardian may incur. A court may release the bond and discharge the surety only upon the consent of all parties.

S. TERMINATION OF GUARDIANSHIP

The relationship between a ward and a guardian terminates under several circumstances. For example, upon restoration of a ward to competency, a court terminates its jurisdiction and discharges the ward's guardian.

Restoration is a legal determination that individuals who have been adjudged incompetent are now able to manage adequately their business and personal affairs. The law, however, presumes persons who are adjudicated incompetent remain incompetent. In order for wards to regain competent status, they normally either must vindicate themselves in a separate judicial proceeding or, in a few states, be discharged from a mental institution.

Additionally, the relationship between a ward and his or her guardian ends upon the death of either party. Furthermore, a guardianship ends when the ward's domicile changes to a different state, where the ward retains his or her property, and a court appoints a new guardian in that state.

Without explicit statutory authority, a guardian may not resign. However, a court has discretion to remove a guardian from his or her responsibilities upon proof of misbehavior or unfitness. The grounds for removal are designated by state statute.

CHAPTER 12

COMPETENCY TO STAND TRIAL

A. THE CONCEPT OF COMPETENCY TO STAND TRIAL

The requirement that a defendant be present at trial and mentally able to take part in providing a defense are fundamental requirements of a fair trial; as the Tennessee Supreme Court observed in *Jordan v. State* (Tenn.1911), at the beginning of this century: "[i]t would be inhumane, and to a certain extent a denial of a trial on the merits, to require one who has been disabled by the act of God from intelligently making his defense to plead or to be tried for his life or liberty." By the end of the nineteenth century federal courts were clear that a proceeding against a person who is incompetent to stand trial violates due process. For example the United States Court of Appeals for the Sixth Circuit in *Youtsey v. United States* (C.C.A.1899), stated it was "not 'due process of law' to subject an insane person to trial upon an indictment involving liberty or life." This view was reformulated by the United States Court of Appeal for the District of Columbia in *Sanders v. Allen* (D.C.App.1938) which stated: "trial and conviction of a person mentally and physically incapable of making a defense violates certain immutable principles of justice which inhere in the very idea of a free government." Therefore, a defendant who is incompetent to stand trial cannot be tried, sentenced, convicted, or executed.

The United States Supreme Court held in *Drope v. Missouri* (S.Ct.1975), an incompetent defendant lacks the capacity to confront witnesses, testify on his or her own behalf, decide on a defense, assist counsel, understand the trial, or comprehend the reason for assigned punishment. Thus, trial proceedings are accurate only when the defendant can mentally assimilate all the facts relevant to the case, understand the substantive options available to him or her, and understand his or her punishment and the reasons for receiving it.

B. DEFINITION OF COMPETENCY TO STAND TRIAL

A defendant is competent to stand trial if the defendant has the current ability to assist in his or her defense, and to understand the nature of the charges which have been brought and all aspects of the trial process. By contrast, issues of insanity or aspects of the defendant's mental capacity that are part of a defense that relate to a defendant's criminal responsibility are limited to aspects of the defendant's past mental condition at the time of commission of the crime.

To determine a defendant's competency to stand trial, the United States Supreme Court held in *Dusky v. United States* (S.Ct.1960) the trial court must determine whether the defendant has sufficient present ability to consult with a lawyer with a reasonable degree of rational understanding, and whether the defendant has a rational as well as factual understanding of the proceedings being brought against him. In *Dusky,* the Supreme Court did not require establishing that an incompetent defendant has a mental illness or defect. However, most states currently require a finding of mental disease or defect to declare a defendant unfit to stand trial. Furthermore, the Court did not indicate specific guidelines to determine whether a defendant is incompetent or unfit to stand trial.

Since *Dusky,* a New York court in *People v. Swallow* (Sup.Ct.1969), held that a defendant who is competent to stand trial must have "some depth of understanding, not merely surface knowledge of the proceedings." Generally, **the following standards are used by courts to determine a defendant's competency to stand trial:** whether the defendant: (1) is oriented as to time and place; (2) is able to perceive, recall, and relate; (3) has an understanding of the process of the trial and the roles of judge, jury, prosecutor and defense attorney; (4) can establish a working relationship with his attorney; (5) has sufficient intelligence and judgment to listen to the advice of counsel and, based on that advice, appreciate (without necessarily adopting) the fact that one course of conduct may be more beneficial to him than another; and (6) is sufficiently stable to enable him to withstand the stresses of the trial without suffering a serious prolonged or permanent breakdown.

C. COMPETENCY TO PLEAD GUILTY

A defendant's competency to stand trial requires that the individual be able to decide how to plead to a charge. The United States Court of Appeals for the Ninth Circuit held in *Sieling v. Eyman* (9th Cir.1973) that a hearing is required to determine the defendant's ability to plead guilty when an issue is raised about the defendant's current mental capacity.

D. COMPETENCY TO WAIVE COUNSEL

A person who is competent to stand trial is not necessarily competent to waive his or her constitutional right to counsel. If a defendant wants to proceed without counsel, the trial court must initially decide whether the defendant is competent to stand trial. Moreover, the United States Supreme Court held in *Westbrook v. Arizona* (S.Ct.1966), that the trial court must separately determine whether the defendant is competent to waive his or her right to counsel. Clearly, there is a distinction between a defendant's ability to assist his or her counsel and a defendant's ability to proceed *pro se*. Thus, if a court determines that a defendant is not mentally competent to represent himself, defendant should not be able to proceed *pro se,* rather the court should appoint an attorney to represent the defendant. Even if the court permits the defendant to proceed *pro se*, the court often appoints a stand-by counsel who may be brought into the defense if the situation requires the expertise of a trained lawyer.

E. PROCEDURE TO DETERMINE COMPETENCY TO STAND TRIAL

A defendant's competency to stand trial may be raised anytime during the trial. The defendant may raise the issue. However, a defendant's failure to raise the issue does not waive his or her right to due process. An incompetent defendant can not knowingly and intelligently waive his or her right to have the court determine his or her ability to stand trial.

Occasionally, a defendant prefers to go to trial without an inquiry into his or her competency, because he or she would rather accept a definite sentence from a conviction rather than be held under an indefinite commitment to a mental health facility. Regardless of a defendant's desire to raise the issue of his or her competency to stand trial, a prosecutor or a court may also raise the issue.

Courts apply various standards in determining whether an evaluation is necessary to determine a defendant's competency to stand trial. Many lower courts apply the "bona fide doubt" standard. (*Pate v. Robinson* (S.Ct.1966)). If there is a "bona fide doubt" of a defendant's competence, the trial judge must raise the issue *sua sponte* and hold a hearing with sufficient procedures to reasonably assess the defendant's competency according to medical and legal standards. (*Holmes v. King* (5th Cir.1983)).

Alternatively, the trend in the federal courts is that a judge must have a "reasonable doubt" of a defendant's competence before the judge orders an evaluation of the defendant. A defendant's irrational behavior, his or her demeanor at trial, and any prior medical opinion with regard to a defendant's competence to stand trial are relevant to determine whether a court must inquire further. However, a full competency hearing is not necessary each time a court finds some evidence of incompetency. Instead, when a judge has a "reasonable doubt" of a defendant's competence, the majority of jurisdictions provide statutory authority for the judge to commit the defendant for an examination by an expert or at a hospital. In a minority of states, a jury may determine the issue instead of a judge. However, a defendant does not have a constitutional right to have the issue decided by a jury.

After the examination of a defendant, the trial court must decide whether the defendant is competent to stand trial. Usually, the prosecution has the burden to prove competency after the issue is raised. Alternatively, some statutes dictate that the burden of proof is on the movant.

Most states apply the preponderance of the evidence standard of proof. Thus, a defendant is mentally competent to stand trial when a court finds that the prosecution has established the defendant's competency by a preponderance of the evidence. In some states, the court relies solely on the expert's report. If either party or the court disagrees with the expert's report, the court must conduct a hearing. However, the court usually follows the recommendations of the expert after the hearing.

F. EVALUATION TO DETERMINE COMPETENCY TO STAND TRIAL

When a judge has a "reasonable doubt" of a defendant's competency to stand trial, due process mandates that the defendant receive a mental evaluation. Usually, the defendant receives a competency evaluation at the hospital to which the court committed the defendant. A defendant may remain in the hospital for thirty to ninety days.

Alternatively, some state statutes require a court to determine, on an individual basis, the appropriate placement for an incompetent defendant. The trend in many state statutes is to require competency evaluations on an outpatient basis in court clinics, rather than in hospitals. Outpatient evaluations are usually sufficient to determine a defendant's capacity to assist his or her counsel and to understand the trial proceedings. Moreover, outpatient evaluations are cost efficient.

State statutes specify who must conduct the evaluation and the amount of evaluations required. Approximately one-half of the states require that a psychiatrist must perform the evaluation. Other states allow a clinical psychologists with a doctorate in psychology to perform the evaluation, or otherwise direct the state mental health agency to conduct competency examinations. Typically, evaluators conduct one interview of a defendant within several days after he or she enters the hospital. Often, the prosecution or the defense requests additional evaluations by a second expert. Evaluators do not apply standard evaluations since most states do not require an evaluator to specifically report the methods used to support his or her conclusions.

A few of the types of evaluations used to determine a defendant's competency include:

(I) A standard instrument for determining competency to stand trial is the Competency to Stand Trial Assessment Instrument (CSTAT). However, this test is often criticized because the CSTAT's definitions do not eliminate possible examiner's prejudice, resulting from the examiner's presumptions, when he or she interprets the defendant's responses. The CSTAT includes measurement of thirteen "ego functions" related to what is demanded of a defendant to protect himself or herself in a criminal proceeding. The thirteen criteria include:

1. Appraisal of available legal defenses;

2. Unmanageable behavior;

3. Quality of relating to an attorney;

4. Planning of legal strategy including guilty pleas of lesser charges where pertinent;

5. Appraisal of role of (a) defense counsel, (b) prosecuting attorney, (c) judge, (d) jury, (e) defendant, (f) witnesses;

6. Understanding of court procedure;

7. Appreciation of charges;

8. Appreciation of the range and nature of possible penalties;

9. Appraisal of likely outcome;

10. Capacity to disclose to an attorney available pertinent facts surrounding the offense including the defendant's movements, timing, mental state, and actions at the time of the offense;

11. Capacity to realistically challenge prosecution witnesses;

12. Capacity to testify relevantly, and

13. Self-defeating versus self-serving motivation (in a legal sense).

(II) An alternative instrument used in determining competency to stand trial is the Competency Screening Test. This test determines whether a defendant requires a further examination to determine his or her competency to stand trial. The test identifies defendants who are clearly competent and who do not require additional comprehensive competency examinations. The examination contains twenty-two incomplete sentences which the defendant must complete.

(III) A third instrument is the Interdisciplinary Fitness Interview. The purpose of the test is to balance psychological and legal criteria in the examination. The issues in the examination include:

1. Capacity to appreciate the nature of the alleged crime and to disclose pertinent facts, events, and motives

2. Quality of the relationship with one's current attorney

3. Quality of the relationship with attorneys in general

4. Anticipated courtroom demeanor and trial conduct

5. Appreciating the consequences of various legal options

6. Primary disturbance of thought

7. Primary disturbance of communication

8. Secondary disturbance of communication

9. Delusional processes

10. Hallucinations

11. Unmanageable or disturbing behavior

12. Affective disturbances

13. Disturbances of consciousness/orientation

14. Disturbances of memory/amnesia

15. Severe mental retardation

16. General impairment of judgment or insight

G. EFFECT OF INCOMPETENCY TO STAND TRIAL

Each year, approximately twenty-five percent of the defendants who raise the issue of competency to stand trial are adjudicated incompetent. If a defendant is incompetent to stand trial, the court suspends the criminal proceedings and usually commits the defendant to a mental institution until he or she recovers. If a defendant recovers after a long commitment, a court may dismiss the charge either because it would be unjust to resume the proceedings, or because critical witnesses are no longer available. If a defendant does not recover, he or she is never tried.

Alternatively, if a court finds a defendant competent to stand trial, the trial proceedings continue.

H. COMMITMENT FOR INCOMPETENCY TO STAND TRIAL

When a defendant is incompetent to stand trial, the following problems of unfairness to the defendant may arise:

First, a court usually commits a defendant to a mental hospital until he or she is competent to stand trial. Accordingly, a court may commit a defendant for a longer period than the sentence that would have been imposed on the defendant had he or she been convicted of the crime. Thus, an incompetent defendant's hospitalization may have the same effect as a criminal sentence, even though the court never found the individual guilty of any criminal charge.

Second, most jurisdictions commit a defendant to an institution without following the procedures for a civil commitment. Typically, civil commitment procedures require a court to determine whether a defendant is dangerous to society or unable to care for himself or herself. According to the United States Supreme Court in its decision in *Jackson v. Indiana* (S.Ct.1972) the procedures and standards to commit a defendant who is incompetent to stand trial must be similar to those for a civil commitment. In *Jackson,* a mentally retarded deaf mute was charged with robbery. The defendant was found incompetent to stand trial and committed to a mental hospital for an indeterminate period of time. The Court held that the defendant was denied equal protection, because he was subject to a more lenient commitment standard and to a more stringent standard of release than those standards generally applicable to all other persons confined in a mental health facility who were not charged with an offense.

Additionally, the Court held that the indefinite commitment of a criminal defendant solely on account of his incompetency to stand trial does not meet the Fourteenth Amendment's guarantee of due process. The Court found that it is a violation of due process to commit a defendant for more than the "reasonable period of time" needed to decide whether there is a substantial chance of the individual attaining the capacity to stand trial in the foreseeable future. Thus, a defendant who is charged with a criminal offense and who is incompetent to stand trial may remain committed in a hospital only for the period "reasonably necessary" to decide whether he or she will attain competency. If the defendant does not regain competency within a "foreseeable time," the state must proceed to meet the requirements a civil commitment proceeding or release the defendant. Since the Court did not define "foreseeable" or "reasonable," the guidelines of *Jackson* remain somewhat vague and arbitrary.

Since *Jackson,* many state statutes include similar limits on the time period that a court may confine an incompetent defendant in a hospital. Yet, fifty percent of the states permit indefinite hospitalization as "reasonably necessary" based on a defendant's incompetency to stand trial. Other states permit hospitalization of incompetent defendants for limited periods as determined by his or her ability to recover or by the maximum period that the defendant could serve if sentenced.

Some courts traditionally committed a defendant who was incompetent to stand trial and suspended all criminal proceedings until he or she recovered. However, this view impinges a defendant's Sixth Amendment rights to a speedy trial, ability to confront his or her accusers, and capacity to assist in his or her defense. The Sixth Amendment guarantees a defendant's speedy trial, because a person charged with crime is presumed innocent. Arguably, a court should not detain a defendant until he or she is proven guilty.

Several states permit a trial for an incompetent defendant. However, courts only enforce a verdict of not guilty. Courts do not enforce a guilty verdict. Instead, a guilty verdict is set aside and the court commits the incompetent defendant until he or she recovers. For example, *People v. Lang* (Ill.1986), involved a deaf mute who was incompetent to stand trial for murder. The state proved that the defendant was guilty beyond a reasonable doubt. The Illinois Supreme Court found that the dismissal of the defendant's criminal charge, with leave to reinstate, did not release the defendant from the indictment. However, the court held that the defendant's incompetence tolled his Sixth Amendment speedy trial concerns since the conviction of an incompetent defendant violates due process. The defendant was subsequently involuntarily committed in a civil court.

An incompetent defendant may present pretrial motions and preliminary defenses. Additionally, state statutes incorporating relevant provisions of the Model Penal Code allow an incompetent defendant to pursue "any legal objection to the prosecution which is susceptible of fair determination prior to trial and without the personal participation of the defendant." The trend is for states to follow the latter approach. Some states permit the presentation of evidence for matters in which the incompetent defendant's presence is not critical. Other states require a hearing to determine probable cause before a court commits an incompetent defendant to a hospital.

I. CONSTITUTIONAL PROTECTIONS AND A FINDING OF INCOMPETENCY TO STAND TRIAL

1. Self–Incrimination and the Incompetency Evaluation

According to the Fifth Amendment to the United States Constitution, "no person … shall be compelled in any criminal case to be a witness against himself." However, when a defendant raises the issue of competency to stand trial, a court does not violate the defendant's privilege against self-incrimination when the court compels the defendant to submit to an examination. During a defendant's competency evaluation, a defendant's statements may relate to the charges against him or her. A judge or a jury may eventually receive a report including statements of the defendant made in the compulsory psychiatric examination ordered to make a determination of the defendant's fitness to stand trial. The concern arises whether a defendant's statements made in connection with a fitness determination may have adverse consequences for the defendant's privilege against self-incrimination.

Some courts admit the statements made by a defendant during the defendant's evaluation for the purpose of determining fitness. Often, courts rely on statutory authorizations which allow a waiver of a defendant's privilege against self-incrimination when his or her competency to stand trial is raised as an issue. For example, some state statutes provide that a defendant's compulsory psychiatric evaluation does not impinge on his or her right against self-incrimination if the defense, the prosecution, or the court uses the results of the evaluation solely to determine the defendant's competency to stand trial or to impeach the defendant in the fitness proceeding.

Many state statutes and judicial opinions such as that rendered by the United States Courts of Appeals for the Third Circuit in *United States v. Alvarez* (3d Cir.1975), explicitly prohibit anyone to use statements that a defendant made during his or her competency examination to establish the defendant's guilt. The United States Supreme Court in *Estelle v. Smith* (S.Ct.1981), held that a trial court may not use the results of a defendant's competency evaluation to decide the defendant's criminal responsibility, or to sentence, unless the defendant was told of his or her Fifth Amendment right against self-incrimination and knowingly waived that right. However, when a defendant requests an examination and presents psychiatric evidence, the United States Supreme Court held in *Buchanan v. Kentucky* (S.Ct.1987) that the prosecution may rebut the evidence with the report of the defendant's examination without violating the fifth amendment.

The American Bar Association Criminal Justice Mental Health Standards strictly limit the use of information received from an incompetent defendant. The ABA standards provide that any information elicited from the defendant at a competency hearing, or any information derived from the record of a competency hearing, or any testimony of experts or others based on information elicited from the defendant, should be considered privileged information and used only in a proceeding to determine the defendant's competence to stand trial.

2. The Bail Requirement and a Finding of Incompetency

The Constitution does not guarantee a defendant's release on bail in every circumstance. In most states, courts deny or revoke a defendant's bail during the competency evaluation. Arguably, a court should not deny or revoke a defendant's bail when the evaluation is performed on an outpatient basis.

3. The Speedy Trial Requirement and a Finding of Incompetency

Under the Sixth Amendment, in any criminal prosecution a defendant has the right to a speedy trial. Thus, the United States Supreme Court in *Barker v. Wingo* (S.Ct.1972) found that an incompetent defendant's prolonged hospitalization violates the defendant's right to a speedy trial, because such hospitalization is oppressive and increases the defendant's anxiety. The right to a speedy trial prevents oppressive pretrial incarceration of the defendant.

However, the Speedy Trial Act provides that "[a]ny period of delay resulting from the fact that the defendant is mentally incompetent" is not included in computing the period when the trial must begin.

J. SPECIFIC MENTAL CONDITIONS AND THE DETERMINATION OF INCOMPETENCY TO STAND TRIAL

1. The Effect of Mental Retardation on Competency

Mental retardation is a significant subaverage intellectual functioning which exists concurrently with deficits in adaptive behavior. A defendant with a significant degree of mental retardation is incompetent to stand trial. However, if a defendant's intelligence level is below normal, his or her low intelligence does not make the defendant incompetent to stand trial.

Therefore, an examination that confirms a defendant's general mental retardation is not sufficient to establish that the defendant is incompetent. Instead, the evaluator must apply the results of the examination to the defendant's ability to meet the legal standard for competency to stand trial.

2. The Effect of Amnesia on Competency

A defendant suffers from amnesia when he or she has a general memory loss that encompasses more than the defendant's forgetfulness of a few details. Expert testimony is critical to verify a defendant's amnesia. The United States Supreme Court in its decision in *Drope v. Missouri* (S.Ct.1976) found a defendant who is competent to stand trial must be able to provide his or her counsel with information relevant to prepare a defense. A defendant's loss of memory from amnesia, which hinders the defendant's ability to provide counsel with the facts of the offense, is not sufficient to find the defendant incompetent to stand trial. Thus, amnesia alone does not render a defendant incompetent.

Instead, a court must decide the following facts about the person's amnesia in order to establish it as a basis for a finding of unfitness to stand trial: whether a defendant has the amnesia, the extent of the amnesia, and the effect of the amnesia on the defendant's ability to aid his or her attorney. The following factors are used to determine whether the amnesia affects the defendant's competency so that the defendant is not fit to stand trial: (1) the extent to which the amnesia has affected the defendant's ability to consult with and assist his lawyer; (2) the extent to which the amnesia has affected the defendant's ability to testify in his own behalf; (3) the extent to which the evidence relevant to the case could be extrinsically reconstructed without the help of the defendant's; (4) the extent to which the state can assist the defendant and his counsel in that reconstruction; (5) the strength of the prosecution's case; and (6) any other facts and circumstances which would indicate whether or not the defendant had a fair trial.

3. The Effect of Medication of Persons Otherwise Incompetent to Stand Trial

Although the Supreme Court has raised the issue of whether an incompetent defendant must accept medication against his or her will in order to make the defendant competent to stand trial, the Court has not resolved the issue. In *Riggins v. Nevada* (S.Ct.1992), the United States Supreme Court considered the propriety of forcibly medicating a criminal defendant to restore competency. Ultimately, the Court focused on the effect of over medication on a defendant's ability to stand trial. The Court found that evidence showed the medications may have diminished the fairness of the defendant's trial and remanded the case for a determination of whether the defendant suffered actual prejudice.

Most courts, as exemplified in the decision by the United States Court of Appeals for the Fifth Circuit in *United States v. Hayes* (5th Cir.1979), have found that a defendant is competent to stand trial even though he or she is legally competent only when medicated. According to this view, although a state may compel medication of an incompetent defendant, if a defendant by choice becomes incompetent to stand trial because of refusal to take properly prescribed medication, the defendant may waive his or her right not to be tried while incompetent.

While most courts have held that a physician may medicate an incompetent defendant to make the defendant competent to stand trial, the United States Court of Appeals for the Fourth Circuit in *United States v. Charters* (4th Cir.1987) held that an incompetent defendant could refuse the forced administration of medication. According to this view, forced medication is not justified unless the defendant presents an immediate threat of violence that can not be avoided through less restrictive means. In *Charters*, the defendant had been found incompetent to stand trial and had been committed to a federal facility for treatment in order to make the defendant fit to stand trial. Since the defendant's incompetency to stand trial did not preclude his medical competency to decide his own care, the court held that the defendant could refuse medication unless he was found medically incompetent.

K. REHEARING ON COMPETENCY TO STAND TRIAL

The majority of states require a court to review the status of incompetent defendants during his or her treatment. Typically, the review is given on a semi-annual basis.

CHAPTER 13

MENTAL CONDITION AND CRIMINAL DEFENSES

A. THE RELATION OF MENTAL DISORDER TO CRIMINAL DEFENSES

Mental disorder is relevant to a criminal charge in two significant ways. First, the determination of the presence of mental disorder is relevant to establishing that a defendant had the requisite intent at the time of the commission of the criminal act. Under the criminal law, an individual may only be criminally punished if he or she has the requisite intent to commit the offense. Mental disorder may affect the individual's capacity to form the requisite intent.

Second, the mental condition of a criminally accused person may be invoked in relation to recognized criminal defenses. One of the most discussed defenses is that of insanity. The law in most states provides that a defendant may not be convicted of a criminal offense if the defendant was insane at the time of the commission of the offense. The standard for establishing an insanity defense differs among the states. Other defenses related to mental condition may also be raised. For example, during criminal trials, psychiatrists and psychologists may be asked to testify about the defendant's condition at the time of the crime, not only to establish insanity, but also in order to establish such defenses as: automatism, diminished capacity, self-defense, duress and provocation.

B. MENTAL CAPACITY AND THE JUSTIFICATION FOR CRIMINAL PUNISHMENT

In order to understand why the insanity defense, along with other defenses relating to criminal responsibility is recognized, it is essential to understand the theoretical purposes for criminal punishment. While there are various justifications for criminal punishment, including: retribution, general deterrence, specific deterrence, incapacitation, and rehabilitation; retribution is the basic underpinning of any system of criminal punishment. A person is punished because, as a responsible person, he or she has been found to have violated the law. Under retribution theory, punishment is sanctioned, because the defendant as a responsible person acted in such a way that he or she deserves to be punished for violating a rule of law that provides that the consequence of a violation will be the imposition of criminal punishment. Liability for criminal punishment presupposes that a defendant is capable of knowing and conforming to the rules of law. However, if a person is so mentally disordered that he or she lacks the capacity to understand what the law requires, then it would seem unjust to punish a person for behavior that violates the law. A person may lack this capacity to understand, because he or she is subject to psychotic delusions at the time of engaging in the conduct that provides the basis of the criminal charge. Punishment is inappropriate, unless the defendant is blameworthy. Blameworthiness attaches to a person who has the capacity to conform to rules of law, but instead violates those rules. The capacity to conform is not present in persons who are so mentally disordered, because of insane delusion or other mental disorder, that they do not understand what the law forbids or requires.

C. THE INSANITY DEFENSE TESTS

English criminal law did not consider mental disease legally significant until the twelfth century. Initially insanity did not bar convictions. Instead, insanity was considered a ground upon which English kings could pardon murderers. During subsequent centuries, the insanity defense slowly evolved. As late as the mid-nineteenth century, neither the United States nor England had settled the law of the insanity defense. However, in this period, two major developments occurred. The first was the publishing of a treatise on the Medical Jurisprudence of Insanity by Isaac Ray, an American studying human mental functioning. This treatise had significant influence on American judicial thinking about criminal responsibility. The second was M'Naghten's Case (Eng.1843).

1. The M'Naghten Rule

Daniel M'Naghten pled insanity as a defense to charges brought against him for the attempted assassination of the English Prime Minister and for the shooting death of the Minister's Secretary.

M'Naghten based his defense on a claim of mental disorder; he apparently suffered from delusions of persecution that are symptomatic of paranoid schizophrenia. M'Naghten was acquitted of the charge of murder based on the trial court finding him insane at the time of the shooting.

Following the acquittal, the English House of Lords were asked to set out rules for the defense of insanity. The Lords announced what has come to be known as the M'Naghten Rule: "To establish a defense on the ground of insanity, it must be clearly proved that, at the time of the committing of the act, the party accused was laboring under such a defect of reason, from disease of the mind, as not to know the nature and quality of the act he was doing; or if he did know it, that he did not know he was doing what was wrong." Today, this test is accepted generally in English and some American courts.

The two most significant words in the M'Naghten Rule are "know" and "wrong." Some courts confine the meaning of "know" to a purely cognitive standard; was the defendant capable of being aware of the existence and the terms of the law. Other courts ask whether the defendant had an "affective" understanding of the law. Under a purely cognitive approach, to know only requires that the defendant be able to correctly perceive the existence of the law and the nature of his actions. Under the "affective" approach, to know means whether the defendant was able to appreciate the meaning of the law and the significance of his actions.

Similarly, "wrong" is defined either narrowly or broadly depending upon the court. Under a narrow approach, "wrong" means whether the defendant knew or was capable of knowing his actions constituted a crime. Under a broad approach, "wrong" means whether taking into account the defendant's idiosyncratic beliefs, the defendant knew the act was prohibited or illicit.

Two major criticisms of the M'Naghten test exist. First, the M'Naghten test is deemed incomplete. The test only focuses on the individuals' cognitive impairment. According to Sir Isaac Ray, the defendant's ability to control his or her actions must also be considered. Second, it is argued that the test is too rigid. A strict application of the test should rarely lead to an acquittal. Only the most extremely mentally disturbed would come within the terms of the test.

2. The Irresistible Impulse Test

In response to criticism of the M'Naghten rule that it focused to narrowly on cognitive impairment, a new basis of finding lack of criminal responsibility emerged—the irresistible impulse test. It is unclear whether the early proponents of the test meant for it to be an elaboration of the M'Naghten test or a separate defense. However, today it is considered a separate defense. One of the first courts to adopt the irresistible impulse test was the Alabama Supreme Court in *Parsons v. State* (Ala.1886). Under the irresistible impulse test, a defendant is not legally responsible for his or her actions if: (1) by reason of the duress of such mental disease, the defendant had so far lost the power to choose between the right and wrong, and to avoid doing the act in question, as that the defendant's free agency was at the time destroyed; (2) and if, at the same time, the alleged crime was so connected with such mental disease, in the relation of cause and effect, as to have been the product of the mental disease. Basically the irresistible impulse test provides that a person is not criminally responsible if as a result of a mental disease or defect, the defendant has lost the ability to control his or her actions.

The irresistible impulse test draws its justification from both the retributive and deterrence justifications of punishment. If a person is truly unable to control his or her behavior, then that individual cannot be blamed for his or her actions. Similarly, if the individual cannot control his or her conduct, then criminal sanctions could not deter the individuals' actions.

The irresistible impulse test has been met with criticism. First, it is argued that the irresistible impulse can be feigned; and may, therefore, lead to improper acquittals. Second, it is argued that the cognitive and volitional elements of behavior are not distinct. That when a person claims to be unable to control his or her actions, it is likely that the person does not fully understand or accept the characterization of their action as wrongful. And third, like the M'Naghten test, the irresistible test is criticized for being too rigid. In a rigid application, the test only leads to an acquittal if the individual was totally unable to control their behavior and conform to the law.

3.   The Durham Rule

In 1954, a third test—the Durham rule was developed by the United States Court of Appeals for the District of Columbia in *Durham v. United States* (D.C.Cir.1954). The Durham test sometimes referred to as the "product" test, emerged partially a result of the criticisms directed against both the M'Naghten rule and irresistible impulse test. Under the Durham rule, "an accused is not criminally responsible if his unlawful act was the product of the mental disease or defect."

The Durham test was never widely used. The test is criticized, because the court failed to define either mental disease or product. Further, the test proved difficult to apply and was abandoned by the District of Columbia Court of Appeals in 1972. The only jurisdiction now using the "product" test for insanity is the state of New Hampshire.

4.   The American Law Institute Test

Dissatisfaction with the existing standards for determining criminal responsibility, another test emerged, the American Law Institute (ALI) test that was incorporated into the Model Penal Code. Under the ALI test, "a person is not responsible for criminal conduct if at the time of such conduct as a result of mental disease or defect he lacks substantial capacity either to appreciate the criminality of his conduct or to conform his conduct to the requirements of the law." The language of the ALI test combines the chief features of both the M'Naughten Rule and irresistible impulse test. However, the ALI rule makes it clear that a defendant's cognitive or volitional impairment at the time of the offense need not be total, rather it need only be "substantial" to establish an insanity defense.

The ALI test, has not been free of criticism. First, it is argued the test relies too much on the medical model. Under the test, a mental disease of defect is a medical diagnosis. Secondly, it is argued the test focuses too much on a volitional behavior. The volitional prong makes the administration of the test too difficult, and is subject to the charge that without cognitive impairment, individuals should be held accountable for their behavior. In response to criticism of the volitional prong of the ALI test, the United States Congress simply abolished "capacity to conform" as a defense to criminal charges in federal courts in the Insanity Defense Reform Act of 1984. The federal statute provides: "It is an affirmative defense to a prosecution under any federal statute, that at the time of the commission of acts constituting the offense, the defendant, as a result of severe mental disease or defect, was unable to appreciate the nature and quality or the wrongfulness of his acts. Mental disease or defect does not otherwise constitute a defense."

All existing insanity tests require establishing the existence of a mental disease or defect. However, there is lack of agreement about what constitutes a mental disease or defect. Significantly, analysis of what constitutes a mental disease or defect changes depending upon whether the basis for a defense of insanity is cognitive or volitional.

One approach to defining mental disease or defect is to use a psychiatric diagnosis. This requires reliance upon the DSM IV. A second approach is to accept any mental abnormality, without regard to whether it is a psychosis, neurosis, organic or congenital, as sufficient if the abnormality causes an impairment that meets the requirement of the relevant test for insanity.

Courts differ on who has the burden of proof of establishing insanity. In most jurisdictions, insanity is an affirmative defense that needs to be raised by the defendant. In some states, the defendant needs only to present some evidence of insanity, and the burden shifts to the prosecution to prove that the defendant was sane at the time of committing the offense. A minority of courts place the burden on the defendant to establish insanity. Most states, regardless of where the burden falls, require that the defendant inform the court of the intention to raise the insanity defense.

D. THE AUTOMATISM DEFENSE

Most crimes require an *actus reus* (the physical conduct of the crime) and *mens rea* (the intent). In order to obtain a conviction, the prosecution must establish that the defendant committed the forbidden act with requisite intent. Moreover, the act of the defendant must be voluntary as reflected in such defenses as coercion and duress that are not related to mental disorder.

The automatism defense focuses on the degree to which a defendant's actions were involuntary because of the defendant's mental condition. Some otherwise criminal acts may be considered noncriminal, because they were committed while the actor is subject to automatism resulting in involuntarily action. Several conditions that bring behavior within the category of automatism include: sleepwalking, epileptic seizure, hypoglycemia attack, or acts occurring during unconsciousness.

Courts have strictly limited the application of the automatism defense. Many courts disallow the defense if the defendant has previously experienced the conditions and did not take reasonable steps to prevent the criminal occurrence.

The defense of automatism differs from an insanity defense in several ways. First, insane individuals are generally conscious of their actions. Automatism is only invoked where the defendant is unconscious of his or her acts. Second, with insanity, courts differ on who holds the burden of proof. With automatism, the burden of proof is on the prosecution, because proof of a voluntary act is an element of a crime the prosecution must establish in order to obtain a conviction. Third, insanity requires the finding of a diagnosed disease or defect. Automatism does not require such a finding.

E. DIMINISHED CAPACITY DOCTRINE

Approximately one half of the states allow a defendant to present evidence that the defendant "acted" under a diminished capacity. While this does not result in a not guilty plea (as in the insanity defense), the defense may result in a reduced charge. Under the Model Penal Code, "evidence that the defendant suffered from a mental disease or defect is admissible, whenever it is relevant to prove that the defendant did not have a state of mind that is an element of the crime." It is essential to identify the requisite mens rea in order to determine if the defendant had the proper state of mind.

Historically, criminal law divided *mens rea* into two categories: specific intent and general intent. Specific intent refers the intent of the actor to bring about the act and its consequences. General intent refers to the intent simply to perform the act, or to engage in an action. The Model Penal Code abandoned the classifications of specific and general. Instead the Model Penal Code establishes four categories of intent: purposeful, knowledge, recklessness, and negligence. "Purposeful" requires establishing that the defendant acted with the objective of producing certain results. "Knowledge" requires proof that the defendant was aware that the conduct would or was likely to produce a certain result. "Recklessness" requires proof that the defendant consciously disregarded a substantial and unjustified risk that the act would produce a certain result. "Negligence" requires proof that the defendant should have been aware of the substantial and unjustifiable risk that the act would produce a certain result.

Where allowed, the diminished capacity defense reduces specific intent crimes to lesser offenses. Under the Model Penal Code, lack of mental capacity, may establish the defendant was not capable of the level of mental function necessary to establish the requisite level of intent. The defendant only needs to introduce evidence of a mental impairment that negates the required intent. The prosecution has the burden of establishing that the defendant had the requisite mental state.

Diminished capacity is most often used as a defense in murder cases. For example, first degree murder requires the intent to perform the act plus intent to cause a death. A showing of lack of capacity to form such a purposeful intention would establish a successful defense that would reduce a first degree offense to second degree murder.

Opponent's of the diminished capacity defense argue that the diminished capacity doctrine allows too broad a range of psychiatric testimony. This defense allows testimony of psychological impairment to establish the defendant's capacity for responsible action was diminished, but not fully eliminated, as a result of mental disorder. Thus, recognition of this defense may undermine the very notion of criminal responsibility that can be viewed as an all or nothing matter.

Generally, state courts are cautious in accepting a defense based on diminished capacity. Most states impose three restrictions on the use of expert testimony to establish diminished capacity. First, the diminished capacity must be associated with a mental disease or defect similar to that required for the insanity defense. Second, the testimony may only address the capacity of the defendant to harbor the required mental state, not whether the defendant had the mental state. Third, the evidence is restricted to certain crimes. Some states only permit expert testimony on the issue of diminished capacity where the charge is a form of intentional homicide. Other states limit the testimony to crimes requiring specific intent.

F.   SELF–DEFENSE

Psychiatric expert testimony may be offered when the defense is self-defense. Traditionally, one who is not the aggressor in an encounter is justified in using a reasonable amount of force against an adversary when he or she reasonably believes that there is an immediate danger of unlawful bodily harm from the adversary. In addition, the use of such force must be necessary to avoid danger, and not be excessive. Most states allow a person to use deadly force to repel an attack that is reasonably believed to be deadly, even if safe retreat is possible. However, a minority require retreat where one can completely retreat to safety; however, retreat is not required when an unprovoked attack takes place in the home. A successful self-defense case will result in acquittal.

The battered spouse syndrome has recently been introduced into the courts as a form of self-defense. This defense most often is raised by women who have killed their husbands following a long period of abuse. The testimony usually includes evidence that the wife suffers from low self-esteem, and passivity, resulting from inculcation of traditional societal attitudes about females. The defense aims to establish that the battered female defendant feels powerless, at blame and helpless in face of physical and psychological abuse by her husband. The defense asserts that the woman feels that there is no escape from the husband's abusive behavior except by violent action that incapacitates the husband. Often these women defendants kill their husband when the husband is asleep or following a plan of ambush. The states are divided as to whether testimony of battered spouse syndrome should be accepted as a basis for self defense.

G. DEFENSE OF PROVOCATION

Psychiatric expert testimony is presented to establish adequate provocation as a defense. Provocation is only available as a defense to a charge of homicide. An effective provocation defense reduces murder to voluntary manslaughter. In order to establish provocation, the defendant is required to establish the following: (1) the homicide was in reaction to provocation that would cause a reasonable person to lose control, (2) that defendant was in fact provoked, (3) a reasonable person would not have cooled-off prior to the homicide, and (4) defendant did not in fact cool-off prior to the homicide.

H. DEFENSE OF DURESS

The defense of duress often involves psychiatric testimony. The defense of duress is available when a person's unlawful threat(s) caused the defendant to reasonably believe that the only way to avoid imminent death or serious bodily injury is to engage in criminal conduct, and the defendant acts upon that belief. This defense, unlike provocation, is not available for homicide. The defense of duress requires that the defendant chose the lesser of two evils; homicide is not considered a lesser evil.

Under the Model Penal Code, the defense is not available when the actor has recklessly placed himself in a situation in which it was probable that he or she would be subjected to duress.

I. GUILTY BUT MENTALLY ILL

The guilty but mentally ill plea was developed, in part, to reduce the number of insanity pleas and resultant acquittals. A minority of states allow the finder of fact to return a verdict of guilty but mentally ill.

Generally, under the guilty but mentally ill plea, the defendant pleads not guilty by reason of insanity. The fact finder makes the determination of whether the defendant is not guilty, guilty, not guilty by reason of insanity, or guilty but mentally ill.

A person found guilty but mentally ill is subject to the same disposition as individuals found guilty of the charged crime. The defendant may be sentenced to any term appropriate for the offense. However, the finding of "guilty but mentally ill" is intended to provide the convicted individual with an increased opportunity for treatment in a mental hospital during the period of incarceration.

Those favoring the guilty but mentally ill plea maintain that it may increase the likelihood of treatment of mentally ill offenders. Opponents point out that finding the offender was mentally ill at the time of the offense is not useful in determining the offender's current mental condition, nor the person's current treatment needs. Moreover, every state already requires that prisoners be provided needed medical treatment, including mentally ill prisoners who are to be provided needed mental health treatment. Additionally, the "the guilty but mentally ill" verdict does not lead to special treatment of the person subject to this finding.

J. ABOLITION OF THE INSANITY DEFENSE

The insanity defense continues to be the object of skepticism. Alternatives to the insanity defense, such as the finding of "guilty but mentally ill" have been established. Also, there have been strong arguments made for abolition of insanity defenses. One alternative to the insanity defense is limiting psychiatric testimony to the *mens rea* issue. Moreover, states have adopted bifurcated trials in order to enable the jury make findings of fact about the alleged commission of a criminal offense without being subject to confusing psychiatric testimony related to an insanity determination.

A few states have adopted *mens rea* alternative. Under this approach, the accused may be acquitted if as a result of mental disability, the defendant lacked the *mens rea* necessary for commission of the offense. The defense of insanity is abolished, and other evidence of cognitive or volitional impairment due to the mental disability is only admissible at sentencing. At sentencing, if the accused was suffering from a mental disease or defect which rendered him unable to appreciate the criminality of his conduct or to conform his conduct to the requirements of law, the accused may be sentenced to an appropriate institution. The sentence may not exceed the maximum term of imprisonment for the offense with which the individual was convicted. Supporters of this approach argue that it may lead to a more realistic appreciation of the relationship between mental impairment and criminal behavior.

Moreover, the *mens rea* approach would make expert testimony on volitional impairment irrelevant, and diminish the scope and importance of psychiatric testimony relating to cognitive impairment.

Opponents of the *mens rea* approach maintain that the *mens rea* defense would permit conviction of a defendant upon a showing that the person knew what he or she was doing at the time of the offense, and possessed the intent to commit it, no matter whether the individual acted under an impairment such as delusional psychosis. For example the person who killed under the delusion he or she was ordered by God to do so, would be guilty of the offense of murder.

Another approach to reducing concerns about the insanity defense is bifurcation of trials. The first stage of the trial is the adjudication of guilt. The second stage of the trial addresses the determination of insanity. The bifurcation method has been proposed to (1) alleviate jury confusion by restricting or eliminating psychiatric testimony at the first phase of the adjudication, (2) eliminate insanity verdicts out of sympathy for the defendant, and (3) conserve judicial resources where the defendant is acquitted at the fact finding stage. Some courts have found the bifurcation scheme unconstitutional to the extent that it precludes psychiatric evidence that is relevant to establishing lack of the requisite *mens rea*. Additionally critics point out that inevitably much of the evidence considered at the first stage of the trial will be duplicated during the second phase of the adjudication.

CHAPTER 14

MENTAL CONDITION AND SENTENCING

A. MENTAL DISABILITY AND SENTENCING

After conviction, an individual is subject to the sentencing process during which the decision maker must consider evidence of mental disability if applicable. The tension between evidence of a mental disorder and an appropriate sentence for the crime committed is most evident in the contexts of capital sentencing, and in the sentencing of those deemed to be "mentally disordered sex offenders."

B. CAPITAL SENTENCING

The irreversibility of the death penalty has resulted in intense scrutiny of the procedures for imposing with reference to both the Eighth Amendment's ban on cruel and unusual punishment and the Fourteenth Amendment's due process clause.

The United States Supreme Court in *Furman v. Georgia* (S.Ct.1972), reviewed the Georgia death penalty statute. The statute granted virtually unguided discretion to the jury in imposing the death penalty. The result was a record of imposition of the death penalty of a "freakish nature, with no rhyme nor reason." In overruling the statute, the Supreme Court did not require one specified method for determining whether the death penalty should be imposed; but, instead, held that unbridled discretion was not allowed under the Eighth and Fourteenth Amendments.

In response to the decision in *Furman,* almost all states redrafted their death penalty statutes. The new statutes took two general forms: (1) elimination of jury discretion, and (2) allowance of jury decision making follow clearly established guidelines as to how jury discretion was to be exercised, specifically identifying various aggravating and mitigating factors.

The United States Supreme Court has since overruled all mandatory death sentencing statutes. The deficiency of mandatory statutes was their failure to provide for consideration of the "individuality of each death penalty case." The result of the Supreme Court's decisions on the death penalty is that while a jury is not to be given unlimited discretion, a state may not prevent the jury from considering information relevant to the offender that has relevance for determining the appropriateness of imposition of the death penalty. The Court noted in *Lockett v. Ohio* (S.Ct.1978), that: "The Eighth and Fourteenth Amendments require that the sentence, in all but the rarest kind of capital case, not be precluded from considering, as a mitigating factor, any aspect of a defendant's character or record any of the circumstances of the offense that the defendant proffers as a basis for a sentence less than death."

Today, most state statutes provide that before a defendant can be sentenced to death, the fact finder must find the existence of at least one aggravating circumstance without any mitigating circumstance. Examples of aggravating factors are: murder of a police officer; killing for pecuniary gain; killing while in the commission of another felony crime such as robbery or rape; and, significantly, from the perspective of mental health law, a finding that the person is considered "dangerous."

Typical mitigating factors include a finding that: the defendant was a juvenile at the time of the murder; the defendant acted under duress or domination by another; and, again significantly, from the perspective of mental health law, whether the killing was committed while the defendant was under the influence of extreme mental or emotional disturbance, the defendant could not conform his or her conduct to the requirements of the law as a result of a mental disorder or defect, or that the defendant believed the murder was morally justified.

In balancing mitigating and aggravating circumstances most state statutes allow imposition of death in a capital case if the aggravating circumstances outweigh the mitigating. Some states allow imposition if there are no mitigating circumstances sufficient for leniency or, in one state, imposition of death's available only if no mitigation is found.

C. MENTAL ILLNESS AND AG-GRAVATING AND MITIGAT-ING CIRCUMSTANCES

Usually, psychiatric evidence of mental disability as an aggravating circumstance at a sentencing hearing goes to the individuals "future dangerousness." Admissible evidence at the sentencing hearing must relate to the defendant, or involve responses to hypotheticals at the sentencing hearing posed to expert witnesses.

The United States Supreme Court held in *Barefoot v. Estelle* (S.Ct.1983), psychiatric testimony can be admitted at a sentencing hearing on the issue of dangerousness. The Court concluded that psychiatric testimony on the subject of dangerousness was not unreliable; moreover, the Court determined that a qualified fact finder, and the adversary system itself, are competent to uncover, recognize and take due account of any shortcomings of psychiatric testimony. As for hypothetical questions, the Court held there was no constitutional barrier to applying ordinary rules of evidence to this type of testimony. The essential component of the sentencing hearing, according to the Court, was that the fact-finder have all the relevant information before it in order to make the ultimate determination of whether the death penalty should be imposed.

There are usually four mitigating circumstances recognized in state statutes that relate to the capital offender's mental state: (1) whether the defendant was under duress or under the domination of another person, (2) whether the defendant was suffering from extreme mental or emotional disturbance, (3) whether the capacity of the defendant to appreciate the criminality (wrongfulness) of his conduct or to conform his conduct to the requirements of law was impaired as a result of mental disease or defect or intoxication, and (4) whether the murder was committed under circumstances which the defendant believed to provide a moral justification or extenuation for his conduct.

Not all evidence of mental illness is appropriate for consideration of the existence of a mitigating circumstance at the sentencing hearing. The Supreme Court has held that restriction of mitigating factors is impermissible, because this creates a risk that the death penalty will be imposed despite the presence of factors that call for less severity. However, the Court observed that "nothing in this holding limits the traditional authority a court has in excluding evidence not bearing on the defendant's character, prior record, or the circumstances of his offense." This suggests that courts may refuse consideration of frivolous claims of mental illness presented for the purpose of mitigation. The United States Supreme Court in *Skipper v. South Carolina* (S.Ct.1986), did hold, however, that consideration that a defendant does not pose a danger must be considered for purposes of potential mitigation and may not be excluded from the sentence decision making.

A separate question of admissibility of evidence of mental illness as a factor for mitigation arises in regard to whether particular evidence meets the relevant statutory mitigation criteria. The importance of fitting particular mitigating evidence within the statutory criteria becomes extremely important where the statute establishes the requirement of balancing statutory established mitigating factors against statutory aggravating circumstances to determine the sentence. Similarly, fitting the evidence of mental disorder within a specific statutorily authorized mitigating criteria becomes important where the statute will not permit the imposition of the death penalty if "any statutory mitigating factor is present." Moreover, most courts do not interpret the statutorily established factors broadly; therefore, fitting evidence of mental illness into a "category" within the terms of mitigating criteria takes on even greater importance.

Categorization of aggravating mental illness into statutory criteria is of importance as well. In one Florida case, a trial judge concluded that since a defendant had an incurable and dangerous mental illness, and since the sentence of "life in prison" did not mean that the defendant would actually spend life in prison because of the possibility of parole, the judge imposed the death penalty. The use of the defendant's mental state as an aggravating circumstance was not part of the Florida statutory aggravating circumstances listed. The Florida Supreme Court, in *Miller v. State* (Fla.1979), reversed the trial judge noting that the use of this nonstatutory aggravating factor as a controlling circumstance improperly tipped the balance in favor of the death penalty. According to the Florida Supreme Court the aggravating circumstances specified in the statute are exclusive, and no other factors may be used as aggravating circumstances; this view is required in order to guard against unauthorized aggravating factors being brought into the equation that might tip the weighing process to favor of death.

D. MENTAL RETARDATION AS A MITIGATING FACTOR

The United States Supreme Court in *Penry v. Lynaugh* (S.Ct.1989), has held that when mitigating evidence of mental retardation is offered, juries must, upon request, be given instructions that allow them to give effect to that mitigating evidence in determining whether to impose the death penalty. The Court has held that a state cannot, consistent with the Eighth and the Fourteenth Amendments, prevent the sentence decision maker from considering and giving effect to evidence relevant to the defendant's background or character, or to circumstances of the offense that mitigates against imposing the death penalty.

The Supreme Court, however, did not find a categorical ban on capital punishment of the mentally retarded. The Court has noted that the Eighth Amendment was adopted when the common law banned cruel and unusual punishment. The common law prohibited punishment of "idiots" which term described "persons totally lacking reason, understanding, or the ability to distinguish between good and evil." Thus, the Supreme Court has ruled that it may be cruel and unusual punishment to execute those "profoundly or severely" mentally retarded, because they wholly lack the capacity to appreciate the wrongfulness of their actions. However, some mentally retarded individuals are not so profoundly retarded, and these persons not only know their action is wrong but could conform their conduct to the requirements of the law. For such individuals, the court has ruled it is constitutional to execute, so long as their capacity to understand the wrongfulness of their actions is not "wholly lacking."

Personal culpability is the touchstone of these cases. Punishment of a capital offender must be based on the individual's culpability in relation to the crime. Individuals who come from disadvantaged backgrounds or have emotional or mental illnesses are generally less culpable. Since imposition of punishment is related to the personal culpability of the defendant, the decision maker must be allowed to consider and give effect to mitigating evidence that is relevant to the defendant's background, character and crime. Moreover, consideration of all mitigating factors enhances the reliability of a jury's sentencing decision.

E. MEDICAL EVALUATION AND EXECUTION OF SENTENCE

In *State v. Vickers* (Ariz.1989), the United States Supreme Court denied a writ of certiorari to decide the issue of whether a state has a duty to provide psychiatric testing necessary to determine the sanity of a condemned defendant before sentencing. Vickers was convicted of murdering a prison inmate and was sentenced to death. His only defense at trial was insanity. Vickers claimed that he suffered from a brain disorder causing violent behavior rendering him unable to appreciate the nature and wrongfulness of his acts. Vickers' court-appointed psychiatrist determined that Vickers suffered from "definitive dissociative reactions, possibly due to temporal lobe epilepsy." Based on this evaluation Vickers requested that the trial court provide access to diagnostic testing. Vickers included, with his request, affidavits from three psychiatrists who testified that strong evidence indicated that Vickers suffered from a mental disorder which impaired his capacity to make rational judgments, but that diagnostic testing was necessary before a firm conclusion could be reached. The trial court denied the request. Before sentencing, Vickers again requested diagnostic testing to establish the brain disorder as a mitigating circumstance; the court denied his motion.

Justice Marshall dissented from the denial of the *writ of certiorari* for review of the state supreme court's affirmance of the denial of the defendant's request for psychiatric testing. Marshall noted the Supreme Court previously had held in *Ake v. Oklahoma* (S.Ct.1985), when an indigent defendant demonstrates to the trial judge that his sanity at the time of the offense is a significant factor, the state must assure the individual's access to a competent psychiatrist who will conduct an appropriate examination and assist in evaluation, preparation and presentation of a defense of insanity. According to Justice Marshall the right to a competent psychiatrist necessarily includes the right to adequate psychiatric tools of evaluation. Marshall noted that an indigent defendant is not entitled to every scientific procedure that will remotely bolster his defense; but when a defendant demonstrates that his sanity is at issue and his psychiatrist makes a plausible showing that certain testing is necessary, that testing must be considered materially necessary to building an effective defense and the state must provide access to such testing.

The denial of writ in *Vickers* and the holding of *Ake* are inconsistent. Under *Ake* the state must provide a competent psychiatrist to make an "appropriate" examination in preparation for the defense of insanity. To deny a right to the tools for an appropriate examination is inconsistent with *Ake*. Moreover, a psychiatrist may only be as competent as the tools he can obtain. A denial of diagnostic testing works to undermine the right secured by *Ake* for the mentally ill condemned.

F. NONCAPITAL SENTENCING

Sentencing outside the capital punishment setting has historically been dominated by objectives of retribution, deterrence, incapacitation and rehabilitation. Retribution determines the culpability of the defendant and the appropriate punishment, while the other concerns lead to imposing punishment in order to confine or reduce the criminal propensities of the offender.

Most of the states and the Federal Government require "fixed or presumptive" sentences, or permit sentences within narrow ranges for most offenders. Variance of sentence is permissible in most schemes depending upon the individual offender's culpability.

Under the predominate approach to sentencing in use today, only those aspects of mental disability relevant to "blameworthiness" are to be considered in determining a criminal sentence. In most statutes which reflect this approach, the relevant aspects of mental condition or disability are identified as aggravating and mitigating factors. Under the now somewhat discredited "rehabilitation model" all aspects of an individual's mental disability would be relevant.

G.   PSYCHIATRIC TESTIMONY AND SELF–INCRIMINATION

Psychiatric testimony based on the psychiatric evaluation of a defendant can be detrimental at sentencing. For example, if the psychiatric report reveals that the defendant feels no regret for the crime, the judge may feel obligated to impose the harshest punishment available.

The United States Supreme Court in *Estelle v. Smith* (S.Ct.1981), stated that the Fifth Amendment's privilege against self incrimination applies to the sentencing phase of trial, as well as the guilt-determination phase. Moreover, the Court has held that a criminal defendant, who neither initiates a psychiatric evaluation nor attempts to introduce any psychiatric evidence, may not be compelled to respond to a psychiatrist if his statements can be used against him at a capital sentencing proceeding. The Court has yet to determine whether there is an applicable right in the non-capital sentencing context.

An analogous issue that the Supreme Court has addressed is the Sixth Amendment right to counsel in the context of a psychiatric evaluation. Here the Court has concluded that in cases involving possible imposition of the death penalty, a defendant should not be compelled to be involved in such an important matter without the "guiding hand of counsel."

H. MENTALLY DISORDERED SEX OFFENDER STATUTES

1. MDSO Statutes

Statutes dealing with "mentally disordered sex offenders" (MDSOs) are typical examples of an in-capacitation and rehabilitation model of sentencing. The initial impetus for the laws was a desire for an alternative to criminal punishment for a specific group of offenders. The laws were designed to re-move from society sexually dangerous individuals and, if possible, to treat them.

The procedures of MDSO statutes vary considerably. Commitment proceedings are initiated after a conviction for a sexual offense. The common feature of most statutes is that the defendant has been convicted, has plead guilty to, or has had a prior record of sexual offenses. Most statutes are specially concerned with those committing sexual crimes against children.

The MDSO statutes come into play at the time of sentencing. The standard to be applied is one of "dangerousness" and the imposition of treatment is done as an alternative to sentencing to prison. Standards for release after commitment is usually a medical finding that the person is "fully recovered" or improved sufficiently so that they no longer present a danger to others.

The MDSO statutes are civil in nature, thus, statutory definitions of applicable offenses that trigger a commitment hearing are not as burdensome as those required for initiating a criminal proceeding.

The United States Supreme Court in *Specht v. Patterson* (1967), found that while MDSO statutes may be ostensibly civil in nature, the reality is they can lead to indeterminate institutionalization. The possibility of such institutionalization entitles a person subject to MDSO proceedings to certain fundamental protections, including the right to be represented by counsel, have an opportunity to be heard, be confronted with witnesses have the right to cross-examine and to offer evidence. The Court went further to hold that "sound logic and fundamental justice would seem to dictate the applicability of the constitutional procedural safeguards normally applicable in a criminal case to sexual psychopathy proceedings, despite the civil nature of the latter."

2.   MDSO Commitment Standards

Most MDSO commitment statutes require that a mental disease or defect be found. However, this requirement is not always followed prior to commitment. One study found that 49% of those admitted as MDSOs were diagnosed merely as having some variant of "sexual deviation." Thirty-six percent suffered from "personality disorders" and only eleven of the 260 MDSOs received any psychotic diagnosis.

Another requirement is that a MDSO must be determined "dangerous" prior to commitment. Most courts have interpreted this statutory language extremely broadly. For instance, the Wisconsin Supreme Court in *State v. Hungerford* (Wis. 1978), held that a prediction of physical harm is not required, and that "moral" harm alone might by sufficient.

Courts have taken various views respecting the standard of proof required in proceedings under MDSOs commitment statutes. Some courts have taken the view that the requisite standard of proof is by a preponderance of the evidence, or the greater weight of the credible evidence. Courts taking this view emphasize that guilt is not a factor, rehabilitation or treatment is the goal, as opposed to criminal punishment. Other courts take the view that where the statute provides for imprisonment of anyone convicted of a specified sex offense for an indefinite term of one day to life, the standard of proof required in the hearing to determine sentencing is by clear, unequivocal, and convincing evidence. Finally, other courts have held that the standard of proof beyond a reasonable doubt is required in proceedings for the commitment of a MDSO reasoning that due process mandates this standard given the loss of liberty entailed by proceedings and the attendant stigma if one is found to be a MDSO.

3. Constitutional Problems with Lack of Treatment for MDSO's

When the MDSO statutes were initiated the goal was to treat a group of "sex offenders." However, "sexual psychopaths" as these individuals are often called today, constitute a broad category of personalities. They vary in dangerousness, frequency in committing their acts, and the type of victims they choose. There is no one treatment to help all designated MDSOs.

The MDSO statutes find their validity in the isolation of the individual, in the opportunity for treatment. The persistence of uncertainty in identification of MDSOs and doubts about the possibility of effective treatment have eroded confidence in the appropriateness of treating MDSOs as separate group under sentencing schemes. This question of separate consideration of MDSO's arises where the individual is committed for an indefinite period as a result of being deemed an MDSO, where the individual would have spent less time incarcerated if sentenced under the criminal law.

Since the justification for longer incarceration is premised on the chance for rehabilitation and since this objective is seldom realized, MDSO laws have been subject to constitutional attack.

CHAPTER 15

THE RIGHT TO REFUSE AND CONSENT TO PSYCHIATRIC TREATMENT IN THE CRIMINAL CONTEXT

A. USE OF PSYCHOTROPIC MEDICATION IN THE CORRECTIONS SETTING

Introduction of psychotropic drugs in the 1950s had a dramatic effect on the treatment of the mentally ill. The most marked benefit was the amelioration of the symptoms of mental illness. Today, antipsychotic medications are commonly used in almost all treatment plans for the mentally ill.

In the prison setting, however, the findings of beneficial use of psychotropic medication often has been counterbalanced by reports of abuse. Institutional staff have used medication not only to treat, but also to control and punish. Sometimes, over use of psychotropic medication occurs as a response to under-staffing. Because of the possibility of abuse, and the frequent occurrence of severe side effects with psychotropic medication, efforts have been taken through litigation to enforce a right of prisoners to refuse medications.

To establish a right of persons in correctional institutions to refuse medication, advocates often relied on the Fourteenth Amendment's due process clause and the constitutionally based rights to privacy and protection of bodily integrity. Irreversible side effects, such as tardive dyskinesia, were presented as a factual basis for recognizing a right of refusal of psychotropic medications.

Advocates for prisoners not only urged a right to refuse medication or drug treatment, but also a right to refuse to undergo invasive procedures such as electroconvulsive therapy (ECT) and psychosurgery. ECT is the inducement of a seizure by use of an electric current. Psychosurgery is the surgical cutting, destruction, or removal of brain tissue with the intent of altering emotions or behavior.

B. INDIVIDUAL AND STATE INTERESTS UNDER CONSTITUTIONAL ANALYSIS

There are substantial state interests inherent in the operation of a correctional facility. One goal of the criminal law is to remove dangerous individuals from society. To accomplish this goal, individuals convicted of criminal offenses can be placed in correctional institutions. Although convicted individuals do retain some of their constitutional rights, these rights are limited by virtue of their incarceration. Correctional authorities are permitted to treat individuals differently than other citizens can be treated by state authorities.

When considering the Fourteenth Amendment right of a prisoner to refuse medical treatment, the Supreme Judicial Court of Massachusetts in *Commissioner of Correction v. Myers* (Mass.1979), held that a prisoner could be forced to undergo hemodialysis and medication. The court noted that, although the defendant's incarceration did not divest him of his right of privacy and interest in bodily integrity, it did impose limitations on those constitutional guarantees because of the state interest "in upholding orderly prison administration."

Washington v. Harper (S.Ct.1990), is the most significant United States Supreme Court opinion examining the right of a convicted prisoner to refuse medical treatment. The case involved a prisoner who refused to take anti-psychotic medication because of the "irreversible chemical effect it had upon his brain." The prisoner was being compelled to take medication under a prison policy that permitted compulsory administration of antipsychotic medication when an inmate "suffers from a mental disorder and as a result of that disorder constitutes a likelihood of serious harm to himself or others and/or is gravely disabled."

The Washington Supreme Court had held that Harper was entitled to a judicial hearing prior to involuntary administration of antipsychotic medication. The United States Supreme Court reversed holding that, although there was a liberty interest present in being free from "arbitrary administration" of psychotropic medication, substantive due process was satisfied by limiting compulsory administration of such medication to those inmates who were mentally ill and gravely disabled, or who represented a danger to themselves or others. Furthermore, the Court held that a judicial hearing was not required, and that procedural due process was satisfied when a mental health professional, instead of a judge, decided the medication issue. Finally, addressing the issue of "alternative treatments" through which the state could realize its goals, the Court rejected the prisoner's claim to the less restrictive alternative of restraints or seclusion, instead of forced medication. The Court reasoned: "Nor are physical restraints or seclusion 'alternative[s] that fully accommodat[e] the prisoner's rights at *de minimis* cost to valid penological interests' .... respondent has failed to demonstrate that [these alternatives] are acceptable substitutes for antipsychotic drugs, in terms of either their medical effectiveness or their toll on limited prison resources."

Even though the Supreme Court has not found a right of refusal of psychotropic medication by prisoners, a number of state courts have recognized such a right based on the Fourteenth Amendment (liberty and privacy interests in freedom from bodily intrusion), the Eighth Amendment (prohibition of cruel and punishment) and the First Amendment (guarantee of freedom of religion). The right to refuse, psychotropic medication by a prisoner, however, has never been viewed as absolute. As is always the case with convicted criminals, prisoner's individual interests are to be balanced against those of the state correctional institution.

It is generally recognized that correctional inmates have a right to physical medical treatment when a "serious medical needs arise." In *Estelle v. Gamble* (S.Ct.1976) the United States Supreme Court held that the Eighth Amendment obligates the government to provide medical care for prisoners, but only to the extent necessary to avoid "deliberate indifference to serious medical needs of prisoners." Courts have interpreted "serious medical needs" to encompass psychiatric or psychological problems as well as physical medical needs. Therefore, when a prisoner's right to refuse psychiatric treatment is recognized and exercised, institutional authorities are in a dilemma between recognizing the right of refusal and the obligation to treat. This problem is furthered exasperated when the administration of psychotropic medication involves an effort to control a prisoner's behavior rather than primarily to treat. In *Keyhea v. Rushen* (Cal.1986) a California appeals court considered a case where a prisoner was involuntarily medicated as a result of an effort to control, rather than to treat, the court held that the prisoner had stated a valid claim for relief for violation of a liberty interest as protected by the due process clause of the state constitution. Furthermore, the court stated that even, if the prisoner was compelled to take medication for treatment purposes, if the process of administering forced medication was not in compliance with institutional established procedural safeguards, there was a basis for a claim of violation of procedural due process.

Most state courts recognize the need for involuntary treatment in the prison context at some level, but stress procedural safeguards to protect individual rights. Normal procedural safeguards mandate a hearing to review the propriety of compelled medication and, where appropriate, a hearing to determine the prisoners competency to refuse such treatment. A violation of procedural due process occurs if institutional procedural rules are not followed when prison officials administer to psychotropic medication against the will of the prisoner.

C. INCOMPETENT DEFENDANTS RIGHT TO REFUSE

In *United States v. Charters* (4th Cir.1987), the United States Court of Appeals for the Fourth Circuit was faced with an incompetent defendant's right to refuse treatment. The court rejected the state's assertion that it could impose medication on an incompetent defendant in order to restore the defendant to competency. The court reasoned that the significant risk that antipsychotic drugs might cause serious injury to the defendant far outweighed the state's interest in the mere possibility that the administration of forced medication might restore the defendant to competency, and allow the state to proceed to trial. The court was also concerned with the fact that psychotropic drugs could create a misimpression by the jury as to the defendant's mental state. The common side effects of the medication the state proposed to use included agitation and restlessness, or apathy and lack of emotion. As a result the court feared that administration of the medication might result in the defendant appearing in a false light to the jury. Finally, the court addressed the defendants liberty interest, holding the government's interest to try the defendant "does not permit such a draconian invasion of the individual's freedom and the risk of permanent physical injury."

The *Charters* opinion generally has not been followed. Most states permit forcible medication to restore competency, as well as permit medicated defendants to stand trial. These states attempt to handle the "demeanor perception" problem, noted in *Charters* in one of two ways. Some states allow either party to introduce evidence regarding the treatment or habilitation and its effects, and to require the court to give the appropriate instructions to the jury. The second approach was outlined by the New Hampshire Supreme Court in *State v. Hayes* (S.Ct.1978). In Hayes, the court permitted the state initially to compel medication of an incompetent defendant. However, if a defendant by voluntary choice, after being restored to competency after being medicated withdraws from medication with the result that he or she becomes incompetent to stand trial, such defendant may be deemed to have waived his right to be tried while competent.

CHAPTER 16

FITNESS TO BE EXECUTED

A. THE DOCTRINE OF "FITNESS TO BE EXECUTED"

Under the doctrine of "fitness to be executed" a condemned person must be competent at the time of execution. Only those persons who understand that they are to be executed and why they are to be executed, may be put to death. If before, or at the time of execution, a person is condemned to death is determined to be incompetent, that prisoner must be treated, most usually with medication, to regain competency. Roughly half the states have enacted provisions proscribing execution of the incompetent. Other states have transfer procedures providing for the moving of an incompetent condemned person to a state mental hospital for treatment until the person is rendered competent. A few states have adopted, by case law, the common law prohibition of execution of those deemed presently incompetent.

B. CONSTITUTIONAL PROHIBITION ON EXECUTION OF THE MENTALLY INCOMPETENT

In *Ford v. Wainwright* (S.Ct.1986), the United States Supreme Court decided the issue of whether a state could execute an incompetent person. *Ford* involved a defendant convicted of murder and sentenced to death. At the time of his trial and at sentencing, there was no indication that the defendant was incompetent. However, awaiting imposition of the death sentence, the prisoner began to manifest gradual changes in behavior. Examining psychiatrists found the prisoner incompetent having determined he suffered from paranoid delusions. Pursuant to state law, the governor appointed a panel of three psychiatrists to examine the prisoner to determine whether he was capable of understanding the nature of the death penalty, and the reason it was being imposed on him. The experts reported their agreed finding that the prisoner understood his situation and the nature of the death penalty. The state court found the prisoner fit to be executed. The governor, subsequently, rejected the defense counsel's attempts to submit additional information including the previous psychiatric reports, and signed the death warrant for the prisoner.

In reversing the state court, the United States Supreme Court held that the Eighth Amendment requires adherence to the common law rule that an insane prisoner may not be executed. The Court identified six rationales that serve as the basis for the rule that a person must be competent prior to execution. According to the Court: (1) an incompetent person might be unable to provide counsel with last minute information leading to vacation of the sentence; (2) madness is punishment in itself; (3) an incompetent person cannot make peace with God; (4) execution of an incompetent person has no deterrent effect on the population; (5) such execution "is a miserable spectacle . . . of extreme inhumanity and cruelty"; and (6) the retribution meant to be realized by execution cannot be exacted from an incompetent person.

C. PROCEDURE FOR DETERMINING COMPETENCY TO BE EXECUTED

The United States Supreme Court went on in *Ford v. Wainwright* to consider the proper procedure for determining competency of a person prior to execution. The Court determined that a full-scale trial was not required. The Court observed that the issue of "executing the incompetent" arises only after an individual is convicted of a capital crime and sentenced to death. The question, the Court stated, was not "whether to take the prisoner's life, but when." The Court concluded that a state may properly presume that a prisoner remains sane at the time of execution (after having been sane through trial and sentencing) and may require a substantial threshold showing of insanity merely to "trigger the hearing process."

In reaching its decision in *Ford*, the Supreme Court relied on its earlier decision in *Solesbee v. Balkcom* (S.Ct.1950), where the Court faced the issue of whether it was a denial of due process under the Fourteenth Amendment to allow a state governor, assisted by medical professionals, to determine whether a condemned prisoner has become insane after sentence and, if so, whether he should be committed to an insane asylum or executed. The governor's review was not subject to judicial review; and there was no adversary hearing where the condemned could appear, present evidence, or cross examine. The Court held that the process it was considering did not involve a violation of due process. The Court first noted that the discretionary power of clemency is rarely subject to judicial review. The Court drew a distinction between trial procedures and sentencing, ruling that a state cannot be compelled to hold an independent hearing upon "every suggestion of insanity ... to protect itself society must have the power to try, convict and execute sentences." The court concluded it did not violate due process to leave the question of a condemned's mental capacity to the state's highest executive with aid of skilled professionals.

In *Ford,* the decision of "incompetency" was initially decided by the governor. Although the Court did not overrule *Solesbee,* the Court noted that when it had decided *Solesbee* it had not considered the possible existence of a right under the Eighth Amendment. Moreover, at the time of the *Solesbee's* decision, the Eighth Amendment had not yet been applied to the states; the sole question in *Solesbee* had been whether the state's procedure for determining sanity effectively prevented the execution of an insane person. The Court's opinion in *Ford* makes it doubtful that a process limited to a decision of the governor's sole discretion, without the possibility of judicial review of the question of sanity and execution would be upheld. *Ford* clearly mandates that a hearing, although not necessarily a formal hearing, must be made available to the condemned prisoner for the purpose of determining sanity before the state can execute a capital sentence.

D. FORCED COMPETENCY AND EXECUTION

The United States Supreme Court considered the issue of whether a state could forcibly medicate a condemned prisoner for the purpose of execution in *Perry v. Louisiana* (S.Ct.1991). In *Perry,* a prisoner argued that forced medication is an impermissible device to circumvent the holding of *Ford v. Wainwright.* The prisoner also argued that, under the holding of *Washington v. Harper,* a state may only forcibly medicate an offender for purposes of genuine treatment, or in the alternative, for protection if the offender is dangerous to himself or others. The prisoner claimed there was no evidence that he was dangerous. In essence, the prisoner's claim was that forced medication, for purposes of execution, constitutes cruel and unusual punishment prohibited by the Eighth Amendment.

The prisoner also argued that forced medication of an incompetent capital offender solely to make him fit him for execution violated those "evolving and contemporary standards of decency" that are at the core of the prohibition against cruel and unusual punishment.

The state responded in *Perry* by establishing that it was obligated, under the Eight Amendment, to treat the prisoner's condition. Deliberate indifference to serious medical needs of a prisoner would constitute unnecessary and wanton infliction of pain that is prohibited by the Eighth Amendment. The state also claimed that forced medication of the prisoner was not "cruel and unusual", because the prisoner's mental condition actually improved as a result of the medication. The fact that the prisoner experienced side effects, according to the state, did not alter the fact that the medication was for treatment, and not punishment.

The Supreme Court remanded the case in light of its decision in *Washington v. Harper* holding that the Due Process Clause permits the State to treat a prison inmate who has a serious mental illness with antipsychotic drugs against his will, if he is dangerous to himself or others and the treatment is in his medical interest.

E.   INFORMED CONSENT

The doctrine of informed consent mandates that a medical professional make a patient aware of the risks, discomforts, and side effects of proposed treatment. The professional must also inform the patient of possible benefits and any alternative treatment.

Informed consent, in the context of the mentally disabled prisoner condemned to death, means that the medical professional must inform the patient of the possibility that treatment will make the inmate competent to return to death row, and subsequently be executed. The inmate also should be informed that competency will allow a better understanding of his impending execution.

It should be noted that a finding of unfitness of a prisoner for execution does not by itself render a prisoner incompetent to make treatment decisions. Nor does the fact that the prisoner may not have a right to refuse the treatment in the first place negate the obligation of the treating professional to inform the prisoner as to the reasons for, and nature of, the treatment to be given.

F.   ETHICAL ISSUES

By taking the Hippocratic Oath physicians vow to preserve life. As a result, involvement of physicians in the process of making a mentally incompetent or disabled person "fit for execution" by use of medication gives rise to ethical issues. With psychiatrists, the issue may even be more troublesome. The refusal of a physician to take part in any execution by serving as the expert declaring the prisoner dead after execution, or by administering the lethal injection that effectuates the execution would not prevent an execution from taking place since other persons may be employed to perform these various functions related to the process of execution. By contrast, the participation of psychiatrists in treating a condemned prisoner, in order to render the prisoner fit for execution, may help effectuate an execution which might not otherwise occur. Psychiatrists find themselves initially involved in a process that may delay an execution, but then find themselves involved in administering treatment that will make the execution possible. Psychiatrists may find a prisoner incompetent during the process of determining lack of fitness to be executed, thus, forestalling the execution. However, the psychiatrist is also involved in bringing about an execution that would not occur but for the treatment of the prisoner by the psychiatrist that renders the prisoner fit for execution.

The American Medical Association's Ethics Committee takes the view, even though a psychiatrist may be opposed to capital punishment, that a psychiatrist must treat an incompetent inmate, even for purposes of execution, since a failure to do so would violate a psychiatrists duty to evaluate and treat the mentally ill.

Another view taken by psychiatrists involved in treating prisoners is that their professional activity involves evaluation of a patient who happens to be a prisoner, diagnosing the patient's mental disorder and treating it. These psychiatrists take the view that they are not involved in the legal decision to execute. Treatment is for medical, not legal, purposes; and the decision to execute is a legal, not a medical decision.

Other psychiatrists view their function as a mixed medical and legal one since they provide a diagnosis of competence and provide an opinion regarding competency for execution. This method was in fact used in *Ford v. Wainwright* where psychiatrists used medical terminology in providing a diagnosis, but also offered a legal opinion based on the statutory standard for competency.

G. MENTALLY RETARDED PRISONERS

The United States Supreme Court has held that, when mitigating evidence of mental retardation is presented, it must be given effect in determining whether to impose the death penalty. However, the Supreme Court held in *Penry v. Lynaugh* (S.Ct. 1989), the Eighth Amendment does not categorically prohibit the execution of mentally retarded capital murderers. The Court has stated that the Eight Amendment's ban on cruel and unusual punishment applies to practices condemned by the common law at the time the Bill of Rights was adopted, as well as to punishments which offend our society's evolving standards of decency as expressed by objective evidence: juries' verdicts and legislative enactments.

Under the common law, punishment of "idiots", or those "totally lacking in reason, understanding, or the ability to distinguish between good and evil", was prohibited. Thus, it may be cruel and unusual punishment to execute persons who are profoundly or severely retarded and, therefore, lacking the capacity to appreciate the wrongfulness of their actions. It should be noted, however, that some mentally retarded individuals know their conduct is wrong and are capable of conforming their behavior to the requirements of law. Therefore, execution of mentally retarded capital offenders is constitutional so long as their capacity to understand their wrongfulness is not "wholly lacking."

CHAPTER 17

PROTECTION OF THE MENTALLY DISABLED FROM EMPLOYMENT DISCRIMINATION

A. FEDERAL PROTECTION AGAINST DISCRIMINATION

The Rehabilitation Act of 1973 and the Americans With Disabilities Act of 1990 represent substantial federal efforts toward providing the mentally ill with care, treatment, rehabilitation, and community services. In addition, both statutes play an important role in protecting the mentally disabled from discrimination in employment. While the Rehabilitation Act provides protection only to employees of the federal government and employees of federal government contractors, the Americans With Disabilities Act provides protection to employees in the private sector.

1. Rehabilitation Act Of 1973

Title V of the Rehabilitation Act of 1973 prohibits employment discrimination against handicapped persons. The provisions of Title V are similar to the discrimination prohibitions found in the 1964 Civil Rights Act, and amendments, which protect other minority groups.

Section 504, the most significant part of Title V relating to prohibition of discrimination in employment against the mentally disabled, provides in part that: "No otherwise qualified individual with handicaps ... shall, solely by reason of her or his handicap, be excluded from the participation in, be denied the benefits of, or be subjected to discrimination under any program or activity receiving federal financial assistance or under any program or activity conducted by an Executive agency or by the United States Postal Service...." This section provides broad protection against discrimination by agencies of the federal government, federal contractors and entities that receive federal funds.

Section 501 of the Rehabilitation Act mandates that each federal agency establish and implement affirmative action programs providing "adequate hiring, placement, and advancement opportunities for handicapped individuals." Section 502 empowers a special board to investigate and oversee efforts to make public buildings and transportation accessible to all handicapped persons. Section 503, governing employment under federal contracts, states that, in any contract with the federal government exceeding $2,500, the contracting party "shall take affirmative action to employ and advance in employment qualified handicapped individuals."

2. Americans With Disabilities Act

Upon discovering that nearly forty three million Americans suffered from either physical or mental disabilities, and that little legal remedy was provided for discrimination against them, Congress adopted the Americans With Disabilities Act of 1990. While the Rehabilitation Act primarily protected the disabled against discrimination in the federal government federally funded activities, the Americans With Disabilities Act, invoking the Fourteenth Amendment, extends protection by prohibiting employment discrimination by "any employer of fifteen or more people."

The purposes of the American With Disabilities Act of 1990 includes: (1) providing a clear and comprehensive national mandate for the elimination of discrimination against individuals with disabilities; (2) providing clear, strong, consistent, enforceable standards addressing discrimination against individuals with disabilities; (3) ensuring that the federal government plays a central role in enforcing the standards established in this Act on behalf of individuals with disabilities and; (4) invoking the broad sweep of congressional authority, including the power to enforce the Fourteenth Amendment and to regulate commerce, in order to address the major areas of discrimination faced daily by people with disabilities.

The Americans With Disabilities Act defines disability as: (1) a physical or mental impairment that substantially limits one or more of the major life activities of such individual; (2) a record of such impairment or; (3) being regarded as having such an impairment. As a general rule the Act states: "No covered entity shall discriminate against a qualified individual with a disability because of the disability of such individual in regard to job application procedures, the hiring, advancement, or discharge of employees, employee compensation, job training, and other terms, conditions, and privileges of employment."

The Act, however, makes exceptions for corporations, associations, educational institutions or societies of a religious nature. Religious groups are not prohibited from preferentially hiring individuals who are members of the particular religion, so long as the employment is connected with serving the religious group.

The Act excludes, from the definition of "qualified individual with a disability," coverage of any employee or applicant who is currently engaged in the illegal use of drugs. However, the Act does cover disabled employees who have successfully completed, or are engaged in, a treatment program and are not using illegal drugs.

Other conditions not covered by Act include: (1) homosexuality, bisexuality, transvestism, pedophilia, exhibitionism, voyeurism, gender identity disorders not resulting from physical impairments, or other sexual behavior disorders, (2) compulsive gambling, kleptomania, pyromania, (3) psychoactive substance use disorders resulting from the current illegal use of drugs.

The language of the Rehabilitation Act of 1973 left uncertain whether a state, invoking the Eleventh Amendment to the Constitution, was exempt from the duties mandated by the Act. The American

With Disabilities Act of 1990, however, specifically addresses this issue providing: "A State shall not be immune under the Eleventh Amendment to the Constitution from an action in Federal or State court of competent jurisdictions for a violation of this Act." In any action against a State for a violation of the requirements of the American With Disabilities Act, remedies are available in an action brought against a state agency for such a violation to the same extent as such remedies are available for any other violation in an action against any public or private entity.

The powers, remedies and procedures of the Americans With Disabilities Act of 1990 are the same as the powers, remedies, and procedures set forth in the Civil Rights Act of 1964. These powers are supplied to commissions given authority to deal with alleged discrimination, the Attorney General, or to any person alleging discrimination on the basis of disability in violation of any provision of the Act.

B. CONSTITUTIONAL CLAIMS TO PROTECTION FROM EMPLOYMENT DISCRIMINATION OPPORTUNITIES

The United States Constitution provides only limited protection against employment discrimination. If an individual can establish an entitlement or expectation of employment in a government job, for example tenured employment at a state university, a mentally disabled individual may challenge a denial of employment, limitation of benefits, or dismissal under the due process clauses of the Fifth or Fourteenth Amendments. Due process is violated by state action creating an irrebuttable presumption of unfitness because of mental disability, or by inflexible policies denying employment to the mentally disabled. Due process mandates that individuals must not be denied an employment opportunity consistent with their ability to demonstrate their capacity to perform the job competently.

Equal protection challenges have generally not been successful for the mentally handicapped. Declining to apply "strict scrutiny" analysis, most courts have not found the mentally disabled to be members of a "vulnerable and insular minority" entitled to special protection under the Constitution. Nor have these courts found employment to be a "fundamental concern." Generally, a lower level of scrutiny is applied where employment is at stake. Moreover, when lower scrutiny is applied, the "intermediate and rational relationship test" challenges generally are not successful. Both equal protection tests have been interpreted to give the state the benefit of the doubt as to the legitimacy of any claimed governmental objective. Moreover, the United States Supreme Court made clear in *City of Cleburne v. Cleburne Living Center* (S.Ct.1985), strict and heightened scrutiny is not applicable to claims of discrimination by mentally disabled persons.

The status of a particular employer accounts for differing legal results in cases interpreting the relevant federal statutes. Public employers are generally more responsive to the employment needs of the handicapped than most private employers. This results from two main factors, the less competitive employment setting of the public sector, and the long standing recognition of the Rehabilitation Act with its attendant obligations. The obligations imposed upon private employers by the Americans With Disabilities Act over time are likely to create similar awareness among private employers of the needs of the handicapped.

C. STATE LAW PROHIBITIONS AGAINST EMPLOYMENT DISCRIMINATION

State laws protecting the handicapped can generally be divided into two broad categories: (1) general prohibitions against specified kinds of discrimination, and (2) eligibility criteria for workers' compensation.

Most states prohibit discrimination on the basis of handicap or disability. However, only about half of these states specifically protect persons with mental disabilities. Some state statutes prohibit discrimination against any individual undergoing mental health treatment. Others state statutes prohibit, generally, any discrimination based on any handicap. A third group of statutes limits protective coverage to the physically handicapped and the mentally retarded. Many state statutes specifically limit coverage to the physically disabled. Usually receipt of federal funds brings forth protections against discrimination under federal laws. Most state antidiscrimination statutes provide protection against discrimination; moreover, these statutes usually encompass both private employment as well as employment with the state, or by entities receiving state funds.

State workers' compensation statutes grant compensation for loss resulting from any injury, disablement, or death resulting from an industrial accident, casualty or disease. Worker's Compensation laws share two basic features: providing no-fault compensation regardless of tort liability, and compensation based upon a loss of earning power.

Worker's compensation benefit awards for claims involving a mental disorder are usually limited to disorders resulting from a physical injury. However, there is disagreement about coverage of the Worker's Compensation Laws where the mental condition originates from work related "stimuli" or stress. Traditionally, a claimant must establish the existence of a physical basis for the condition in order to receive compensation. Increasingly, however, compensation, although limited, has been provided if the cause of the stress or stimulus is of a psychological nature. For example, unjustified badgering of an employee may lead to compensation. The rationale is that compensation should not depend upon the cause of a condition, but should relate to the nature of the disability experienced by the disabled person. There is a consensus, however, that normal, everyday stress, even if disabling, either should not be compensated or should be compensated only when causation can be established by clear and convincing evidence.

D. WHO IS HANDICAPPED OR DISABLED?

In all discrimination cases brought under the Rehabilitation Act or the Americans With Disabilities Act, the plaintiff must be "handicapped or disabled." The Rehabilitation Act defines handicapped as "a physical or mental impairment which substantially limits one or more of such person's major life activities." The Americans With Disabilities Act in defining "disability" adds, "a record of such impairment" and "being regarded as having such an impairment" to this definition. This makes an individual who presently does not have a specific tangible and identifiable handicap, yet nonetheless is "impaired," protected from discrimination.

Applying these provisions in particular cases requires a court to determine the existence of a handicap or disability, and then to consider the relationship of the handicap or disability to the particular work requirement in order to make the ultimate finding of discrimination because of disability.

Discrimination against a person with a handicap or disability, and discrimination based on a false "perception" that a handicapped individual is incapable to perform a job are targets for elimination

by the federal anti-discrimination laws. The federal
Acts do not deem a refusal to hire to be "discrimination" when such refusal is based on the reality
that the handicapped individual, as would be the
case with many nonhandicapped individuals, is not
suited for the specific job at issue.

E.   PRE–EMPLOYMENT INQUIRIES AS TO HANDICAP

Under regulations promulgated pursuant to the
Rehabilitation Act, recipients of federal funds may
not make pre-employment inquiry of an applicant
as to whether the applicant is a handicapped person
or as to the nature or severity of a handicap of a job
applicant. Pre-employment inquiries must be limited to questions about the applicant's ability to
perform job related functions. The Americans With
Disabilities Act has a similar provision. These laws
are construed by courts to prohibit questions directed to a job applicant designed to elicit information
about whether he or she has been treated for a
mental disorder. The purpose of these laws is to
ensure an employer will base the hiring decision on
an applicant's actual job qualifications, rather than
on any perceived limitations.

F.   THE OTHERWISE QUALIFIED REQUIREMENT

As seen both under the Rehabilitation Act and
the Americans with Disabilities Act, an employer
may refuse employment to a handicapped individual

where the handicap significantly impinges on the capacity of the employee to carry out the normal tasks associated with the employment. This justification for discrimination is tempered, however, by provisions in the laws that define a "qualified handicapped person" as one "who with **reasonable accommodation,** can perform the essential functions of the job in question." Reasonable accommodation involves those modifications of the job or workplace that can be accomplished without undue hardship to the employer.

An employer's duty of reasonable accommodation under the Rehabilitation Act is created by regulation. In the Americans With Disabilities Act of 1990 the duty to reasonably accommodate the disabled employee is imposed by the statute itself. An employer's failure to "make reasonable accommodations to the known physical or mental limitations" of a qualified handicapped applicant or employee constitutes discrimination, unless to do so would involve an unreasonable burden to the employer.

G.   CATEGORIES OF DISABLED SEEKING SPECIAL TREATMENT

1.   Alcoholic Employees

Courts generally have held alcoholism is a handicap for purposes of the Rehabilitation Act of 1973. The reasonable accommodation requirement has been construed to require federal employers to exert substantial affirmative efforts to assist an alcoholic employee toward overcoming this handicap, and to assist the employee in seeking treatment, before firing the employee for performance deficiencies related to drinking. Some courts hold the alcoholic employee must be offered an unpaid leave of absence to enable the seeking of in-patient treatment. These courts note federal statutes and regulations impose substantial obligations upon federal employers to assist alcoholic employees, including providing disability retirement benefits.

2. Compulsive Gambling

In *Rezza v. United States Dep't of Justice* (E.D.Pa. 1988), a federal district court found a cause of action could be brought under the Rehabilitation Act of 1973 by a compulsive gambler who was dismissed from his federal employment. Noting that compulsive gambling is a recognized mental disorder, the court found that whether the plaintiff was otherwise qualified (*i.e.*, is qualified if reasonable accommodations were made) raised issues of material fact persuading the court to deny the government's motion for summary judgment.

H. REASONABLE ACCOMMODATION IN PRIVATE SECTOR EMPLOYMENT

The Americans With Disabilities Act extends protection from discrimination to applicants and employees in the private sector. The statute provides that: "A qualified individual with a disability is an individual with a disability who, **with or without**

reasonable accommodation, can perform the essential functions of the employment position that such individual holds or desires." The Act's coverage is broader than the Rehabilitation Act in that the duty of reasonable accommodation may not be limited, altered or omitted by regulation. There are, however, limits to the reasonable accommodation requirement as reflected in the courts decision in *Pesterfield v. Tennessee Valley Authority* (6th Cir. 1991). The Sixth Circuit found a plaintiff with anxiety neurosis was not qualified, because a stress-free work environment is not feasible.

I. JUDICIAL REMEDIES

1. Scope of Judicial Remedies

Section 505 of the Rehabilitation Act extends to the disabled the remedies available under the Civil Rights Act of 1964. The Civil Rights Act provides a private right of action to persons aggrieved by discrimination. Damages are usually limited to back pay in employment situations, but reasonable attorney's fees may be awarded to the prevailing party.

State agencies receiving federal financial assistance fall within the scope of the Rehabilitation Act, the Americans with Disabilities Act, and the Civil Rights Act. The Americans With Disabilities Act explicitly extinguishes any state claim to immunity under the Eleventh Amendment.

2. Nonjudicial Remedies

Non-judicial remedies are available to persons filing claims under the Rehabilitation Act or the Americans With Disabilities Act. Section 706 of The Civil Rights Act of 1964 authorizes the Equal Employment Opportunity Commission to take administrative action against a federal agency. When an aggrieved individual has filed allegations with the EEOC, the Commission can either dismiss the charges or decline to file a civil action. Such an individual, however, is not precluded from filing his claim, if the EEOC refuses to file a claim. An aggrieved individual can file a claim in a federal district court on his or her own behalf. The EEOC, or in certain cases, the Attorney General, is also authorized to file a civil action on behalf of an aggrieved individual.

J. AFFIRMATIVE ACTION PROGRAMS

Section 501 of the Rehabilitation Act of 1973 mandates that each federal agency promulgate "an affirmative action program plan for the hiring, placement, and advancement of individuals with handicaps." This affirmative action requirement extends only to federal agencies, and not to entities receiving federal funds.

Once an affirmative action plan has been implemented, however, persons hired through the plan are presumably to be accorded similar treatment as those hired under normal procedures. In *Allen v. Heckler* (D.C.Cir.1985), a federal district court held that where a government agency hired under an affirmative action program and then treated those employees as inferior in benefits and protections "this defeats the clear command of the statute ... any distinctive treatment must be related to legitimate work place needs." According to the court, this result is detrimental to the cause of the mentally disabled.

CHAPTER 18

HOUSING AND ZONING

A. HOUSING THE MENTALLY DISABLED

A great deal of controversy has surrounded efforts to provide housing to the mentally disabled. Objections are often raised to allowing the mentally ill to reside in districts zoned for single family residences. Such objections are based on fear of mentally ill individuals coming into contact with children, fear for safety that residents feel stemming from the perceived dangerousness of the mentally ill, and fear of a decrease in property values resulting from the presence of the mentally ill in the neighborhood.

Unfortunately, the consequences flowing from failure to provide adequate housing to the mentally ill are not widely appreciated. In an era of deinstitutionalization, placing the mentally ill in an outpatient or community treatment setting is difficult without the cooperation of community residents. Furthermore, the normalization of the lives of the mentally ill is hindered when the mentally ill are not allowed to interact with community residents on a daily basis. Fortunately, courts and legislatures have contributed effectively to the development of standards for the introduction of the mentally ill into housing in residential communities.

B. JUDICIALLY IMPOSED STANDARDS FOR EVALUATION OF RESIDENTIAL PROGRAMS

Perhaps the greatest advances in housing rights for the mentally ill have been developed from the United States Supreme Court's ruling in *City of Cleburne v. Cleburne Living Center* (S.Ct.1985). *Cleburne* involved a private individual who purchased a house to lease to Cleburne Living Center as a residence for thirteen mentally retarded individuals. The purchaser was told a special use permit was required to operate a group home. The purchaser's application for a permit for a special use to establish the group home was denied by the city's Planning and Zoning Commission, as well as by the city council. The Center filed suit, alleging the ordinance was facially invalid, because it discriminated against the mentally retarded in violation of the Fourteenth Amendment's equal protection clause.

The Supreme Court found no rational basis existed to support the City's assertion that a group house and presence of the mentally retarded residents would pose any threat to Cleburne residents. The Court rejected the City's objections to the Center's location across from a high school, by pointing out many mentally retarded children already attended the school. The Court rejected the City's argument that property values would decrease as a result of the presence of mentally ill individuals in the community. Finally, the Court rejected the City's argument that the purpose of the ordinance was to avoid over concentration and overpopulation of the neighborhoods. The Court pointed out the living center would have no greater impact on the population than do currently existing apartment buildings, fraternity houses, and hospitals.

The Supreme Court emphasized only legitimate municipal interests could prevent the establishment of community centers for mentally handicapped individuals. Certainly, a valid concern for the safety of city residents qualifies as a legitimate interest. However, the dangerous propensities of the mentally handicapped may be difficult to establish, particularly when close supervision of residents is provided. In *Cleburne* the Court's decision focused only upon the mentally retarded, but the decision has been extended to the provision of housing for other mentally handicapped or disabled individuals as well.

C.   THE FAIR HOUSING AMENDMENT ACT

The Fair Housing Amendment Act of 1988, makes it unlawful "to discriminate in the sale or rental, or to otherwise make unavailable or deny, a dwelling to any buyer or renter because of a handicap." However, the statute excepts property owners from making dwellings available to "those individuals whose tenancy would constitute a direct threat to the health or safety of other individuals, or whose tenancy would result in substantial physical damage to the property of others". However, as indicated in the Court's opinion in *Cleburne*, the degree of imminence of danger needed to pose a threat to the community is one which may be difficult to establish. Given the subjective nature of such a perception, and given the various means for eliminating such danger through appropriate supervision, imminent danger will rarely be found to be a valid reason for restricting the access of the mentally disabled to housing in a particular community.

The Fair Housing Amendment Act's coverage extends to rentals, as well as sales, of multifamily housing. Discrimination under the Act includes alteration in the terms and conditions of the leased or sold property, and outright denial of sales and rentals. The Act may be enforced either by private action for equitable relief or damages, including punitive damages, or by a public action brought by the Attorney General. The Secretary of Housing and Urban Development (HUD) may implement conciliation proceedings at either the federal or local level.

D. THE TREND TOWARD COMMUNITY MENTAL HEALTH TREATMENT

Mental health treatment increasingly involves placement of patients in community settings. This approach encourages normalization by placing patients in a community setting facilitating a regular daily routine.

E. THE HOMELESS MENTALLY ILL AND THE RIGHT TO SHELTER

1. Factors Contributing to Homelessness

Community mental health treatment is particularly effective for patients who can return to or adapt to daily lifestyles following institutional treatment. Unfortunately, deinstitutionalization has been a major factor contributing to homelessness. Deinstitutionalization is but one of several factors leading to homelessness. The shrinking housing market has left individuals with limited financial reserves unable to afford housing. Moreover, the reduction in governmental benefits for the mentally impaired has left many former psychiatric patients with inadequate financial means to afford housing.

2. The State's Obligation to Provide Shelter

Courts have begun to find that the state has an affirmative obligation to provide shelter for the homeless. In *Callahan v. Carey* (N.Y.Sup.Ct.1981), a court found New York City was required to provide shelter for homeless males. The court's ruling was extended to females in a subsequent case. Following establishment of a right of the homeless to shelter, courts also have begun to make determinations on the adequacy of the shelter provided. For example, another New York case found placement of the homeless in certain hotel rooms to be "inadequate" housing.

3. The Need to Provide Aftercare

Court determinations of the need to provide aftercare housing have also been made, and are currently the subject of legislation. Aftercare housing involves residential placement of a patient after completion of a course of institutional treatment. In one New York City case, *Klostermann v. Cuomo* (N.Y.1987), involving the homeless mentally ill, a court ruled "failure to provide suitable adequate treatment cannot be justified by lack of staff or facilities." New York has also enacted legislation requiring emergency relief for the homeless.

4. The Right to Housing Under Discharge Plans

Perhaps the greatest advance in civil rights of homeless mentally ill patients came in a New York appellate court's decision in *Heard v. Cuomo* (N.Y. 1988), ruling that homeless mentally ill patients are entitled to receive housing under prepared discharge plans. Prior to discharge from a mental health care facility, all patients are entitled to receive the following: 1) a statement of the patient's need, if any, for supervision, medication, aftercare services and assistance in finding employment following discharge or conditional release; 2) a specific recommendation of the type of residence in which the patient should live and a listing of the services available to the patient in the residence; and 3) a listing of organizations and facilities, including those of the department of mental health, that are available to provide services in accordance with the patient's need.

F. ZONING

City residents objecting to the placement of mentally ill individuals into residential communities often act by encouraging their city councils to enact zoning laws prohibiting establishing group housing for the mentally ill within specific areas of a city. The term "zoning" in itself implies some limitation on property use. Although zoning is a valid exercise of state and local police power, constitutional limitations have been found to restrict the application of zoning ordinances. Most of the controversy has centered around the establishment, through zoning ordinances, of single family residential districts in efforts to restrict opportunities to provide mentally handicapped individuals with housing.

1. Single Family Residential Districts

In the past, municipalities successfully have barred the establishment of community living centers by zoning districts as single family residential. This zoning strategy prevented groups of unrelated individuals from residing together in single family residential districts. However, courts have been invalidating the use of such zoning ordinances to deny mentally ill persons the right to reside in group centers. The most restrictive ordinances define "family" as a housekeeping unit related by blood, marriage or adoption. Other ordinances simply limit "family" to mean a designated number of unrelated persons living together under a common roof. Some ordinances combine the above definitions of "family". Because foster or group homes licensed to serve the mentally handicapped are maintained by state funds, cities claim group facilities to be business uses of property and attempt to limit such facilities to commercial and industrial zones.

Courts have been persuaded to recognize new interpretations of the term "family". Municipalities are encountering increasing difficulty in blocking the establishment of group centers through the use of single family residential districts. Increasingly, residents of single family areas, who attempt to bar housing for the mentally disabled, are unsuccessful in convincing courts of the need to exclude such housing in order to maintain a "family" atmosphere. A Colorado appeals court decision in *Greenbrier-Cloverdale Homeowners Association v. Baca* (Colo.App.1988), rejected a homeowners association objection to the establishment of a group home for developmentally disabled adults, holding covenants restricting land use to single family dwellings do not bar group homes for persons with mental disabilities. The court stressed the need for establishing group homes in single family zoned districts in order to provide a family type living experience for the mentally disabled. In another Colorado case, the Colorado Supreme Court in *Hessling v. City of Broomfield* (Colo.1977), found land use covenants which did not define the term "family" or express an intent to limit occupancy to those related by blood or marriage necessarily permitted establishment of group homes in single family residential districts.

Group home operators are unsuccessful in challenging limitations under single family zoned districts when ordinances refer specifically to regulations applicable to group homes. In a recent challenge by a community living center to a Pennsylvania ordinance prohibiting two group homes within one mile of each other, the ordinance was upheld. A Pennsylvania court in *Verland v. Zoning Hearing Board of the Township of Moon* (Pa.1989), concluded the center did not qualify as a single family residence but fell within the zoning ordinance's definition of a group residence facility. The court also determined the zoning ordinance's distance requirement was constitutional since the requirement's purpose was to open zoning districts to group homes while preserving a family atmosphere.

2. Zoning Challenges Under the Fair Housing Amendment Act

Challenges to single family zoning ordinance prohibitions on group homes have also been brought under claims of violation of the Fair Housing Amendment Act of 1988. An Ohio federal district court in *Ardmore, Inc. v. City of Akron, Ohio* (N.D.Ohio 1990), issued a preliminary injunction barring the City of Akron from interfering with the establishment and operation of a group home for five adults with mental retardation. Plaintiff withdrew the application for a conditional use permit for operation of a group home, alleging the application process was burdensome and a direct violation of the Fair Housing Amendment Act. The court found requiring the plaintiff to go through with the application process would discriminate against those who wish to open group homes and be unduly burdensome by subjecting them to an unacceptably lengthy application process.

CHAPTER 19

EDUCATION OF MENTALLY HANDICAPPED

A. FEDERAL LEGISLATION DEALING WITH EDUCATION OF THE MENTALLY HANDICAPPED

Education of the handicapped is governed primarily by federal law. The Federal Education of Handicapped Act grants funding to states that provide free appropriate public education to handicapped children. The Act establishes guidelines and procedural safeguards for states to follow. However, what constitutes free appropriate public education is shaped largely through case law.

1. Education of Handicapped Act

The Education of Handicapped Act of 1975 provides federal funding to states and local agencies for the education of handicapped children. Congress enacted this statute in order to meet the special educational needs of handicapped children. At the time the Act was enacted Congress estimated that eight million children in the United States were handicapped. Of those eight million, more than half were not receiving appropriate educational services enabling them full educational opportunity, and one million were entirely excluded from the public school system. Congress also found that advanced knowledge existed in teachers' training, diagnostic and instructional procedures, and methods that could meet the needs of handicapped children. Thus, Congress determined that with proper funding, states and local educational agencies could provide adequate special education.

The Education of Handicapped Act emphasizes provision of special education and related services designed to meet the handicapped child's unique needs. The Act is designed to ensure handicapped children free appropriate public education.

The Act defines handicapped to include the mentally retarded, hearing impaired, deaf, speech or language impaired, visually handicapped, seriously emotionally disturbed, orthopedically or otherwise physically health impaired, and children with specific learning disabilities. The Act includes all handicapped children between the ages of three and twenty-one. In essence, the Act protects only children who require special education.

In order for the state to receive federal funding for a child, the child must be classified as handicapped under the Act. However, classifying a child as handicapped is not always a simple matter. First, the Act only recognizes certain disabilities. For example, the Act does not protect children who simply find learning to be difficult. Second, the Act requires placing a label on a child. Children risk being permanently harmed through being labeled; or they may rebel against the special treatment given to them. Third, some children may be borderline; a child may fall into either category of handicapped or non-handicapped. Finally, some children may require private programs. Yet funding is limited by the discretion of the public school system.

The Education of Handicapped Act provides federal funding to states that comply with the provisions of the Education of Handicapped Act. Before receiving funding, each state must adopt a policy that assures all handicapped children the right to a free appropriate education.

No state is required to accept federal funding; and, therefore, no state is required to comply with the Act unless it receives federal funds for special education. All states, however, must meet the needs of handicapped children under the Equal Protection Clause of the Fourteenth Amendment of the United States Constitution.

2. Requirement of Free Appropriate Public Education

The cornerstone of the Education of Handicapped Act is free appropriate public education. Free appropriate public education is special education and related services, provided at public expense and under public supervision that meet the standards of the state's educational agency. This special education includes preschool, elementary and secondary school education. In order for a child to receive free appropriate public education, the child must be evaluated and identified as handicapped. The educational system must then design a special individualized educational program, which it must then implement.

The first step in providing free appropriate public education is identification of the child as handicapped. Identification of handicapped children is not the responsibility of the parent. The responsibility of identifying handicapped children is upon the service provider.

Identification procedures vary among service areas. Identification may include taking a census, community surveys, public awareness activities, and screening school age children. Additionally, referrals by parents, teachers and doctors are often made to those responsible for providing free appropriate public education. While parents have the right to object to identification measures, parental consent is not necessary.

After a child is identified as possibly handicapped, the service provider must evaluate the child. Evaluation is two fold. The first purpose is to determine if a handicap exists. The second purpose is to obtain information necessary to create an individualized educational program. Evaluation usually includes gathering information about the child's family, social and economic situation. Also, evaluated are the child's physical and mental health, educational and social background, test scores, parent and teacher interviews, and home and school observations. The Act requires that an evaluation of a handicapped child be repeated at least every three years.

Prior to evaluation, parents must be notified. Further, the parents consent to their child's evaluation must be requested. If parental consent is refused, the service provider may ask for a hearing to determine whether an evaluation is appropriate. If the hearing officer determines that the child is in need of evaluation, the parents have only two choices. First, the parents can grant the evaluation. Second, the parents may place the child in a private school, or a home instruction program.

The Act ensures handicapped children the right to special education designed to meet the unique needs of the handicapped child. Special education includes classroom instruction, physical education, home instruction, and instruction given within hospitals and institutions. Vocational education is considered a form of special education when specially developed as a method of instruction. The child is not guaranteed the best educational techniques, services, or materials. Rather, the child is guaranteed an individualized plan so that learning may occur.

3. Provision of Related Services

The handicapped child's individualized educational program extends to services related to education. Related services are those that assist a handicapped child to benefit from special education. Related services may include transportation, developmental or corrective services, and supportive services. However, the United States Supreme Court placed limits on special services in *Board of Education of the Hendrick Hudson Central School District v. Rowley*

(S.Ct.1982). In *Rowley*, a deaf child was performing at an above average level in her classes, but below her potential. The parents requested a sign language interpreter be assigned to assist the child during class. The denial of the interpreter was appealed to the Supreme Court. The Court found the sign language interpreter was not a necessary related service. The Court held that as long as the child was provided with personalized instruction sufficient and supportive services to permit the child to benefit from the instruction, the child was receiving free appropriate public education.

Similarly, in *Polk v. Central Susquehanna Intermediate Unit 16* (3d Cir.1988), the United States Court of Appeals for the Third Circuit addressed the issue of whether a retarded child was "receiving some educational benefit." *Polk* involved a severely retarded child who's education consisted of learning basic life skills—feeding, dressing, and using the toilet; from a physical therapist. The school, however, discontinued the direct therapy and instead used the therapist to instruct the child's teacher on how to integrate physical therapy with education. The child's parents appealed. The court held that the Education of the Handicapped Act requires that "any educational benefit be more than *de minimum*." The court left the decision of whether this was *de minimis* to the trier of fact.

4. Required Individualized Educational Programs

Most educational programs are based upon a 180 day school year. Parents and specialists challenged the limited school year and successfully argued that children who are severely and profoundly retarded or emotionally disturbed regress significantly during the long summer breaks. As a result, some handicapped students are unable to progress educationally. In *Armstrong v. Kline* (E.D.Pa.1979), a federal district court in Pennsylvania held that if a handicapped child requires additional schooling, then special education could not legally be limited to a normal 180 day school year.

After an individual educational program is developed and agreed upon, the child must be appropriately placed as soon as possible. Placement is not dependant upon already existing programs; nor may children be placed on waiting lists. Rather, programs must be designed to fit the needs of the individual child.

5. Limitations on Separate Programs

Placement may be in either public or private facilities as long as the child is placed in the least restrictive environment. Under the Act, the handicapped child must be educated with non-handicapped child to the extent possible. The Act does not mandate mainstreaming. However, the Act does limit separate programs to situations where the handicap is such that education with non-handicapped children cannot be satisfactorily provided.

6. Procedural Issues Under the Education of the Handicapped Act.

In assuring free appropriate public education, the Act imposes procedural requirements upon the states. The school must notify the handicapped child's parents or guardians prior to any change in identification, evaluation, or educational placement. Unsatisfied parents or guardians have the right to bring a complaint regarding any matter relating to identification, evaluation, or placement. During the resolution of the complaint, the child if possible, must remain in the current educational placement.

Complainants are given a hearing before an impartial hearing officer. During the hearing, parties may present evidence confront witnesses, and be advised by counsel. After a local hearing, appeals may be brought before the state educational agency. In addition, parents may file a civil action suit. Under the Act, the court may determine the appropriate relief. Appropriate relief, at a minimum, means injunctive relief. Money damages may be awarded in extreme circumstances, for example, if the school acts in bad faith or places the student's health at risk.

Under the Act, the state has the primary responsibility for identifying and evaluating handicapped children, as well as developing and executing educational programs. However, the Act ensures state compliance by authorizing the withholding of federal funds if the state or local agency fails to satisfy the requirements of the Act.

B. STUDENT RECORDS

In 1974, Congress enacted the Family Educational Rights and Privacy Act, also known as the Buckley Amendment. This Act guarantees the right of parents and students to (1) view the contents of their records, and (2) restrict third party access to school records. This Amendment have special significance for handicapped children. First, handicapped children are exposed to more tests, evaluations, and observations than nonhandicapped peers. Second, parents are able to determine if their handicapped child is receiving adequate and appropriate education.

Parents, guardians and eligible students have the right to examine the student's records. Eligible students who have access to these records are defined by the child's age, severity of disability and type of disability. Third parties also may have access to a child's student records if written permission is obtained. However, written permission is not needed to examine a handicapped student's records by some educators, financial aid counselors, research organizations, the United States Comptroller General and the Secretary of the Department of Education. Additionally, courts do not need consent to subpena records.

However, not all student records are accessible. Inaccessible records include those records in the sole possession of the educator, records maintained only for law enforcement purposes, employment records, and records created by physicians, and psychiatrists, psychologists during treatment.

Parents may request an amendment of their child's file when inaccurate or inappropriate information is included. If the request is denied, the parents may appeal. The appeal is held before a hearing officer. If the hearing officer determines the material is inaccurate or inappropriate, the information will be withdrawn.

C. DISCIPLINE AND SPECIAL EDUCATION

Schools have a limited right to discipline students who violate school rules. The United States Supreme Court limited a school's ability to suspend students in *Goss v. Lopez* (S.Ct.1975). In *Goss*, the court held education was a constitutionally protected liberty interest that could not be infringed upon without due process of law. The court held that prior to expulsion for greater than a trivial amount of time, the student is guaranteed the right to notice and an informal hearing. This right extends to handicapped children. In *Pennsylvania Association for Retarded Children v. Pennsylvania* (E.D.Pa. 1972) a federal district court in Pennsylvania held any suspension or expulsion of a mentally handicapped child is a change in educational assignment. Therefore, suspension on exclusion requires notice and a hearing.

A school's ability to expel students is even more restricted. Courts have interpreted the Act to hold that a handicapped student may not be expelled until it is determined whether the child was appropriately placed at the time of the misbehavior, and whether the misbehavior was a manifestation of the child's handicap. Where the misbehavior is a manifestation of the handicap, one federal court ruled the student may not be expelled. In *Stuart v. Nappi* (D.C.Conn.1978) a federal district court in Connecticut held expulsion denied the student the right to free appropriate public education, the right to remain in current placement until a more appropriate placement was determined, the right to education in the least restrictive environment, and the right to procedural safeguards. The court concluded that while the child could not be expelled, the child could be placed in a more restrictive environment. However, the expulsion of handicapped students has been upheld in other cases.

CHAPTER 20

SOCIAL SECURITY DISABILITY BENEFITS

A. SOCIAL SECURITY BENEFITS FOR THE MENTALLY DISABLED

Many private and public organizations provide disability compensation to mentally disabled individuals. However, Social Security is the principle provider of federal benefit awards to the physically and mentally disabled. Eligibility for benefits under Social Security depends upon a determination of the existence and continuation of a physical or mental disability. Social Security benefits are only available to individuals who have contributed sufficiently to Social Security or to individuals who are financially needy.

B. DISABILITY UNDER THE SOCIAL SECURITY ACT

1. Definition of Disability

In order for an individual to receive federal Social Security benefits, the individual must qualify as mentally or physically disabled as defined by the Social Security Act. The Social Security Act defines the term disabled by reference to what an individual cannot do. In order to be found mentally disabled, an individual must be unable to engage in any substantial gainful activity by reason of a medically determinable physical or mental impairment. Additionally, the impairment must be expected to result in death or serious injury if the individual continues to engage in the work activity, or the impairment must have lasted for more than twelve months, or the impairment can be expected to last continuously for more than twelve months.

In sum, the individual bringing a disability claim must be so severely impaired that the individual is unable to satisfactorily perform his or her prior work. In addition, the individual must be unable to perform any other substantial gainful work. The age, education, and work experience of an individual are all considered in determining whether the individual is capable of other gainful employment.

To establish a disability claim, the physical or mental disability must be an impairment that results from an anatomical, physiological or psychological abnormality. This abnormality must be detectable by medically accepted diagnostic techniques and supplemented with objective medical evidence. However, providing objective medical evidence is difficult in the case of some psychiatric disorders.

2.   Burden of Proof

Impaired individuals have the initial burden of establishing that they are unable to perform their prior work. Once this burden is satisfied, the burden shifts to the government. To deny a claim, the government, then, has the burden of establishing the existence of other substantially gainful specific activities that the claimant would be able to perform.

The government must prove the disabled individual is able to meet the age, educational, skill and specific requirements of the employment in order to support a conclusion that the individual is capable of other specific substantial gainful employment. The government's findings must be expressed in specific acceptable job types, not within broad categories of employment. The government must present specific findings to demonstrate that the individual has the physical and mental capacity necessary for the specific types of employment.

3. Retroactive Application

The Social Security Act places a twelve month limitation on retroactive benefit awards. Therefore, claimants may only receive compensation for the twelve months prior to filing the claim and for continuing disability. Equal protection challenges against this limitation have met with little success. Courts generally employ the rationale that the care provider acting on behalf of the severely impaired individual should have great incentive to file the claim on a timely basis. Additionally, Congress allows for a twelve month grace period to avoid penalizing disabled workers who fail to file on a timely basis. Finally, courts also have rejected an equal protection argument; because all claimants, regardless of the severity of their disability, must file within one year of the disability in order to receive full compensation.

C. DISABILITY BENEFITS PAYMENT

The Social Security Act provides compensation through two different programs: the Social Security Disability Insurance program and the Supplemental Security Income program. In addition, various state programs also provide compensation.

1. Social Security Disability Insurance

Social Security Disability Insurance (SSDI) grants benefits to mentally disabled individuals who contributed to the Social Security fund through their tax payments. Claimants who earn enough yearly quarters of coverage are automatically insured for physical and mental disabilities. Compensation for a disability, is equal to the amount claimant would be entitled to in old age benefits if claimant were sixty-two years of age.

2. Supplemental Security Income

The Supplemental Security Income (SSI) program grants benefits to aged and disabled individuals in need of financial assistance. Supplemental Security Income is not based on past payments to the government. Rather, payments are dependant upon the claimant's income and available financial resources. Any individual qualifying for SSI also qualifies for Medicaid.

3. State Compensation Programs

States also provide compensation benefits to physically and mentally disabled individuals. One area for compensation is workers' compensation, another area is public aid based on financial need.

D. TERMINATION OF BENEFITS

Social Securities benefits are not guaranteed to last for the life of the claimant. Theoretically, the benefits are only provided to individuals who are unable to maintain substantial gainful employment. If an individual regains his ability to maintain gainful employment, Social Security benefits will end.

In the 1970's and 1980's the Social Security administration began mass termination of benefits to thousands of psychiatrically disabled. The decision to terminate benefits was the result of a finding that many groups of disabled had shown medical improvements. However, at that time individual assessments were rarely performed, and many mentally impaired lost their disability compensation.

The Social Security system terminated benefits to many mentally disabled individuals in New York resulting in many disabled persons being rendered homeless or left awaiting release from mental hospitals. In *City of New York v. Heckler* (2d Cir.1984), the city brought suit on behalf of its residents for a violation of provisions of the Social Security Act. The City charged the federal government with failure to use an appropriate evaluation process to determine eligibility for benefits. One step of the evaluation process called for an assessment of the individual's residual functional capacity, including the capacity to engage in basic work activities, and a decision whether the claimant's residual functional capacity permit the individual to engage in their prior work. In implementing this evaluation process, the agency presumed an individual's ability to function. As a result, the claimants with less severe mental impairments were presumed to retain a residual functional capacity sufficient to perform at least unskilled work. In reality, this presumption denied coverage to many needy individuals. The United States Court of Appeals for the Second Circuit found the government's procedure invalid. In response to the courts opinion, Congress enacted the Social Security Disability Benefits Reform Act of 1984. The Act required a revision of the criteria for determining the existence of a mental disability and a claimant's ability to work.

*

MENTAL HEALTH AND DISABILITIES INDEX

References are to Pages

349

MENTAL HEALTH AND DISABILITIES 361
References are to Pages

Employment Discrimination—Cont'd
Federal protection, 306
Judicial remedies, 318–319
Pre-employment inquiries as to handicap, 315
Qualified handicapped person, 316–317
Reasonable accommodation, 316, 317–318
Refusal to hire, 315
Rehabilitation Act of 1973, 306–307, 312–315, 316
State law prohibitions against, 312–314

Etiology, 27

Evidence
See also Testimony
Admissibility, 47
Bifurcation of trials, 272
Clinical psychiatric, 46–64
Conclusion testimony, 64
Constitutional issues, 61–62
Competency, 57–58
Demographic, 55–57
Diagnostic reliability, 49–50
Expert evaluation, 59–60
Expert testimony, 46, 58–59
Frye test, 53
Hearsay, 62–64
Jury comprehension, 54
Lay opinion, 48
Medical certainty test, 53
Modern rules, 51, 58, 64
Prima facie case, 53
Propensity, 54–56
Scintilla, 53

Execution of Mentally Incompetent, 296–305

Factitious Disorder, 39

Fair Housing Amendment Act of 1988, pp. 323–324, 330

Family Educational Rights and Privacy Act, 338–339

Federal Tort Claims Act (FTCA), 75

Fitness to be Executed
Constitutional prohibition, 296–298
Cruel and unusual punishment, 301
Doctrine, 296

†